DOERS
OF THE
WORD

MORAL THEOLOGY FOR
THE THIRD MILLENNIUM

Terence Kennedy, C.Ss.R.

TRIUMPH™ BOOKS
Liguori, Missouri

Published by Triumph™ Books
Liguori, Missouri
An Imprint of Liguori Publications

Library of Congress Cataloging-in-Publication Data

Kennedy, Terence, 1942–
    Doers of the word : moral theology for the third millennium / Terence Kennedy :
foreword by Bernard Häring. — 1st American ed.
        p.   cm.
    Includes bibliographical references and index.
    ISBN 0-89243-918-1 (pbk.)
    1. Christian ethics—Catholic authors. 2. Catholic Church—Doctrines. I. Title.
BJ1249.K46   1996
241'.042—dc20   96–1043

© 1995 St Pauls, Slough, United Kingdom
First published in the United Kingdom by St Pauls, Slough
This edition published 1996 by special arrangement with St Pauls, Slough, United Kingdom

00 99 98 97 96   5 4 3 2 1
Printed in the United States of America
First U.S. Edition

NA-2086

Contents

SECTION II
SOURCES OF A CHRISTIAN VISION OF ACTION

SECTION III
A CHRISTIAN VISION OF ACTION

SECTION IV
MORAL DIMENSIONS OF THE GOSPEL VISION

A WORD OF APPRECIATION

This volume has been a number of years in preparation. Its appearance now is a result of the support and encouragement of my family, colleagues and confrères. I wish to thank Father Patrick Corbett, Provincial of the Australian Province of the Redemptorists, and the presidents of the Alphonsian Academy in Rome, Fathers Séan Cannon and Bruno Hidber. I am particularly grateful to those who assisted me during my sabbatical year while I was gathering material; the Redemptorist communities in Melbourne; San Francisco; Chicago; Esopus, New York; and Geistingen, Germany. Mrs Joan Durand, librarian at Mount St Alphonsus, Esopus, rendered invaluable assistance obtaining books and articles, otherwise unavailable to me. Father Bernard Häring has been a constant inspiration to complete this task. The community of Sant'Alfonso in Rome, my fellow professors, the librarians, staff and students of the Alphonsian Academy have been good companions on my journey. I wish to thank my publishers, and the community of the Society of St Paul, Slough, for their hospitality, patience and expertise. They kept me to the proper deadlines and were thoroughly professional in preparing the manuscript for publication.

Foreword

Many years ago I encouraged my confrère Terence Kennedy to write a volume on fundamental theology in view of the situation in the world and Church today. Now the text is ready: *Doers of the Word.*

The two main poles of the Christian life are (1) listening to the Word, and (2) doing what the Word demands. Moral theology is aimed at changing our life for the better. This book is written for people who are yearning to do the right thing for the benefit of our world, of themselves and of others, to the honour of God.

The very desire to become what God intends for us and to act according to his plan of salvation urges and obliges us from within to be ever better listeners, learners. We listen at the same time to the revealed Word of God, turning with heart and mind to Christ, knowing that there is no master besides him and like him. We listen to the saints, who are the very best images of Christ. We never fail to listen to those in authority in the Church, and we shall never neglect the expertise found in the humane sciences. In order to be fruitfully "doers of the Word", we surely listen to the cry of those in bitter need, acknowledging their right to be loved, honoured and whenever possible helped. Enormous and urgent is the need to cooperate in creating a healthier world, healthier human relationships and healthier structures in the Church and world.

The reader of this book will surely be greatly helped to understand better his/her overall human and Christian vocation, to discern the signs of the times. It is an encouragement to become doers of the Word in a healthy, healing and liberating commitment, and with competence.

My hope is that this book of Terence Kennedy will find the readers it deserves.

Bernard Häring, C.Ss.R.

Introduction

In a season of renewal for Church and world the Gospel is our ultimate rule and criterion of life. We look to it as the Word of Christ to light our path through the darkness. Thirty years after the Second Vatican Council the evangelical call sounds more urgent and in a different tone. "But be doers of the Word, and not merely hearers who deceive themselves" (Jas 1:22). This text has been chosen as the title of this manual because it puts a challenge to us to pass from theory to practice, from preaching to life, from orthodoxy to orthopraxis. The great temptation for enthusiasts of renewal is to clasp the truth to themselves without "doing the truth in love". St Paul expects the Christian strengthened by the Gospel to "bear fruit in every good work" (Col 1:10).

A *doer of the Word* is one who transforms the world in expectation of the coming of the Kingdom. The idea proposed here is that we as agents can shape the world and with it our own identity according to the Word of God. He created us in the image of his Son. In the same way we are to shape our existence in the universe by becoming *doers of the Word*. Human activity is our way of indwelling the universe as a common home with God.

This volume moves according to the logic of the Conciliar Constitution on the Church in the Modern World: from the facts of our experience reflected on in faith to the discovery of Christ the Lord of history. This logic will move in four phases. The first is to situate us and our destiny in a created universe. This confronts the critical question of finding and establishing the basic truths of morality. The ultimate foundation of action is in God who shares his love with the whole universe; the proximate foundation is an integral conception of the human person; the result is a Christian view of morality. The second phase uncovers the sources of this vision in Scripture and the Church's living tradition. The third phase explains its essential elements: the meaning of action, the purity of conscience, education to a fully rounded character in a truly human culture, and lastly how evil contradicts all this when sin and guilt invade our lives. The fourth phase projects this vision into history in the twin dimensions of a Christian understanding of law according to the Gospel and in Christ's final coming to take possession of the Kingdom in glory.

A living faith is not just a matter of hearing the Word of God, but of putting it into action in love. Christ was the first Doer of the Word by becoming man for our salvation. Like him we fulfil the Father's will by acting as *doers of the Word* for the world's salvation.

SECTION I
Foundations

1

God, our focus on destiny

At the very moment that people feel the future of the planet earth is at stake, whether by nuclear holocaust or the wilful destruction of the earth's ecological system, the leading question is, where and how do we fit into nature? This is essentially a moral challenge. Our power over nature now makes us responsible not only for our personal future but for all humankind and even for the universe itself. The fact is, we are inseparably linked together. Is there a truly human destiny for us in this universe? Any account of Christian living today must pay very deep and serious attention to the whole human community and the universe in which it dwells.

1. Meaning as a concern of the twentieth century

The late twentieth century is one of the unique moments in history when the very foundations of morality have been called into question. There is no starting-point for ethical reflection that cannot be called into doubt. Among periods that parallel our own was ancient Greece three centuries before Christ, when Socrates, Plato and Aristotle battled to overcome the challenge of the Sophists and the Cynics. What they bequeathed us is the conviction that we all want a fully human life called happiness. They proposed life in the Greek city, the life of leisure, of understanding, of contemplation of the truth, as the most fulfilling. Aristotle argued that there must be one activity to make us happy and that was contemplation. ONE THING MUST MAKE US HAPPY. The second time the foundations of morality were believed to be unsound was the twelfth century of the Christian era when the Aristotelian idea of beatitude seemed to rock Christian convictions about life's meaning and purpose. Thomas Aquinas fused the Christian conviction of blessedness through the evangelical Beatitudes with Aristotle's idea of happiness. Our life's fullness consists in attaining God finally in beatific vision and joy; here on earth our only treasure is charity, to be united with him as friend. Today the abstractness and impersonality of the old ideas no longer hold our adherence; we want a personal answer, an authentic way of life. Where does that axis of love that holds the whole universe together run through my heart? How can I find love that overcomes "man's inhumanity to man"?

Wisdom is a grip on ultimates, the certainty about the basics on which we build our lives. There is one golden thread through the whole history of Christian morality and we call it by many names: God's personal providence for us his children, his cosmic love expressed in a personal call; the purpose and surety of a love that could create us and make the universe our home, that has bent down to heal and restore us when we moved away from his good intention; the conviction that God has all in his hands from beginning to end. Now, if such a purpose is revealed by the wonder of our cosmos unfolding itself, especially by what God has achieved for us in salvation history, if grace and nature form one story of divine wisdom and abundant love, what must be our response? How does this mysterious reality live and move within us? How do we know what we are made of, for what purpose and why? The one word that stands between us and cosmic destruction, ecological ruin, personal senselessness and even suicide is a love big enough to embrace everything that may ever occur. Such a love must be infinite; to create from nil, to save from senselessness, to conquer death. Morality starts at a level deeper than explicit reflection, where within ourselves we are swept along by and go along with this one universal drive to goodness. We realise that it becomes personal within us, for in our decisions about our life's direction we cannot but cooperate with this drive toward goodness; we must want God above all, as our all. Christian wisdom sees morality not as the restraint of law on our doing good, but as good attracting us to possess the perfect good that fills our emptiness with his fullness, meets our poverty with his richness, clothes our nakedness in his finery, and attains all from him who can give all. The question of morality is a God-question. Not whether we can prove his existence! No! Not whether we can discern his hand in human affairs! No! These truths are too obvious. But, what is he doing with me, my life, my community, my destiny? Where am I going because he is calling me there? How am I going to move because he has moved me? Morality starts in the recognition that we as persons are not grains of sand in a senseless cosmic sea; we are the sparks of love to make the universe glow with divine love.

2. Love is the force uniting the universe

Our vision of morality is one of purpose and sense built from the collaboration of faith and reason. It is a unified panorama of nature and grace. Before these two were crudely hacked apart by warring theologians they were nuanced parts of God's unified plan that all he had created and done for us should reach its one goal in himself. The Christian vision is suffused with unsurpassed beauty that embraces reality because it glimpses the artistic purpose in the plan of its Creator. The first assertion is about the absolute God before whom all else is relative and dependent. His providence for his creation has only one purpose in view, to glorify him simply by what it is, to manifest his goodness. Modern cosmology leads directly to the God-question; could all of this order, even the rational patterns in what appears to us as chaos, could all of this be for naught? No! It has its own sense, it can be understood, it works to its own goals. The anthropic principle shows that the construction of the cosmos is so measured and determined that it is made for the emergence of the human, it is made, designed and patterned so as to be a home for the human race. We see that this human purpose is open to meaning, even one that could transcend its own existence. Women and men are the authors of myth and magic, of art and science because they look upwards toward transcendence. Religion is the greatest human achievement: to organise life in worship of God. But the greatest thing is not only that we stretch up to meaning, to the infinite, but that the infinite has rendered itself accessible to us, descending to become an active agent in our history so

as to raise us above our failures to ascend to God. Theologians
have expressed this all-embracing sense of direction, of a
world permeated by a divine purpose and love, firstly as
God's providence; then as human responsibility to realise in
mental effort, love, freedom and human labour the divine
purpose. Thomas Aquinas says that we are mediators of God's
purpose to creation for we are the agents in salvation history,
as well as the mediators of creation to God by building a new
world that will truly only find perfection in God's final Kingdom. Humanity is truly IMAGO DEI. As the image of God a
person has providence over his or her own life by deliberate
thought and freedom of choice. Human being reflects God's
awareness and liberty in his creative act by having freedom,
dominion and autonomy over life and destiny. Persons move
dynamically from the depth of their being toward God who
summoned and energised them into existence not by flinging
them down senselessly, as Sartre thought, but by calling with
the sound of his own voice that still echoes in the sanctuary of
their being. This voice is a direction-finder, for the human
person cannot resist being attracted by infinite love. Persons
are that part of the universe that is free and conscious of itself;
they recognise in themselves the historic movement of an
ongoing cosmos whose destiny hangs on their decisions. They
recognise that they are part of the ONE HUMAN RACE, that most
developed part of the cosmos that has achieved its aim by
being centres of intelligence and freedom, values to be defended against all irrationality and tyranny. Once this dynamism is recognised, it is clear where the pull toward goodness
is leading. Indeed it tugs at the human heart, giving people
strength to go on not by rote but because of meaning. Who is
pulling at us, lifting us above the surrounding situation, challenging us to reach out to a future, has a personal name, God,
Alpha and Omega, beginning and end, Creator, Saviour and
reward to come. This state of affairs is not something we
created for ourselves; what we were given is what we confirm
and opt for in freedom. This attraction that we cannot quiet
within ourselves has been called the natural desire for God. A
yearning that awakens our heart to how as creatures we are
dependent in total openness on God. We are open to receive,

ready to move into the mystery of God if and when he should beckon to us with his graciousness. The natural desire for God is necessary since God in his providence created us for himself: there is only one utterly final goal to life, to exist totally to be with him because that is what he willed by creating the race in grace at the very beginning. Karl Rahner has an enlightening manner of expressing this. God created the universe so that it could be the place of his self-communication. God created humankind to be the partner of his self-manifestation, those to whom he could unveil his existence as being, "HE WHO IS". So we were made *capax Dei*, with a nature that could open itself through grace to receive God communicating himself to it by sharing his being and his nature. Our very essence is to be open to God, not only because our intellect and will want to know and to love, but because knowledge and love of him alone can ever satisfy them.

3. The desire for God

Henri de Lubac, in his magisterial *The Mystery of the Supernatural*, a book that changed the shape of theology in the twentieth century, sees humanity less as a natural creature than as one who consciously desires God and is thereby the spiritual heart of the universe. De Lubac says of our human searching,

> My finality, which is expressed by this desire, is inscribed upon my very being as it has been put into this universe by God. And by God's will I now have no other genuine end, no end really assigned to my nature or presented for my free acceptance under any guise, except that of seeing God.[1]

This desire for God, this finality of humanity sets us apart from all other created natures with their natural drives. Nor is this drive or desire like other created appetites that are capable of finite fulfilment; the desire for God is a transcendental drive that stretches beyond the limits of finite, temporal fulfilment.

Such is the human paradox: "man cannot live except by the vision of God" – and, as St Iraeneus says, that vision of God depends totally on God's good pleasure. Grace is given gratuitously and where grace is not recognised or where grace is rejected human life falls short and is truncated or deformed. We now see that the axis of love around which the universe was created runs most intensely through humanity because each person has a transcendent destiny to be worked out in God.

Here we contact the restlessness, the drive into the darkness, the wish to discover that unsettles the heart of every human person conscious of who they are. "My heart was made for You, O God, and it will not rest until it rests in You", in St Augustine's universally acclaimed formula.

Let us reflect a little on how human purpose gathers up this drive of creation, this silent desire of all that is for its source and fount. It is only in human action as guardianship of the cosmos that this unutterable groaning of creation finds its voice, crying out to return home to God. In the end all must come back to God. This is the magnificent vision of St Paul of the birth pangs of creation (Rom 8), and how it brings forth "a new heaven and a new earth" (Rev 21:1), the eternal dwelling-place of humanity with God. It is this discovery that God will be "all in all" when he is revealed to us face to face in the beatific vision that fills all human action with meaning. If God is not present as the force to sustain our destiny then our acting is in vain. Again de Lubac says,

> Every human act, whether it is an act of knowledge or an act of the will, rests secretly upon God, by attributing meaning and solidarity to the real upon which it is exercised. For God is the Absolute, and nothing can be thought without positing the absolute and relating it to that Absolute: nothing can be willed without tending toward the Absolute, nor valued unless weighed in terms of the Absolute.[2]

This is the God who illumines the mind and moves the will that we might find him, to "seek for him while he may be found", as Scripture says. But what will satisfy and bring our searching home? Here we could reflect on all those objects thought to fill the inner space of the human heart. One fact is beyond doubt in our consciousness, our desires stretch out for ever. Nothing, no-thing can ever fill that infinite space till it opens itself under the coaxing of grace to the only Infinity it knows, God himself.

Now the problems in justifying any sort of belief, a difficulty that has haunted philosophy since Descartes' assault on scepticism with the methods of solipsistic subjectivism and doubt, have spread to ethics and the understanding of moral action. When the sense of purpose penetrating the universe is neutralised and there is no more insight into its unity and its meaning, then the awareness of our desire for God is invalidated and our consciousness of his presence nullified. If we cannot be aware of God moving within our heart, then society, creation and the universe itself seem little more than a sick joke. The obvious consequence is that we also lose contact with Christ as the Redeemer of the world. Here we have uncovered the origins of modern atheism projected on a wide screen. What advantage is there in retaining purpose in the universe? It is precisely in the desire for God that we can discover how the universe's drive toward its Lord is active and present in the human heart. First, purpose weaves all creation in a patterned way in the one direction, pointing it to the one end that attracts and keeps it on course. This is the only point of view that lets us see all of the moral problems that beset us precisely in their formality as moral. "Knowledge of God that comes through the external world is, in itself, in a sense, a revelation", says de Lubac. Beginning with our own personal sense of finality we recognise purpose at work in the very design of the universe. In this way ethics stretches out to cosmic purpose, to the evolution of the cosmos and how the human project of science and technology is answerable for the preservation of nature and in some ways even for the future of the planet and the human race. We are responsible for our cosmic destiny, to make the human race's future sure on this planet and in this universe. Our properly human responsibility is expressed by the proper governing and planning of how human history should progress. We have a responsibility to

history and to future generations to leave them a worthy
human inheritance in the environment, culture and wealth as
their means of well-being and human development. But morality also spreads to social justice and defence of the rights of
the poor. There are as well the most intimate aspects of life
expressed by sentiment, emotion and especially sexuality to
be perceived under the infinite spell of divine love. Here we
must consider the historicity of consciousness, the uniqueness
and dignity of each and every individual person. St Augustine
intuited the divine presence more intimate to our inner being
than we are to ourselves. At the very centre of our being we
know that we were made by and for God, that we issue from
him to return to him. Here is the conducting line of all meaning in our lives, here is our first knowledge of the human
person as *imago Dei*. This likeness or image of God is dynamic
like the creating God himself by working out its intentions
through intellect and will, by becoming a true partner at the
spiritual level with the Creator. Thomas Aquinas begins his
moral theology on the basis of an ontological view of who we
are as icons or images of the Trinitarian God. His morality is
therefore internally consistent and coherent with his theology
of God and what God is doing in the world by creating us, by
calling us in grace and wanting us to share through belief in
Christ in the Kingdom of heaven. "Having spoken of the
Exemplar, God, we must now examine God's image, the
human person, in so far as we are *also* principles of our own
works by reason of our free choice and our power over our
own works."[3] Moral theology is essentially religious because
it takes this relationship with God as the key to all other
relationships so that we see all in God, and we insert all action
into God's action as its mover and its fulfilment. The aspects
of cosmology, of a world governed by the anthropic principle,
of ecology – i.e., of the world as an ongoing home for humanity – of a new international order to secure peace on earth, of
respect and justice in every community, of the most intimate
yearnings of the human heart – the sexual attraction toward
another person who may complement the self by procreating
life in marriage and family – of the vocations to heroism and
prophetic stances against all evil – all of these seem like but

tiny inclinations and indications of deeper meaning. They are in fact the small movements of creation groping its way back to its origin. They need to be viewed as parts or elements in the one total movement of all creation as from-God-back-to-God. Out of this movement arises our awareness of history as salvation history, as the place where God meets our desire to lead us to himself. Now the movement expressed as the deepest desire of the human heart is a given, a fact we recognise as God's gift to us by creation. But it is a given that has to be explicitly discovered, that has to be uncovered.

4. A history of covenant with creation

What has God done to make his attractive power clear and obvious to a rational mind ready to respond in faith? Here we enter the history of the covenants, of the unbreakable pledges that God has struck with us. Each one of these covenants corresponds to one of God's ways of being actively present in the universe. He seals his presence by striking a covenant with each section of the universe in its peculiarity. And so with the cosmos itself we have the covenant of creation, the covenant God made when he saw that all he had created was good and that in spite of human disobedience creation was still to be at the service of humanity. It never lost its radical purity and goodness. The priestly account of creation with all its seven orders leading up to man, with sun and moon, with stars and galaxies, with rain from the heavens and water in the rivers, with fish and crawling things, with fowl and stock, with all the animals, and finally the human being who gives them all their names – this is God's guarantee that the world is a good product, that it is well made. "God saw everything that he had made, and indeed, it was very good" (Gen 1:31). The prophets, particularly Isaiah, meditated much upon creation. When the Hebrews began to wonder whether God would be true to his Word, the prophets would call upon them to observe the rhythm of nature, the cycle of day and night and the sequence of the seasons and the course of the years. These things are stable points of life because God is true to his covenant with the universe so that it serves us humans. These realities testify to the divine veracity. Then there is the covenant with the whole of humanity, made with Noah after the flood when God displayed the rainbow, promising never again to destroy the race by flood. God has sworn by oath to assure the welfare of the whole human race for the whole of its history. And we are bound to him by the observation of the seven Noahitic commandments. These demand respect for life, marriage, sex, family, property, reputation and worship of God himself. These are the basic human values that can never be denied and they are guaranteed to the whole race by God's oath to remain faithful to his Word. God has chosen his people, elected to make them his very own. Here we have the family of faith born of Abraham, our father in faith. It is an oath to make Israel prosper and multiply, to be God's chosen representative among all peoples. And when the Israelites fell into slavery God released them, liberated them from servitude in Egypt, led them out to worship him on Sinai. There he struck a covenant of liberation with them. They would be faithful to him by observing the ten commandments as his words of command. These orders were necessary because the original covenant of creation was no longer securely sealed on their heart as the deepest yearning of their humanity. God's will for them is now declared externally, written on stone so that it can no longer be obscured by the corruption of a mistaken heart. It thus stands in judgement on sin. But the problem of the heart remains: who will cleanse it, make it pure, clear, limpid and receptive of the divine light? "The new covenant" was promised by Jeremiah and Ezekiel as a time when God would change hearts of stone into hearts of flesh on which he would write his law. No one would have to instruct and teach God's faithful people, because they would understand spontaneously and with complete clarity what was required. This instinct for goodness was to be given, implanted by God in the hidden depth of the human heart to satisfy our desire to reach him, to understand his mind, to love him for himself. This new covenant came as the new law, the Beatitudes, the blessings God poured down into our hearts to open their emptiness to his flood of grace; to make us pliable, flexible, ready and uncontaminated instruments of his designs for all humanity. This of course is "the law of Christ", the new covenant effected in his blood when from the Cross he poured out his Spirit as his paschal gift to the new-born Church. The body of Christ is now animated, souled by the Holy Spirit – or, perhaps we could say, when we are all incorporated into this covenant, this unbreakable marriage relationship between God in Christ and the whole race. Christ is now the head and Lord of the body, and the Spirit is her heart and soul. The Fathers of the Church and particularly St Augustine saw the Spirit as the unifier of us all into Christ, the new law of the new covenant. Here the new covenant consists in the Spirit being poured into our hearts so that we can cry "Abba, Father". Our relationship with God is finally clarified and complete; we share the divine life, "sons in the Son" because of the Spirit. Now this covenant is where our consciences are washed clean by the blood of Christ: here in our deepest selves our desire for God turns to prayer and adoration. When we are speechless the Spirit prays in our stead. Morality has been transformed and perfected into the living "spiritual worship" (Rom 12:1) of our whole life; in St Paul's beautiful phrase, "to present your bodies as a living sacrifice". This is where morality as a right relationship with God meets spirituality as the perfection of charity.

What God has done for the world has not yet been fully revealed; it is not perceptible or obvious to the course of secular history and human natural capacities. But this is to be perceived by the eyes of faith. God's final, once for all Word is spoken; he has given his Son and breathed the Spirit into our hearts. Christian morality, unlike the study of ethics, does not begin by observing the patterns of human behaviour from the outside. It starts out from the movement of the Spirit within and seeks to follow his path in remaking the human heart and reconstructing the human family in the world. In this way we have an ethics of the heart that is God-centred and not mere sentimentality. This is also the Spirit promised in Christ's great prayer as the advocate who would abide with us, not abandoning us down the ages, ever ready and unfailing in leading us as the community of Christ's disciples into the living truth of the Master. Now all our external ways of

reaching and striving and researching the truth are so many
instruments in the hands of the Spirit that we may come into
the fullness of the truth, God himself. This means that the
Christian scholar and particularly the moral theologian may
use any method so long as it is authentic and harmonises with
the understanding of faith. In particular the Spirit gathers up
history's wisdom from the past, the challenge of the present
for right decision and discernment, and draws us into his
future by making the most of the gifts he sends us till they
reach completion in the *eschata*. Faith is not yet perfected in
vision, i.e., the beatific union when we shall know God as he
is, "face to face". We therefore still need God's words to
resonate with the harmony of his Spirit within us. We still
need our rationality "to test the spirit". We need our knowledge of the cosmos, of the world and its affairs, but especially
insight of the human heart so that human language may grasp,
however imperfectly, but in our way and at our level how God
is moving us out in mission toward the world. This may be the
little world of our own heart, of family, marriage, community,
right up to the big world of the society of the nation and
the great international community; even to responsibility for
the whole of creation. It is the Spirit as love who unfolds the
mystery of purpose and unlocks the seven seals held by the
Lamb in the Book of Revelation. So the cycle is complete:
God moves us to want him with a natural desire that defines
our created selves as his images and likeness. God does not let
this chance of self-communication go unheeded: he addresses
man in all his covenants till he finally transforms his heart
with a new "soul", his Spirit that links the race together "in
Christ" so that we may return into the heart of the Father
whence we came. The cycle is closed and the story of salvation is done. This circle unites all the aspects of human history
as God's history with humankind in the context of creation.

5. Conversion to God as our "all"

The Christian vision starts in the heart of the believer and
moves outward to embrace the whole universe as it exists in

God's providence. Thus personal adhesion to God means making ourselves participants in this plan. It is precisely the Spirit who puts us into contact with God's purpose for us. In this sense a morality based on how the Spirit moves our heart is a morality of vocation and of conversion, a discovery of God as our all. This is well illustrated by how in every turning to God we find him in our hearts as the Lord of the universe. It is true that as St Augustine struggled against his passions a voice commanded him, "Take and read." This is the turning-point in the *Confessions*. It is true of an internal decision that changed not just the direction of his life but the destiny of so many who have been inspired by him to yield to God's advances.

In AD 627 the monk Paulinus visited Edwin in northern England to persuade him to accept Christianity. He hesitated and decided to summon his advisers. At the meeting one of them stood up and said: "Your majesty, when you sit at table with your lords and vassals, at winter when the fire burns warm and bright on the hearth and the storm is howling outside, bringing the snow and the rain, it happens of a sudden that a little bird flies into the hall. It comes in at one door and flies out through the other. For the few moments that it is inside the hall, it does not feel the cold, but as soon as it leaves your sight, it returns to the dark of winter. It seems to me that the life of man is much the same. We do not know what went before and we do not know what follows. If the new doctrine can speak to us surely of these things, it is well for us to follow it."[3]

These are questions put by every person as she or he comes to maturity. They are questions that form their inner self and respond to their desire to find God as he in whom they can invest their all; what indeed will give sense, meaning and purpose in life if not God's infinite love revealed in Christ? Our faith leaves us with many questions to be answered. How does one reconcile the fullness of life by discovering the inexhaustible beauty of God with life in a highly secularised culture? How does personal faith become social in the communion of saints? And what are we to say of this vision in a

culture where individuals are free to choose freely their style
of life as they see fit? In the wake of Hume, Kant and Hegel
the philosophy of religion has become a recognised discipline
in the universities. It takes religion as a phenomenon for
philosophical study. It treats faith as it finds it, and so it is not
a theological discipline for it does not begin from revealed
principles or what we can understand under grace of what God
has revealed of himself. But in our vision, nature by itself is
not a finished whole; it only comes to perfection when so
enabled and completed by God. And so the perspective of the
philosophy of religion needs the light of faith to discern what
is the sure way to God and what is genuine and pure among
the tremendous variety of religious practices characteristic of
the human race. Principles based on natural religion may still
stand firm in their own right but they have not been able to
satisfy the hunger for the ultimate meaning wakened by our
desire for God. Human answers to the deepest human questions have not been adequate to satisfy the human need for
complete light and truth. Although the philosophy of religion
examines ultimate questions, it is not the prerogative of philosophy as such to evaluate the ultimate claims about our way
to God in Christ. That is the business of faith that opens our
minds to God so that when St Augustine put the only question
the ancient world considered ultimate, that is, "how can I find
blessedness?", he answered that his philosophy was Christ.
Hamlet's intuition is doubly true:

There are more things in heaven and earth, Horatio,
Than are dreamt of in your philosophy.

(*Hamlet* 1.5.166-167)

Religion to be complete needs the supernatural, needs to
be helped by God to grasp the mystery of God himself. It is
precisely at this point that Karl Rahner thinks theology has
changed in meaning because the historical situation defining
our time and era has changed. It is not the horizon of meaning
nor the desire for God but the way faith works in a secularised
society and the place publicly allotted to God that is new.
Where once society itself was sacral so that religion was under

the care of the State, now secular thought and social structures have become autonomous, as has the individual moral subject, so that now each person may choose to believe not because of sociological pressures – social Catholicism – but by personal conviction. Theology has ceased to be an official ideology: it has become a way of contact with and meaningful reflection on the living-out of the mystery. Rahner has shown that where theology had not changed in two centuries this was overwhelming evidence of a separation of faith and life. The specifying characteristic for theology today is the new world with the new condition of humanity to which it is addressed. We may examine Rahner's proposal for a dogmatic theology and find there all of St Thomas' tracts. He rethought philosophical anthropology and found that it leaned heavily on moral presuppositions about humanity's openness to God. Any examination of the status of religion today is a moral question grounded in our approach to the transcendent. In medieval Europe and according to the theology that has prevailed till quite lately the Christian account of destiny as beatitude, that is, as the enjoyment of God, was not questioned. The same obtained for the Jewish and Islamic traditions. Now our societies are multicultural and pluralistic in their religious commitments. Liberalism was precisely a political technique to manage just such a situation of religious tension and diversity: each citizen should enjoy freedom of religion to work out his or her relationship with God or indeed to deny God if he or she would. This was a basic human right which assured that the demands of individual conscience were to be respected. The State should abandon all attempts to impose an established or official religion on the society. Religion and the search for happiness is thus a private affair. Only since the Second Vatican Council has the Church come to recognise this right of religious liberty as a right from God that is also a full civic right, a matter in which the State should not intervene coercively to make an individual or group adhere to this or that belief, saving the rights of the State over public order. It is in fact the growth of individual autonomy and the increased dominion over one's life so that one's fate and destiny are in one's own hands that mark our era and characterise its morality. For the individual this may mean that the choice of a morality may be too great a burden and so there may be a lack of decision or, more often, a confusion before the smorgasbord of choices set before her or him. Our society puts great store in an ethics of authenticity, an almost exclusive emphasis on being true to oneself in every situation. What is needed is true happiness on earth to make final happiness beyond this world credible. What we want more than all else is the evidence of people with such a relationship with God, whose lives are so filled with love that the truth of our destiny with God cannot be doubted. All sincere persons demand our respect. However, it is the saint, from whatever tradition he or she may come, that rises above the flock of humankind and displays what humanity should be. Such persons are a revelation of human destiny because their very goodness shows forth the presence of the Absolute. These are the persons whose lives are truly in focus, who disclose to us its deeper meaning. We must not only be clear on what life is about – more importantly, we must perform this meaning by being *doers of the Word*. Sanctity, wherever it appears in the history of the human race, is the "fruit of the Spirit", the sign that God has honoured the Beatitudes by sending these blessings.

6. Alternatives

The temptation of the twentieth century, because of the unleashed evils of famine, drought and war, and the toll of human misery, is to believe in nothing, to be a nihilist. Some turn their anger on God, denying his rights and finally his existence. It is the experience of evil that has, so to speak, wakened many persons from their religious slumber to undermine their Christian sense of purpose, meaning and destiny. A theologian can find no clearer case of this than Bertrand Russell's account of his taking leave of God and turning to agnosticism:

I may say that when I was a young man and was debating these questions very seriously in my mind, I for a long time accepted the argument of the First Cause, until one day at the age of eighteen, I read John Stuart Mill's *Autobiography*, and there I found this sentence: "My father taught me that the question 'Who made me?' cannot be answered, since it immediately suggests the further question 'Who made God?'" That very simple sentence showed me, as I still think, the fallacy in the argument of the First Cause. If everything must have a cause, then God must have a cause. If there can be anything without a cause, it may just as well be the world as God, as there cannot be any validity in that argument.[4]

Russell's case is of course a caricature of the traditional proof for God's existence, and his lack of logic is horrendous. A little reflection shows that apologetic arguments are usually inefficacious and lead precisely nowhere not because the proofs are not cogent and true, but because they have been ripped untimely from their spiritual and historic context. The biggest lack is any religious conviction at all from which to evoke some deeper thought and reflection. But why are we doing this? As Tertullian queried: why are we asking the Stoa to justify what we should attend to in the porch of Solomon?

Anthony Kenny has provided us with further anecdotal material in his reminiscences *A Path from Rome*. Educated in Rome he became a priest, and later left the priesthood and assumed a position of theological agnosticism. Again and again his mind bends over the difficulties of explaining transubstantiation in the Eucharist, where accidents inhere no substance, and the proving of God's existence. His words are:

> In order to resolve the uncertainties of agnosticism... the most important step... was to examine the proofs of the existence of God to see whether any of them was valid... Having come to have a great respect for St Thomas Aquinas as a philosopher, I decided that the best place to start would be with an examination of the five ways in which he says, in his *Summa Theologiae*, that the existence of God can be proved. If anyone was likely to have offered a really convincing proof of the existence of God, I reasoned,

St Thomas, with all his genius, must surely have done so. So I studied his proofs with great care... None of the arguments, on close examination, seemed to be successful in demonstrating the existence of God... I was surprised and rather disappointed.[5]

What stands out so conspicuously is the lack of any awareness of an infinite horizon to human existence, the complete absence of any religious experience of a God who cares and with whom there is a relationship that awakens our awe and the curiosity of our reason. God will not emerge through reasoning if he cannot already be felt and experienced as lovingly inhabiting the human heart. If there is no involvement with God active in history, if we disallow all signs of his presence, he will not appear by the magic of self-sufficient autonomous reasoning. There seems to be no awareness of the existence of God being a question of religious awe, awareness and belonging, that is, a question with its own infinite dimensions which therefore as such transcends the range of reason. For though reason may assent to his existence, it cannot tell us who he is, till he pronounces his own name, "HE WHO IS", the Father from eternity to eternity, made known in faith by Jesus Christ, his Son, made man through the Holy Spirit inhabiting our hearts. For most people holiness is the touchstone for knowing that God is real and active among us. Why is it that these accounts seem to lack a sense of direction while all around them everything is shouting the message of their purpose so as to render glory to their maker and their goal. There is a lack of feeling and affectivity, a cold rationality dead to mystery. This rationality has viewed the universe as infinite empty space in which humanity is a lost speck of cosmic dust. Society is an *ad hoc* arrangement to prevent chaos in the war of all against all. Ethics then means nothing more than consulting one's own interests at the best price. Popular religiosity should be just this awareness of holiness or sanctity which, Henri Bergson maintained, "must furnish us with the means of approaching, as it were experimentally, the problem of the existence and nature of God".[6]

The problem of modern rationalism is the problem of

agnostic and atheistic reason, i.e., ways of thinking that *a priori* put God beyond the coordinates of the real so that he can be nothing else than a fiction of the imagination; God before the bar of reason where, as C.S. Lewis said, any examination of his existence is foredoomed. And in this account of the world he remains forever invisibly unreal because reason so constructed cannot recognise him. What remains unrecognised is the perception of the one God acting in history and that this immanent God communicates himself in the sending of the Son and the infusion of the Holy Spirit who transforms our awareness precisely so as to confess him. Our experience now discloses to us the one God in three persons. And it is by penetrating this experience that we proclaim ourselves persons in God's image.

Wittgenstein took the strongest exception to Russell and the theologians he called "the parsons". These two are linked together as doing infinite harm because they both believed that philosophical justifications for religious beliefs were necessary before they could be given credence. Both the believer who is driven by his or her rationalism to prove the existence of God and the atheist who scorns the whole idea of any evidence of his existence have fallen into the same trap – what Wittgenstein calls "the idol worship of the scientific way of thinking". Michael J. Buckley S.J. has traced the rise of modern atheism to seventeenth-century theologians like Leonard Lessius and Martin Mersenne who bracketed religious experience of Christ off from the philosophical concern of proving God's existence. Modern rationalism has been built on this divorce from our firsthand experience of the living God and his covenant of love with us. Wittgenstein saw correctly that we cannot totally found religion as an act of faith wholly in rationality or philosophical reflection. Faith demands a moment of personal assent that crosses the boundaries of pure rationality limited by its own strength. Christian religion starts from God addressing us with his Word, and this very speaking asserts his real intervention in our lives, that he has come to exist for us. For the rationalist, the discovery of design in the world becomes a universal scientific method used to ground our knowledge of God. Paul Davies seems to be following the same tactic today with his idea of *God in the New Physics*. Atheism emerged from the frustration of proving God from a set of facts that were never allowed to speak of God. Physics does not provide the warrant for religious belief. The problem of evil when treated rationalistically struck even deeper into the human psyche as a proof not only that God was not but that existence itself was senseless. Once the sense of a personal God with providence over my life as it is inserted in the universe is lost, then any evil is possible and even to be expected. Our knowledge of the world is that of God's creation and thereby affirms that we have already accepted it as his providence. Our way to God is through a healthy recognition of the fullness of our experience, that it does declare an infinite horizon of cosmic love upholding in the universe, a love that has formed a covenant with the human race to preserve it through all ills, a covenant with a chosen people as a way to God, a covenant in my own soul where I am God's image called by him to a vocation of service in the achievement of a destiny uniquely my own.

7. Experience

Experience is not just a reservoir of memory that lets us know the future, nor simply the raw sense material from which we glean our intellectual knowledge of what we can master. Experience is more than acquired skill for gaining a wide range of information on a topic we have sedulously examined. Experience goes beyond the onrush of the empirical to where it has meaning for us personally as the stuff out of which our lives are constructed. In this sense it is strictly moral, for from experience we grasp who we are that we may achieve our true fullness. Experience is not merely passive, but arises out of our deepest activity and doing. Experience is the originating living unity of our being in the world that is structured but not divided. It means that I am alive to and in vital interaction with this world about me. In religious experience we are alive to God by interaction with him through salvation history, through being covenanted to him. In salvation history the abyss of God opens before the human person as the Absolute commanding his or her commitment and attracting the totality of his or her longing for meaning; in this interaction the Christian comes to assent to the living God as his all. Experience in the end is an exchange between God and the person in which we know him as Lord and recognise ourselves as taking our all from him as his image. It is precisely this truth of our status as divine offspring that has been bracketed out by the rationalist search for meaning in the universe over the last few hundred years.

Do not the histories of ordinary Christians witness to this interchange of encounters with God, those moments of life that evoke an unexpected depth from within a person or a community that make the divine reality undeniable? Since experience is concrete and actual, this point needs to be expounded concretely before we go on to theory. We must begin with the reality of exchange between God and a person. Edith Stein was trained in phenomenology as Husserl's assistant. Her academic career had led her from a rabid atheism to a mild sympathy for Christianity. Her journey to God was wakened by her studies in the phenomenological method, the descriptive analysis of the data of consciousness, that of which we are aware in lived experience. The key to her situation was her ability to appreciate the meaning of personal and intersubjective experience. The climax of her journey occurred in 1921 on a visit to the philosopher Hedwig Conrad-Martius when she was left alone to entertain herself for an evening. She picked up the *Autobiography* of St Teresa of Avila and could not put it down. She read it through the night and, as dawn broke on a new day for her, she closed it saying, "This is the truth."

Another fine example is the influence of Leon Bloy on Jacques and Raissa Maritain, recounted by her in *We Have Been Friends Together*. Months passed before she recognised that had Bloy appealed to rational criticism and historical learning he would only have raised insurmountable difficulties for sceptical reason that is programmed to destroy and pull to pieces analytically but not to construct and build the great picture that maps the fullness of life for us. They had studied Plotinus and Pascal and had engaged the best minds in conversation. So, instead of trying to reach a conclusion by argument and inference, he presented them with the lives and writings of the saints and mystics. He exposed them to the experience and holiness of the saints. It was only natural that Raissa Maritain should place the story of their baptism in the chapter entitled "The Call of the Saints". The most forceful and most categorical disclosure of God is in the lives of the saints. In them we see God as our hope and our happiness at work because they are bound to him in the love of charity. We see God in the interaction and the struggle with which the saints move and are drawn toward him, in which their consciousness is transformed by a response which they may not perhaps recognise as divine and grace-filled. It is a tragedy that so much Catholic formal theology has reputed sanctity to be a sign of the genuineness of the Church without linking it to spirituality, morality and practical Christian living.

The aim of this book is to show how holiness transfuses and permeates every aspect of living. It will be necessary at each stage to show how the categories of ethics and moral theory relate to and serve human fulfilment and happiness, that is, how they fit with our going to God as our happiness. One must pass to the theology of the saints such as John of the Cross, who united mystic experience with the expression of his theology in poetry. St Alphonsus expressed the deepest insights of his moral theology in his *Practice of the Love of Jesus Christ*. These saints joined their experience of God with the teaching of Scripture and the Fathers and the formal analytic categories of theology. It was their living awareness of God as their all that enlivened their whole project. Their experience flows into the linguistic resources of the culture to transform it, while it in turn becomes the medium of communication for their experience. The impact of saints is measured by their good fruits in the culture. We can see God somehow in their encounter with the holy. What was it that led them to God so as to make an act of faith if not their absolute dedication to the truth? Their enquiries were filled with a sense of reverence that drew them into the truth that they could finally name as God, or, more concretely, God in Christ. In this way

faith becomes a surrender to the absolute Lordship of Christ.
Here is a summons to obedience that precedes every other
claim. There is no precept or determination or law or other
revelation that is more powerful and binding. There is an
intentional experience of God, a connatural disclosure of the
holy in all that is mediated in everything one confronts. This
can only be called "living by the light", and it brings with it an
interior transformation to sainthood. Here all values of truth,
justice, love, beauty and concern for humanity hold together
in one absolute commitment that orients the whole of life.
This closeness of God in our inner commitments is indeed the
work of the Spirit that conforms us to Christ so that we see in
ourselves the likeness and image of God. This is the encounter
with him in whom all things hold together, Christ the image of
the unseen God. Now all of the disclosures of God in history
are Trinitarian and come to us as manifestations of holiness or
the transcendent. The highest instantiation of holiness is Jesus
of Nazareth, the holy one of God. Even outside the range of
explicitly formulated Christian faith and practice this assertion about sanctity is verified by the experience of sainthood
in world history as contact with God as he who holistically
unifies life and history. And even where he is not personally
recognised, the mystery of a transcendent purpose remains.
It is of course true of all religions that the absolutely transcendent is somehow manifested through them.

8.   Where are the saints for postmodernity?

Dostoevsky was haunted by the prospect of portraying a
wholly good person. "Nothing is more difficult," he said,
"especially in our time."[7] More than ever postmodernity challenges ethicists to say what could be morally sensible when all
systems of thought are jumbled together and seem to fail. It
seems that nothing is proof against the charge that there is no
longer a valid morality, since all morality has been subverted
by the flood of Nietzsche's nihilism so that ethics turns into its
opposite, namely nihilism. But postmodernity is not simply
antinomianism, since it does admit that what is valid must be

verified not by ideas *in abstracto* but by lived experience. Postmodernity does not look to an opposite of ethics, but to life narratives and particularly those of the saints. These at once overturn our conception of morality as a set or code of moral rules, and yet there is an overlap with the greatest values where these rules find their worth. The twentieth century is witness to the violent planned deaths of more people through nuclear, chemical and biological warfare than any other period in history. Edith Wyschogrod has called this new historical horizon "the death event". Previously natural disasters such as floods and earthquakes were spaced and accompanied by a natural sense of awe. But protracted wars in Vietnam or Yugoslavia daily presented on the television have deadened our sensitivity to death, pain and violence. The ills of our world are so horrendous they require extreme measures. Now the world's religious traditions have in the past addressed the problems of the wretched of the earth, in the person of saints, those who put themselves and their lives totally at the service of others. In this sense charity may be found hidden in all traditions, at least to the eye of Christians, though Christian terminology is not used. Here is a concept whose various realisations are capable of sustaining dialogue between diverse religious traditions in their search for the transcendent.

As already said, the antiseptic air of modernism does not allow saints to breathe. In a postmodern view of ethics it is not first a normative discipline but the sphere or area of transaction between the self and the Other that one encounters in compassion. It does not look to traditional philosophical discourse to provide ready answers for human conduct. The narrative of the postmodern self exposes the presuppositions of the discourse of modernity as it runs up against the experience of a disjointed chaotic world. It does this by tuning our experience to the apocalyptic dimension of twentieth-century experience. One cannot help thinking of Vietnam as in the title of the film *Apocalypse Now*. What is typical of postmodernity is that it can leave empty spaces in a perfectly balanced pattern and allow discontinuities and illogicalities in life cycles. It is a combination of pleasure and pain, of good and evil, about which we have become reflexively and acutely aware. It seems that it is worked out without rules, but these only emerge by reflection when the work is done. The rules come to light only after they have been used. Sanctity is seen only in the lives of the saints. In this way the closed thought-structures of the past are broken, and past and future are recognised in their otherness from the present moment. What is proposed here is that since conflicting moral theories land us in an impasse we move to a narrative conception of ethics that highlights the highest achievements of persons in their search for God, namely sanctity. Here we have a multitude of conflicting voices and open-endedness to the issues raised by contemporary experience. There are disruptive fragments and flashbacks that all go into the one narrative. The critical perspective of rational analysis prevents a collapse into sentimentalism, a sort of kitsch of ethical theory. At the same time it should be able to communicate with a wide public. Postmodern writing and works of art are said to be double coded, i.e., they have passed through both the prism of modern rational criticism and the need to have contemporary popular appeal. They have to be analysed and deconstructed as well as resynthesised and newly constructed for life as now lived. This is a conversation of the critical, analytic spirit with contemporary lifestyles and conditions. There will be an amount of necessary eclecticism; from traditional philosophy of Plato, Aristotle and Aquinas to language analysis, semiotics and phenomenology. Altruism is revealed as compassion for the Other because of a passion for transcendence. It is sceptical about all appeals to good and to norms because they have acted as props for powers that did not declare their hand. They were, in short, discourses of power. What stimulates a new search for some anchorage for our ontology and normative standards is the process of planetisation, the fact that this earth has one destiny dependent on our moral decisions. This seems to be the way out of apocalypse back to moral theory. Our postmodern experience has gazed into the abyss of anxiety where all order was gone, the future could not be visualised and all force was swallowed into the black hole of inner emptiness. Against this we must recognise persons and their differences that make them unique and infinitely valuable. It is now the other person who opens

the door to an ethics of the self. This is not so much a conceptual anchorage as a living force. The Other's existence carries
compelling moral weight. Lastly, the existence of the Other is
bound up with physical need and therefore with the materiality
of the body.

By turning to the narrative of saintly life we have criteria
with which to judge ethical theory against the proven quality
of the good. It is a source for a revision, for a rethinking of
ethics. Here the rational, critical perspective of moral theology
contacts a new range of contemporary experience, a new way
of searching after God. The life of a saint originates in and is
nourished by and helps form some community. Irrespective of
the cost to self the saint is dedicated to the Other. The life of
the saint is not normative as setting down a rule for holiness. It
is a force that sweeps people up to follow and to imitate. The
power of compassion is to transform in a godly way all existence down into its roots in bodily being. The body always
pertains to a particular, unique person. It belongs to a person's
total existence and is not merely a part to be set off separately
from the inner spirit. Thus sexual desire, the demands of time
and tiredness etc. go to the making of a saint. Gender plays its
part, and time is lived experience not a chronometer measuring external physical change. Desire leads to ecstasy and
generosity toward the Other. This is the hallmark of sanctity.

What we have established is that we are inflamed with a
desire for God, a drive to transcendence. This is a force whose
highest achievement is sanctity, the perfection of love as compassion for the Other who is overwhelmed by want as a
spiritual and bodily pain that can be soothed and healed by our
compassion, by an ethic of generosity. Our challenge is to
give our moral theology a human face by making our theory
match our experience, by making it truly applicable in our
world. That is our goal.

NOTES

1. *The Mystery of the Supernatural*, trans. Rosemary Sheed, Herder and Herder, New York 1967, 70.
2. *The Discovery of God*, trans. Alexander Dru, J.P. Kenedy and Son, New York 1960, 40.
3. *A New Catechism: Catholic Faith for Adults*, Herder and Herder, New York 1967, 3 from the Venerable Bede's *Ecclesiastical History of the English People*.
4. *Why I Am Not a Christian*, Unwin Books, London 1971, 15.
5. *A Path From Rome: An Autobiography*, Oxford University Press, Oxford 1986, 208-209.
6. *The Two Sources of Morality and Religion*, Doubleday and Co., Garden City, New York 1935, 240-241.
7. From a letter to Maikov, 31 December 1867, as quoted by Edith Wyschogrod, *Saints and Postmodernism*, University of Chicago Press, Chicago 1990, 1.

2

The sense of Christian morality

The intent of Christianity which this book seeks to serve is that of salvation. Salvation is worked by God with our assent and cooperation. It used till recent centuries to be a common assumption for all ethical systems influenced by European philosophy. That is no longer so with the Copernican revolution not only in science but in human awareness. The purpose of ethics is often stated as the self-fulfilment of the individual beginning with the sources of his or her awareness. The self has thereby become the basis of morality, and self-redemption the programme for modern society.

1. Christians in a pluralistic society

Can Christianity find space as a necessary source of meaning in such a society? The greatest challenge for the Church today is to be able to define a Christian stance in a pluralistic society. What is contested is the Christian claim to uniqueness. Are we not all equally human? Do we not all share the same frightful burden of war, famine and injustice? Do Christians really pretend, as Karl Barth did, that when spaceship earth flounders and goes down, the barque of the Church will sail by, picking up lost humanity, wafting it off to the safety of salvation in heaven? Barth thought God was only interested in his Church and did not care to save an evil world. Such an account of Christianity is so unearthly as to be incredible to modern ears. What we are convinced of is that there is only one earth, and that we sink or swim with it. And as a race we are all part of one human history on the face of the one earth. We cannot be safe and sure in our destiny apart from the earth on which we live, move and have our being. If the Church claims salvation as her special competence then she must guarantee this mandate by showing how the future of the planet is secure. The Church is not an alternative destiny to what the world wants and strives for. No! She is the means of being successfully fully human and reaching a perfect fulfilment we could not dream up or plan simply by ourselves.

How do we place the Church in a pluralistic society? We do not put her outside the society. She is not only part of the society, she is immanent to the society in its deepest dynamism and aspirations. In other words she does not have another path to follow than that of what is genuinely human. The present Pope has an expression that puts this truth simply and tellingly: man is the way for the Church. We would say, in inclusive language: humanity is the path for the Church to pursue and follow. This means that this human history as the sum of our moral striving is the story of salvation or of what seems inconceivable, its failure in loss and destruction. We are so very conscious of belonging to the one world and, in a very personal way, of belonging to one another. No one would want to survive and be saved if it were not with every other person. Here is another of our spontaneous convictions: we look forward and long for the salvation not only of the whole world but of the whole of humanity. Now if that be so the Church is for every person the way to meaning and salvation.

2. Renewing Catholic thinking

The Second Vatican Council was not just an occasion for the Church to declare where she stood as regards humanity, its history and its destiny. She did more. She actually changed her place, or better, perhaps, her attitude and stance toward the modern world. By listening to the world that had grown to adult status and come to flourish over the last few centuries the Church saw that it was not so much necessary to proclaim new dogmas as to actualise her truth in the society where she lived. This was no withdrawal from dogmatic truth. No! It was contact with that truth as it needs to be lived today. It was not just proclaiming Christ, but knowing from the intimacy of faith, "for me to live is Christ". He is my very existence so that I define myself by him.

Perhaps the position of the Church in the world was best put by Christ in his parables: the yeast that leavens the dough, the tree in which every bird on the face of the earth has a home, the field in which the harvest of human effort matures... The Council Fathers recognised that any identity, whether of the Church or of humanity, is forged from the fruits of past achievements, present decisions and the defining horizon of the future. Identity knits together constancy and change through the dynamics of transmitting the treasures of the past to the future by human action assisted by the Spirit. Thus the traditional Christian message of salvation has to be actualised for the future.

Pope Paul VI must be credited as the one who saw what needed to be done all in one sweep. His encyclical *Ecclesiam Suam* in 1963 was the vision statement that set the programme for the Council. Paul VI accepted the phenomenological method as a valid methodology to put the Church in contact with contemporary ways of thinking. He thereby submitted his reflection in its very beginning to the data of consciousness and how these formed an awareness of self-identity. In other words he was working within the new universe of thought brought about by the Copernican revolution in philosophy over the last few centuries. This was the novelty in his approach, which was nothing other than the "new treasure" the Gospel speaks of as now being brought into the Church's inheritance. To verify that it belonged to the Church's inheritance it had to be tested against the tradition as a true expression of the Church's thought. The theology of St Thomas Aquinas is a necessary point of reference, as was made clear by the Council. It was necessary to do this for another reason, namely, to overcome the anti-metaphysical prejudices of much of modern thought. This ontology functions as a basic groundwork against which to corroborate newer findings in anthropology, philosophy and the sciences. This traditional ontology has also been rethought and renewed in this century and this provided another stimulus inspiring the Church to reformulate her message for today.

The Church's stance in a pluralistic society is one of dialogue. She wants to be open to all truth from whatever current or corner it may come. Paul VI projected an image of the Church with her identity at the centre and around her, in ever wider-spreading concentric circles, the choirs of humanity. At the very outer rim are those who will have nothing of God either as an idea or a way of life. This is the problem of atheism and it is in fact the biggest challenge the Church faces, because so many atheists were once children of the Church and have now become professedly post-Christian. Its most obvious form was political or state atheism as was imposed in the ex-Communist countries. Since the fall of the Berlin Wall in 1989 this type of system of anti-God belief has collapsed with it. It has, however, left deep marks in the consciousness of the peoples who lived under its hegemony, and this is presently the source of many moral problems. Nor should it be forgotten that such systems still exist, at least in part, in Asia, in China, North Korea and Vietnam. Those who live as if God did not exist may well be the majority of the population if one were to look for consistency between faith enlivened by Christ living in a person's mind and heart and their everyday pragmatic activity. The radical separation of faith and life, of belief and action, is nothing less than atheism in action. It is often the professed faith of a liberal society which wants to keep the Church out of secular affairs because it will put limits on the liberties thought to have been won from repressive religion. Here the Church has been stereotyped as the enemy of freedom. However, it is only a firm grasp on reality and its truth that makes these freedoms real and can lead to the mental conviction of their rightness. The Church makes her appeal to a wider and more genuine understanding of freedom, not as an absolute but as the deepest expression of a person's dominion over self. This means being able to love completely, even unto death and martyrdom for what is utterly right and true were it demanded. Freedom is the way to self-realisation by a donation of oneself and not as an absolutely closed monad sufficient unto itself. It is perhaps ironic that it is in so-called Christian nations that we encounter severely secularised societies. This is true of most of Europe, North America, Australasia and parts of Asia that are strongly developed. In this type of society secular autonomous ethics is often in severe conflict with a Christian vision of the person living in society with an eternal destiny. One of the most penetrating effects of this process is the fact that the idea of salvation has lost its meaning even as a merely human ideal. Such is the force of nihilism in ethics and on popular culture. Even reason itself comes to be doubted in a technological society that, as Jung said, has lost its soul and so proves ever more unsatisfying and vacuous to itself. This emptiness is often filled by spurious forms of religion, by the gnosticism of New Age sects and the fascination with the paranormal and even with dabbling in the diabolic. The Western world is really calling on the Church to show how to give meaning to existence in a new world and a new context.

The next inner circle is that of the religions that do not have revelation from God as their foundation. Here we find the followers of cosmic religions (sometimes called primitive religions), ancestor worship etc. Of special concern are Hinduism, Buddhism, Taoism, Confucianism and all the great world religions that do not depend on revelation. Often they show a balance between heaven and earth or look for a state of illumination that will release us from all earthly passion and thereby from the evil of the world. Quite often the idea of God is either not properly and formally formulated or is not at all clear. Often too there is the ideal of harmony or of illumination, but certainly not what Christians understand by salvation. These religions sometimes are philosophies of life, sometimes they are cultic and even more rarely moral by providing teaching on the sense of right and wrong. They incorporate great wisdom about life and its meaning, but rarely see a strong link between this and moral goodness. The idea of sin remains quite physical or external and undeveloped. Ritual may wipe it away without a deep inner change. Christian ethics can provoke a sense of the person, of responsibility, of being part of an infinite destiny of love for such cultures.

The Church's work here is that of announcing how the human person has infinite worth before God. The integrity of existence demands an inner unity of creed, code and cult that these religions often have not achieved.

The religions of the book are more coherent because they have revelation as the self-manifestation of God as their reason for existence. In this third outer circle God's Word establishes the way of life to be followed. A person becomes pleasing to God by obeying his directions, his revealed will. The three great religions of revelation are historical religions, since they came into being through God's action or intervention in history. In the case of Islam God remains a complete mystery and Muhammad is his prophet. Revelation is understood as an act by which God dictated the Koran to Muhammad. In strict Islamic theology the Koran is literally God's word and cannot be analysed or scientifically studied by the historical-critical method as has been done in the West with the Hebrew and Christian Bible over the last few centuries. None the less, Islamic scholars and lawyers have had to interpret it so as to make it practical for living. They have a long and sophisticated history of casuistry as well of theology that concentrates on their absolute monotheism. There is no distinction or difference in God, so that believers must yield their intellects to his absolute unity. The Jewish people has a finer sense of history. They know that God made himself manifest slowly and by stages as a good guide and educator of his people. They know that he cannot be seen directly but only in darkness as in a cloud, e.g., in the great experience of Moses as the lawgiver for the nation. The prophets taught Israel to await a Messiah. When he came in Christ the revelation of divinity in human flesh was such a strong revelation and communication of God that Christ was a scandal to both Jews and Muslims. The underlying problem is not that God is so hidden but that he has made himself too visible for Jews and Muslims, so that God becoming man is to them tantamount to blasphemy. In common with Christianity these religions of the book conceive of morality as doing the will of God as made known through their sacred books which communicate the will and commandments of the Almighty.

3. The Church's new consciousness of herself

When we come to the inner circle of Christianity we are
faced with the sad fact of division among the followers of
Christ. All Christians agree that he is "the one for the many",
or, in Hans Urs von Balthasar's expression, "the concrete
universal". The centre of Christian belief is that "in him alone
is salvation", and that there is hope in no other. This indeed is
the stumbling-block for our world. Since the Enlightenment
the question of revelation has been the meeting place, the
crossroad where all the tensions of an enlightened, rational
and autonomous culture met. Can God make himself visible,
his help real for us and his will known in the world? Christianity is a scandal not because it speaks about revelation; many
others may do that. Hindus hinge all on the illumination of the
mind; Muslims and Jews believe that God has shone the light
of his truth into the world. But Christianity claims an absolute
revelation which cannot be gainsaid. The West, which has
become embittered with religious strife and discord, which is
disillusioned with its own lack of meaning, keeps asking itself
if Christianity can still renew itself and bring itself back to
life. After all, Christianity has been a cultural force on the
decline over the last few centuries. To throw one's lot in with
Christianity is no longer seen as being on the winning side in
most political and cultural conflicts. In short, Europe in particular has become wearied of Christianity and wonders if the
Church can still do good and renew contemporary culture. The
other great alternative is belief in human self-redemption and
the future that humanity can form for itself from its own
progress by the power of native intelligence and will. It is
against this background that Paul VI and now John Paul II
have called for a "second evangelisation" of the countries that
have considered themselves pillars of the faith but today are
deeply secularised.

The fact is that Christianity has something to say to the
developed countries of the West, something that is decisive
for them and humanity. And if it does not find the strength
and courage to do so there is no other power, ideology or
religion that could ever substitute it, for Christ is the full and

perfect manifestation of God, the Word made flesh; in him God reveals himself and is revealed. He draws together the whole of human history to effect its salvation. Christianity has a unique position that distinguishes it from the other religions whose claims are also based on revelation but which contest its claim to uniqueness. It is the only religion in which revelation is incarnate in a person who presents himself as the living and absolute truth. Christ welcomes in himself all the shades and aspects of truth discovered right down the centuries. He embraces in himself truth's transcendence as propounded by the Platonists; the historicity of truth as discovered by contemporary humanistic studies, and the interiority or immanence of truth so dear to existentialists and personalists. Christ is not just the founder of a religion. He is at one and the same time the Son of God made man, immanent to the history of humanity and yet utterly transcendent to it. He is the one mediator of meaning so as to be called "the sole exegete of the human condition and its problems".[1] It is precisely the function of revelation to help us discover the freshness of this, the first reality of Christianity, the person of Christ. To recognise the specificity and therefore the uniqueness of his person and how it has inwardly transformed the history of the world and with it the meaning of morality is not a mere matter of choice. It belongs to the nature of things for a theology that aspires at the one time to be both contextual and systematic. It is no secret that the bishops at the Second Vatican Council thought that moral theology was more in need of reform than any other ecclesiastical discipline. They called for it to be nourished from the mystery of Christ as revealed in Scripture. That means that Christians partake in the very life of Christ by sharing his paschal mystery of suffering, death and resurrection to become images of God. They wanted this divine life of humanity to be explained systematically with a sound philosophical base. Further, moral theology was to be inserted into the context of today's world so as to bear positive fruit for the upbuilding and benefit of the whole race. With this statement in the Decree on the Training of Priests the Council thereby opened up moral theology to the whole world and its problems. In fact its task became that of encountering the world's problems and seeking solutions to them out of the Church's "treasures new and old". This was a revolutionary change to which moral theologians have not as yet fully readjusted. One must remember that moral theology over the last three or four centuries had developed along the lines of casuistry as a service to priests in their ministry in the confessional. It was the most practical pastoral discipline, not greatly concerned with philosophy or with justifying its principles but with applying them correctly. It had been perfected on the model of jurisprudence where the priest became the accused's advocate with God. It was more important to win the case than to draw up a perfect theory of why this was so. Of course, this practice led to the abuse we know as legalism, i.e., that of thinking of morality as limited to obedience to a code of behavioural rules under the threat of eternal punishment. The Council shifted the emphasis from the individual to the community and to social obligations. Largely as a result of the Council, problems of hunger, population, war and human economic development became the focus of attention, and human rights tended to become the key moral term in moral arguments.

4. Non-believers and moral theology

The challenge that immediately faced Catholic moralists in dialogue with the world was that of finding a common language and understanding even with non-believers. They were asked to give an account of the specifically Christian quality of their morality. This was the theme for the French Catholic Intellectuals' Week in 1966. Their reflections began from the premise that Christian morality was in crisis, and many held that there was a community between Catholics and all others in society and that on this basis the crisis should be faced and resolved. The world in which Christians lived was no different from that of the others; all shared the same problems. Faith evoked a depth and perspective that non-believers could not find inside themselves without the gift of conversion to Christ. This gift revealed what our common humanity should be in its fullness. Christian morality must therefore be presented as basically human in a world that judged moralities by their humanistic qualities. What provoked such attention to a non-believing world was the fact of secularisation, the fact that section after section of contemporary culture was being emancipated from any dependence on or link with the Church and the vision of faith. This was becoming true of education not only in the universities, but in lyceums, secondary schools and even down into infants' schools. There was also a drive to remove explicit mention of Christian values from the civil law so as to ensure that all citizens were completely equal and undiscriminated against.

The movement for reform in moral theology was supported by the neo-scholastics because they recognised that its way of thinking could be assaulted not only from outside, but that it was inwardly vulnerable and weak. They set about correcting the juridical approach that emphasised a casuistry centred on sin that had utterly forgotten social ethics. Since Leo XIII's revolutionary encyclical *Rerum Novarum* the Church's social teaching, although profoundly moral, had grown up outside the narrow concerns of moral theology. The present pontiff, John Paul II, has called for its integration into a renewed and rethought moral theology. The crisis that has typified the last two to three decades in moral theology was precipitated first by rapid change in society and then by a lack of coherence in moral theology's own account of itself. In the midst of this time of difficulty moralists tended to lose confidence in whatever philosophy they had traditionally trusted. St Thomas was definitely out of fashion. They had to find resources with which to answer the questions put by the world.

This need was exacerbated by the debates following the issuing of the encyclical *Humanae Vitae* in July 1968. What was put in question was the Church's authority to teach on matters of natural morality that were perceived to be not of faith as such. It was widely asked: if a teaching is not infallible, how can the Church claim it binds in conscience? This discussion brought forth a debate on the foundation and justification of norms based on the natural law. In other words, how could a coherently rational account of the norms for birth regulation be found. The accounts of natural law with which moralists were familiar were discredited as being physicalist or biologistic. Many of the theories previously invoked had been based on the premise that natural processes dictated moral rules. There was widespread rebellion at this idea, which was commonly but wrongly accepted as what the encyclical taught. What was required were rational arguments to prove that human nature was like this on the basis of human reason without invoking information supplied by faith. This implied that a person who faced the dilemma of contraception was capable by him/herself of deciding its morality and that Church authority had no right of access to personal conscience. Such a person was pictured as autonomous with a thoughtful, adult and mature conscience. It was precisely at this moment that the debate about a specifically Christian ethic became or was absorbed into the new proposal on an autonomous morality. Josef Fuchs put the new position in a neat slogan, "For a truly human morality, moral action means nothing other than 'being human', 'being rational'."[2]

5. The autonomy of morality

Morality was really coming to terms with the tradition of the Enlightenment out of which the modern world had grown. In Germany, in particular, discussions that had been dormant for more than a century were rekindled. The tension between rationalism and fideism flared up again. The person to initiate the new thinking was Alphons Auer, with his book *Autonomous Morality and Christian Faith*. His thesis was formulated as that of an "autonomous morality in a Christian context". He understands morality as our "yes" to the reality of the world and the events that surround us and make up our lives. Faced with these realities we respond rationally and this response is totally human, being recognised as correct because it is based on reason as a self-justifying power. We develop norms and rules of conduct by reflecting on what happens about us and interpreting it humanly by the use of reason. We develop a philosophy of the human which is mediated by the findings of the social sciences. In this way the sciences are integrated into our human self-understanding.

Auer argued that in the Scriptures of both the Old and New Testaments the chosen people did not have a morality that was specifically their own, but did in fact absorb their ethical stance from the surrounding culture into their faith vision. Thus the covenant consecrated and purified the moral customs typical of life in the desert tribes. Even the prophets did little more than recall how that morality was to be applied to settled life in towns and cities as a renewed faith in their saving God. Auer holds further that the Fathers of the Church argued that what Christians did was only what everybody believed was right. It was their faith that gave them the strength to do so. The great medieval theologians also showed how human morality fitted into a scheme of Christian faith without losing its fundamental human characteristics. The Enlightenment brought to the fore the thesis that justified this stance, viz., that morality is autonomous and so needs to be established on its own terms.

B. Schüller supports this position, noting that moral demands must be of their nature intelligible and so communicable to all. Morality in its proper sense is constituted by reason and must be interpreted by reason. Now the faith gives to believers a comprehension of the salvific form of their relationship with humanity in history. Morality is the concrete working out of this relationship in a purely and fully rational way. The faith is a help at the practical level to understand the content and intent of moral rules. Dietmar Mieth says that an atheist would found the autonomy of a purely rational morality only on him or herself and the necessary structures of their thought and action. A Christian would give this autonomy an ultimate sense from their faith. The faith thereby functions as an integrating, stimulating and motivating agent within the horizon of what God has done for humanity. The faith has not contributed a new ethical system to the world but a new "ethos". Beginning from the practice or praxis of morality, autonomy elaborates what is rationally required by way of norms.

6. Challenges to autonomous morality

Autonomous morality among Catholic thinkers was a radical but seemingly balanced attempt to come to terms with the ethical thinking that grew out of Kant's critique of both pure and practical reason. This attempt, like earlier attempts last century, was not successful. These had been severely censured by the magisterium. The encyclical *Veritatis Splendor* mentioned no individual moralist by name, but it did clarify that a radically autonomous ethic could not be reconciled with the doctrine of creation and the fact that God is at the head and source of the moral order. A more immediate reaction to autonomous morality came in the seventies, with what has been named an "ethics of the faith", that is, an ethics that is derived from the faith as an immediate and essential consequent logically and ontologically. The radical cause cited is that reason is so weakened by Adam's fall that it could never hope for, much less realise, the autonomy proposed above. Bernhard Stoeckle held that the ideal of autonomy was always ambiguous. In its manifestations in secularisation, the independence and emancipation of reason to claim an adult status was never able to be fully realised by anybody, let alone by all. It contradicted the human condition and broke every link with God. Konrad Hilpert studied the history of the word's use and concluded that given its connotations of always being independent of God it could not be successfully used in theology. Stoeckle further argued that the rightful subject of autonomy properly understood was the human person and not reason as such. This seemed to make the dignity of the person subject to the law reason imposed, rather than make morality serve the good and growth of the person. Logically, if reason is so absolutely autonomous, a regress to infinity cannot be avoided. It further implies a reduction of the faith to what is human and can be judged solely by human standards. Stoeckle tended toward a fideism that saw revelation as absolutely necessary for reason and human nature to be themselves, so deeply have they been destructively transformed by original sin. So against the exaggerations of autonomy based on pure reason we see the objection that faith and tradition are necessary for humanity to function rationally at all. This is certainly a throw-back to the clash of faith and reason last century and brings us back to solving problems that were never satisfactorily dealt with then. Many authors believe that if we take an autonomous ethic to its bitter conclusion, in fact we arrive at a neo-eudemonianism, or the self-sufficient search for pleasure as its own reward. This has become the style of life typical of the me-generation and the autonomous self. Stoeckle's image of the human is that of a lost and hidden subject deprived of hope because faith and a direct, real and ontological relationship with God has become impossible. Once the faith is abandoned human action lacks the clarity and certitude needed to guide it to the good and the strength needed to actualise the good.

H. Schürmann challenged autonomous ethics as an accurate account of what is given in revelation through the Scriptures. His concern was with the New Testament.[3] He would say that in Christ heteronomous law became the criteria for autonomous law in that all one held in Christian conscience as one's own proper law flowed from the teaching of Christ as the manifestation of God's transcendent will for our salvation. Nor would he agree that the transcendent-categorical distinction was a rightful presentation of the ethics of the New Testament. New Testament imperatives such as the Beatitudes are intended to be brought down and realised in determinate particular actions. They can thus be the rules for universal categorical classes of action. He agrees that morality on the strength of the internal evidence of the New Testament writings is rational, but this in conjunction with and not in opposition to the faith. He believes this holds true of St Paul's treatment of marriage problems in 1 Corinthians 7, where the command of the Lord establishing the indissolubility of Christian sacramental marriage has to be worked out rationally in difficult cases of application.

When New Testament commands thus go back to the words or deeds of the Saviour we still have to show that they were willed by Christ as permanently binding on his Church. This means that such things as women wearing a veil in church or the language to be used in the liturgy were

something historically conditioned and determined. The
apostles and their successors were empowered by the Lord to
interpret authentically these injunctions. This office is continued in the charism of moral teaching exercised by the
successors of Peter and the apostles.

Hans Urs von Balthasar proposes a faith ethic properly so
called. Christian morality is only responsible when performed
in front of, that is, in the presence of Christ who is the "concrete universal" for all morality, and so its ultimate norm. It is
for or against Christ that one makes the fundamental choice
that determines one's whole life. "Christ is the concrete categorical imperative."[4] It is the faith that overcomes the inbuilt
tension between autonomy and heteronomy, for by accepting
God's life in Christ we gain freedom while becoming "slaves
of Christ", as St Paul says. It is only in the inmost intimacy of
the human heart that the Spirit of God can reconcile these two
claims. The heteronomy of the law ceased when God wrote it
on our hearts through his grace. It is the gift of God's grace
that comes from outside ourselves that brings us closest to
ourselves and guarantees our identity. Thus any human contact and communication presupposes our dialogue with God
and with humanity as already established in and by grace. Von
Balthasar thus considers all the types of autonomous ethics as
distortions of our true relationship with God. Instead of waiting with patience as indicated by the Scriptures, the law is laid
down as an absolute, an "ought" that must be obeyed in all
circumstances. He sees such autonomous law as being so
strong-headedly convinced of its own absolute value that it
comes to usurp the place of God in the human heart. No ethic
therefore should abstract from the Word of God, for all moral
activity is only a response to what he has offered in grace. The
objection is that autonomous ethical systems, whether Kantian,
neo-Kantian or even the value system of Scheler, all construct
a self-legislating subject who is self-limiting. The other choice
is to make the law totally external so that it accuses the agent
of acting wrongly and so causes guilt, but without any reference to the dynamics of expectation and hope attached to law
as coming from a faithful, merciful God, as in the Scriptures.

All extra-biblical moralities are then but fragmentary

reflections of what God has revealed. When a person awakens to a consciousness not only of being human but that this implies being moral because he or she is called to a responsible attitude before another person, it is impossible for that person not to raise the question of the moral meaning of the whole of life and reality. In this moment the light of reason discloses to him or her the natural law which as such cannot be absolute and must therefore be open to the transcendent. And to this there corresponds a drive or tendency to unconditioned good, or goodness without limit. This transparency of the image of God that constitutes the human subject is, according to Hans Urs von Balthasar, a memory of our original state at creation. It remains as a preconscious substrate to which the revelation in the Old and New Testaments is addressed. So long as this original intuition of absolute good is not in harmony with our actual responses to goodness there is need of moral norms from outside to guide us. Thus the natural law is an echo of God's original revelation and still stands in need of the clarifying illumination of revelation in Christ.

The fragments of good to be found in non-Christian religions and natural ethics are pointers to the fullness of truth in Christ. This would apply for example to Gandhi or Tagore. Morality is pessimistic when God has not manifested his will through revelation so that humans are left to seek the sense of things through the order they can discover in the world. Christianity brings with it a new liberty, a capacity for spontaneous spiritual action that neither human nature nor order in the world could ever supply. This is the freedom of the children of God accompanying grace. It would seem that a post-Christian ethics founded on an I-Thou dialogue would overcome this impasse. But von Balthasar takes that to mean that a person is indebted to another human and so this ethic is heteronomous. It too finds its foundation in a human subjective consciousness that requires a divine Subject to make sense of and found the relationship of the two human consciousnesses. Death is the last and final destroyer of this integration between the self and social existence. Von Balthasar argues that it is only the resurrection that can guarantee and make that integration successful. His position is that there is no room for autonomy as such.

7. Reason and revelation

As can only be too obvious, there is a polarisation not only
in ethics but in contemporary moral theology as well. The two
tendencies may be described as either full trust in reason and
its autonomy as capable of reaching its own ends, or complete
distrust of reason since it is too weak and distorted to achieve
its inherent goal. As extremes these represent the positions of
rationalism and fideism. The first has given birth to autonomous moral theology or autonomous reason working in a
Christian context; the other to faith ethics where the whole
elaboration of ethics cannot be achieved without the intervention of revelation. The problem is that revelation has been
conceived as not leaving space for reason in its traditionally
proper function. On the other hand, reason can be so strong as
to expel faith and revelation from all the concerns of reason.
This too is intolerable. The debate as we have seen has been
carried on at many levels – anthropological, ethical, scriptural
and even scientific and empirical – and there has been great
difficulty in arriving at common understanding at any one
level, much less across the whole spectrum. For example, at
the historical level Joseph Ratzinger's reasoning leads to a
strong faith ethic while in logic his ethical theory would not
seem to differ radically from Auer's autonomous ethic.

The official Catholic position in papal magisterial statements has historically been hostile to autonomy in the sense of
the ideal set up by Kant and then Fichte. This tendency has
continued with the critique launched against modern systems
of thought that work against the linking of faith and ethics in
life. The idea of a self-enclosed autonomy has thereby been
once again firmly rejected.

8. Moral relativism

If the Catholic community is so intellectually divided over
the interpretation of basic moral notions, the situation is much
more complex and varied among secular thinkers. Rapid social
change has precipitated multiple ways of looking at social and

moral issues. A country such as the United States has been able to reconcile its religious differences for some generations now. The right to religious freedom was assured by the Constitution and it became a strength of the nation, for it accepted that people could be sincere in their religious conscience and should not be legally constrained by an established religion. However, on issues such as abortion, capital punishment, business practices, nuclear arms and aggressive warfare the community seems utterly and irretrievably divided. Today the issues which cause rift and rupture in the social fabric are moral, and as yet there is no consensus on how these issues are to be faced. What results is a multiple account of morality and how to reach the right decision. It is a small move from there to a distrust in reason, saying that reason has to be applied in science where results can be experimentally confirmed, but in ethics it comes down to a case of preference. This is the theory of emotivism that A. MacIntyre so successfully criticised at the beginning of *After Virtue*. What we are threatened with is a situation of moral relativism where each and every person may make choices without regard to common values or a universally binding morality to be acknowledged by all in conscience. Moral relativism holds that there can be no absolute truth binding on all because of the differences in ethos and diverse beliefs over time and between individuals, groups and societies. There is, therefore, relativists say, no way of deciding the differences between ethical codes. They often see ethical codes in a functionalist way as having no other role than the maintenance and defence of society. Terms such as "good", "right" and "ought" vary across time, among individuals and in societies in such a way that two fundamentally different ethical beliefs about what is good, right or what ought to be done can both be true. Radical relativists hold that ethical statements hold no truth value or even that all are equally false. An attitude commonly met is that it is ethically wrong to pass ethical judgement on the behaviour and practice of another individual, group or society with a substantially different ethical code, or that it is wrong to intervene in the affairs of another individual, group or society on the basis of that judgement. This, of course, leads to an ethic of non-judgemental tolerance and non-intervention, but such a universal prescription would become incoherent when applied to societies that interfere in the affairs of others on the basis of ethical judgements. A weaker form of the same is found in contractualism, wherein individuals are required to consent to the principles that govern them. This stance is usually held to require the hypothesis that such consent can be given only by fully rational individuals. This position presumes that one justifies one's treatment of others in a way that they would accept as fully rational individuals. In reality this is a criterion that can never be properly realised; it shows the incoherence of such rationalism and why it must lead to relativism or nihilism.

Moral pluralism is the idea that fundamental moral principles, norms and ideals are so diverse that they cannot be reconciled into any harmonious system of morality. Sir Isaiah Berlin defended this view, "What is clear is that values can clash – that is why civilisations are incompatible."[5] The values of ancient Athens, Renaissance Florence and contemporary China are so different as to be irreconcilable. Berlin added that "the notion of the perfect whole... in which all good things co-exist... is... conceptually incoherent... Some among the Great Goods cannot live together." This view rejects relativism, where values end as merely subjective and matters of preference. There is a real difference between civilisations, in which we do not always find the intellectual means to see these as parts of one vision and so to reconcile them among themselves. However, the fact that we recognise them all as moral visions bespeaks the fact that there is a deeper unity even if we are incapable as yet of describing and analysing it. Moral dilemmas are given as a reason for moral pluralism. Take, for example, the various reactions to people going out on a ledge at a great height to rescue a stranded person. If the ledge will support only one rescuer, many will feel that they should not risk their lives; others will see themselves absolutely obliged. Cases of conflict arising from international law, business practices, direct killing of the innocent, or difficult cases of medical treatment and its withdrawal also provoke a pluralism of moral opinions. Others emphasise conflicting interpretations of the good life. This was something Kant took as a starting-

point in his moral thinking and led to the categorical imperative as a law the agent imposes on himself. Many hold that no
matter how good moral principles are they cannot be applied
in the world as it is. For some Christians this is because reason
has been radically undermined by sin, and conflict must inevitably result. No moral theory can ever be adequate. Another
approach is to say that universal moral principles of justice
and equality apply in the domain of juridical decision, but that
other considerations have priority in the domain of the family.
Michael Walzer's ethics is largely founded on this distinction
of domains. Different social roles require different norms
which may not be coherent among themselves. A psychiatrist
may be justified in not informing the police of a client's evil
intent on the grounds of confidentiality while a co-worker
would not be so justified. Problems of affirmative action
whether in terms of race, colour or sex could also come under
this head.

A. MacIntyre has pointed out that most of these objections
lead to seeing morality from some particular perspective that
excludes all others. The basic error is to posit a perfectly
rational subject who can take a disengaged universal view
from outside history. This type of Cartesian ego, disincarnate
and disengaged from history, is just not real. We always
perceive moral action in its historical dress as involving real
embodied persons. Our moral notions do have universal intent
by discerning what is truly human for any person whatsoever.
This universality is achieved by the power of reason working
and reflecting from within history. We can therefore say that
even our universal notions are historically determined and this
without detriment to their universal character. Their historical
dress flows from the conditions in which we encounter them
and how they are understood over time. This does not deny the
universal worth of values or norms but does take the historicity of the human subject and his or her insights seriously.
Morality is not lived from outside history but from within it.
The consequence of making the human subject the absolute
beginning for all moral reflection and action has been an endless
splitting and sundering in moral thought. Nietzsche foresaw that
nihilism would be the *terminus absolutus* of the Enlightenment.

This is consistent with Pope John Paul's analysis of the contemporary moral condition right at the beginning of *Veritatis Splendor*, n. 1, where, after speaking of sin as weakening and then rejecting the divine light, he visualises a person so conditioned as "giving himself over to relativism and scepticism (cf. Jn 18:38), he goes off in search of an illusory freedom apart from the truth itself."[6]

9. Moral realism

The antidote to this smorgasbord of individual choice just described is moral realism. It is understood to have its foundations in a sound metaphysics of *esse,* which we can describe as the actuality of being, its existence as constituting it outside nothingness. And therefore for believers in the Creator it means understanding created being not just as enjoying existence outside God's mind in this world but more radically as having been brought into being by being thought of and willed in the divine mind in the first place. God is thus the absolute source and origin from which all being comes, to whom it is destined to return because it is attracted to its source, from which it draws its energy and without which it is nothing. It must seek its source and origin because from God flows being, and it clings and strives toward him so as to maintain contact with the source of its energy, outside whom it simply ceases to be a reality.

A Christian metaphysics which is the background and framework for the understanding of Christian morality is a statement of realism both in an ontological and in a moral sense. This unity between ontology and morals was of course sundered by David Hume with his is-ought distinction and the subsequent objections to naturalism in Anglo-Saxon ethics since G.E. Moore. Kant also broke this unity; he founded his ethics in the self which gives itself or imposes on itself the categorical imperative as its law. Ethics does not begin in real existence in the created world but in the mind as conscious of itself. What disappears in both cases is the ontological truth of the creation as absolutely dependent on God. Morality in the Christian vision partakes of the dependence of creation, since the human agent is created directly by God and cannot act to realise itself outside God. Here, the truth of the Gospel is overwhelming. "Without me you can do nothing." That means that without God we are nothing and certainly can achieve nothing.

This doctrine is only recognised in its fullness when our minds are enlightened by the revelation of the Creator. When God revealed himself in the Pentateuch he manifested his name. As he is the source of all, we can never exhaust and catch in our concepts his full reality clearly and exhaustively. "I AM", "I AM WHO I AM" and "I WILL BE WHO I WILL BE" are ways of our getting some idea of God's identity as Creator of the world and destiny of Israel. The Old Testament is full of the awareness of this impenetrable mystery. Moses ascended Sinai to encounter him in the cloud that covered his presence. The prophets and mystics of the old covenant repeated the experience of meeting the Absolute who dominated history in daunting darkness. The New Testament completes our knowledge of God as Being itself, for Christ identifies himself with the Old Testament revelation so often in St John's Gospel, with such a definitive "I AM" that his divine identity and mission cannot be mistaken. He also asserts that he holds this same nature in common with his Father with whom he shares everything and so is "come to do his work". It is not necessary to be caught up in mysticism to realise that Christian thought is grounded in ultimate reality and that our philosophy itself is subject to the light God has thrown on reality by revealing himself as Creator and Redeemer.

This realism has profound repercussions for morality. It presumes that morality cannot wander beyond the limits set by a sound metaphysics. If moral action is directed to building up goodness in our lives this presupposes that there is a metaphysics of the GOOD and that every other individual good as created is nothing but a participation in the absolute GOOD. Participation means that goodness is spread and communicated by God's creative act, since it can arise in no other way and from no other source.

When we speak of moral realism, the inevitable question is what is the moral order. It belongs to the order of being in the sense that human action is an actualisation of our created being, or, in a more visual and pictorial manner, it is a going to God as source from whom we receive being absolutely and through whom by action we increase or grow in personal identity and being. He is the reason, source and dynamism for our existence as ecstasy toward him. The moral order is the order we have to realise by our human action so that we cling to him and return to him as end and fulfilment. Since he created us as agents in the world, it is our responsibility to so structure our existence as we traverse the world that we never lose contact with him or lose sight of him as end. We often say that the moral order is a "given", or that it is established by the law of God. True! It is the capacity inherent in us to realise our selves, to be happy by striving rightly so that we are our true selves in God's plan. The doctrine of creation means that God has thought of us lovingly from eternity: that his plan for us is always to be good toward us — a plan we call providence, whereby God provides for us by his guidance and governance of the universe. That plan is alive and works itself out in our hearts. All of our tendencies and inclinations to goodness are the evidence of his creative love within us. They are activated by his absolute goodness that attracts us back to our origin in him. It is he and he alone who gives true and full purpose and meaning to human existence by being its origin and end.

10. Open to and for God

A fundamental question about order that has tormented the best theological minds in this century has been: how did God intend the human subject when he created it? Did God give us a nature so that we could think out his existence for ourselves, but limits us to the range of natural thought so that our striving would never enter into and penetrate the heart and personality of God himself? This is the doctrine that we could have one natural end or purpose and no other. We would then be restricted by the range of achievements of our natural capacities. Was that how God created us? It could have been, but that was not his known way, intent or purpose. He did give us natural capacities, the light of reason and the force of will. What we recognise spontaneously is that if we know there is a God we want to know him wholly, fully, through and through in the totality of his reality. That is what we call the natural desire for God. It is a great enigma that we who have been made by him, and who want to know him, cannot with our own native power stretch our mind to "the height and depth, the width and breadth" of him WHO IS. So the mind is in fact made for God but cannot achieve what it is made for. What does that mean? Nothing other than that there is an openness, a sort of vacuum, a vague longing where we are attracted to God. When he comes he does so freely, to fill it with his presence by revealing himself. This is the mystery of grace, the sharing of the divine life. We are divinised when we live with God, by God. We have a desire to be divinised and so to realise ourselves ever so fully and completely. This is a natural desire for God or, as we say, for the supernatural. Maurice Blondel was a breakthrough figure who saw that so much philosophy that seemed to be a denial of the faith was at its deepest level the evidence that only the Absolute in person could satisfy us. Apologetics could never prove God but it could lead to a moment of emptiness, of vacuum where the sincerely honest seeker could feel the pull of his origin, the meaning of his existence in the person beyond all naming, the light shrouded in darkness. He did not despair of the wrong ways of modern philosophy but like John Henry Newman saw that even a mistaken conscience that sincerely sought the truth must arrive at God as his end, salvation and spiritual home for eternity.

NOTES

1. See article on "Revelation", in *Dictionary of Fundamental Theology* (ed.) R. Latourelle and R. Fisichella, Crossroad, New York/St Pauls, Slough 1994, 906.
2. In "Human, Humanist and Christian Morality", in *Human Values and Christian Morality*, Gill and Macmillan, Dublin 1970, 116.
3. See "The Question of the Binding Nature of the Value Judgments and Moral Directives of the New Testament", *Readings in Moral Theology*, No. 4, Paulist Press, New York 1984, 95.
4. See "Nine Theses in Christian Ethics", *Readings in Moral Theology*, No. 2, Paulist Press, New York 1981, 190-207, especially 191.
5. "On the Pursuit of the Ideal", Agnelli International Prize Address, Turin, 15 Feb. 1988, 10, 11.

3

The person defines morality

In the battle for the heart and mind of a pluralistic society characterised by any number of moral systems and ethical theories all with different values, ideals, norms and ways of reasoning, one standard has been found to avail for all, namely the worth of the person. It seems that it has been the great discovery of the twentieth century, a discovery that saves humanity from the horrors of totalitarianism on one side and from the exploitation of untrammelled capitalism on the other. The person is not just the middle ground between extremes. The person is the point of reference for every philosophy, social system and political programme because the person is absolute since the person can never be used merely as a means but is always an end to itself since it has value and worth in itself. Catholic social and moral teaching has of course underlined the truth of the person as the one in terms of whom all other values are to be assessed, judged and measured.

1. Christianity and personalism

Revelation furnishes us with a message that puts the person both above and at the centre of creation. The person at once belongs to and transcends the rest of creation. The Genesis account seems to be precisely aimed at showing how God wanted a partner for himself, someone in the world with whom he could share his own mind and love. This means that the human, although infinitely different from God, was willed by God as somehow similar to himself. The creation of humanity is just this capacity of God to find a partner, an image for his own inner life. God did this by breathing his Spirit, that is, his divine life into humanity so that he shares the divine life.

In this one word "image" we realise in ourselves the spiritual capacities of God to know himself and love his own being by sharing it creatively with us. The doctrine that humanity is the image of God has been the linchpin in the Church's approach to the world and its salvation. It has been the ultimate moral claim by which Christians found all the rights that inhere the human subject and which no one should violate. It is the centre-piece in the arch of Christian moral thinking. It is a powerful claim because it is a divine warrant for human identity and its inviolability. In theology it refers back to Christ who is the Son of God by nature, that is, his nature is to be Son generated by the Father. Now we have been adopted into that family circle of Father and Son united by the personal love of the Spirit. It means that our capabilities as intellectual and volitional are social and interpersonal in community with all who share the divine nature by right or by adoption. Here we begin to understand the mind of God, for "Christ is the image of the invisible God." Moral life, like family life, is being caught up into the relationships that make us who we are. It means a life of loving gratitude and adoration, being wrapped in his presence as Jesus was. It also means being introduced into the Trinity as the centre of its *perichoresis*, the circle where all share mutually with each other.

Personalism is therefore the invention of Christianity, beginning with the debates about the Trinity and the inner life of God, then the unity of Christ as a divine person in two natures. From theology, which purified the common notion of person found in Roman law, it was taken up by the philosophers. Today personalism usually means a view of the personal subject in him or herself in a way that makes the self independent in its conception even of God. This is of course the source of the difficulty the Church and theology have with those types of personalism that leave no space for the acknowledgement of God.

Personalism which places the human subject at the centre of the cosmos is in great part a reaction to the scientific study of the human "from below". So we have biology, which certainly can describe the biological processes, laws and configuration of the human, without, however, touching or identifying the human. Physics and chemistry may also analyse the composition of the human species from their respective points of view without saying precisely what is human. The silence about what makes a person in the natural and even in the social sciences is what we call reductionism. It is perceiving the person in terms of scientific determinisms and necessity. But what of thought, freedom and the power to choose? These are qualities that characterise the human and set it off from the rest of creation in this world. We say therefore that humans are superior to animals because the latter may show flickerings of choice and intelligence but only tend that way without fully possessing these capabilities. This makes the person the subject of rights, the centre of society and the one who has dominion over his or her life and destiny.

2. The personalist movement this century

Why was it necessary to wait for the twentieth century to come so consciously and fully to this awareness? Personalism has always been a feature of Jewish and Christian thought. One has only to think of Martin Buber's *I and Thou* as a revelation of how necessary others and in an unconditional way the absolute Other are for my very constitution and conservation as a person. It is the absolute Other who calls me into existence and sustains me in all being and action. St Augustine has furnished the greatest inspiration for Christians to come to theological insight through self-understanding that discloses how God is more intimate to us than we can ever be to ourselves. His *Confessions* show how the return to myself is the way to discover God's light illumining my inner eye of faith and giving sense to my life. So the inward journey when accompanied by Christ leads to transcendent life in the Father's heart to which we are gently guided by the Spirit. There have been other great personalistically inclined theologians who emphasised love as the centre of their philosophy or theology. St Bonaventure's *Itinerarium Mentis in Deum*, that is, the soul's journey to, or better into, God is a classic in spirituality. Pascal also portrayed the majesty and misery in the mystery of human destiny. It was the Renaissance that really brought out the centrality of humanity to all study, or, as students of English literature never cease repeating, in the words of Alexander Pope "The proper study of mankind is man." Pico della Mirandola glimpsed the wonder of creation in the establishment of human dignity in its own right. Henri de Lubac found inspiration in him for his reflections of Christian humanism. Emmanuel Mournier is usually acknowledged as the founder of personalism as a movement. In the political and economic crisis of the 1930s he looked for a new model for basing personal and social life on the Gospel. Rather than a return to the Christendom model from the Middle Ages he latched onto Renaissance humanism and the centrality of the person as his ideal for living out the values of the Gospel. The review *Esprit* was the vehicle for spreading the personalist message, not so much as a philosophical doctrine but as a social and political movement that wanted to forge a third way between the extremes of totalitarianism and individualism. In the totalitarian regimes the individual is swallowed up in the collectivity so that the State in typical Hegelian style absorbs the rights of the individual person, who is reduced to a part in the whole, a cog in the machine. For most Western countries it is the individual who claims rights in such an absolute way that others are denied the very same rights. In other words, only the individual is considered and all others are excluded. In grand part this is the philosophy of consumerism that comes with a radically capitalist system. In opposition to both collectivism and individualism, Mournier and his circle put the emphasis on the person as the source of rights, as the one whom the State must serve and as being able to enter into communication and communion with others. In other words, they believed that there could be a personal and social life worthy of the dignity of the person. Personalism insists on this primary recognition of the dignity of the person, of every person, which is the guarantee of its free and creative exercise. There are in fact many personalisms that come together in their opposition to the two extremes mentioned but they cannot rightly be called a school or even a doctrine. Some are even anarchist, nihilist in the line of Nietzsche, and others are religious and Christian, even explicitly Catholic. Personalism is therefore a widespread movement in the contemporary world that calls for human rights, provides a way of founding them and shows that the person needs to be given prime consideration in our thinking.

3. Types of personalism

There are two fundamental types of personalism, as Armando Rigobello says. Firstly, there is personalism in the strict sense which means the person becomes the theoretical centre-point of all philosophy and theology. This philosophy begins with an intuition of the absolute importance of the person and proceeds to build its theory out of a phenomenology of the experience of the person. It is worth recognising that the very first stirring of a personalist philosophy was in Germany last century in reaction to the pantheism proposed by many idealist philosophers. Schleiermacher adverted to the fact that this is utterly unacceptable since God is personal and has always been worshipped as such by Jews, Christians and Muslims. The person then is the object of the original intuition that in itself grasps the values and significance of the complex deliverances of immediate consciousness. This leads to an existential and historical explanation of the original intuition which is the basis for moral awareness and opens the prospect of action. However, no existential or phenomenological analysis is able to exhaust the value and meaning of the person. This indicates that the person is constituted by transcendence so that every manifestation of its essence and every combination of these manifestations remains but an indication, never a full definition of what it means to be a person. Personalism is thus religious at least in its intent, and logically remains open to transcending all its empirical realisations on the basis of its concrete dynamism as a historical and existential experience.

In the wide sense personalism is but one aspect in the framework of a global approach to philosophy. The person here is not treated as the object of philosophy in its totality so that all somehow derives from the person. Philosophy begins in an awareness of being and not in the intuition of the person which now must validate and justify itself in terms of being. Nor does philosophical analysis begin solely in the context of personal existence but the person is seen as part of the fabric of existence, that is, the person occupies a privileged and indeed unique position in the totality of existence. In the case of a Christian personalism the person holds a central position in regard to values which can only be realised as goals or aims of the person in a meaningful world and a meaningful search for the worth of all that exists and can exist. The unfolding of all philosophical discourse cannot then be reduced to the analysis of the person and its expression. It is not the person that establishes and justifies metaphysics, but the person and its operation is justified in terms of a general or universal metaphysics of existence. In this sense personalism provides an ethical reflection on the basics of metaphysics and provides the foundation for an ethical-political programme in a person-alised culture.

The two types of personalism are reflected in two quite different political approaches. In the first the intuition of the person and its value prevails over all social and political institutions. This is necessary as a guarantee of its absolute conception of the dignity and worth of the person. The con-crete, intensely experienced life of the individual person be-comes the criterion and measure of all social institutions and of the Church and State as well. Often enough, then, intensity of personal experience in an autonomous sense is here taken to be more important than the distinction of levels and types of experience and how personal experience is expressed and institutionalised by social interaction with other personal sub-jects. In a wide sense, personalism provides a way of assess-ing the real worth of social and juridical institutions and of establishing a proper articulation of social institutions that make up the social corpus. The first type can be typical of postmodernism as a position that leaves it wholly to each subject to choose the premises and starting-point of his or her thinking. This starting point may not be the person as related to others and particularly to God. Much postmodernism is reducible to individualism, if not to emotivism, that justifies choice not by its intrinsic rationality but by individual preference. In a personalism based in a solid metaphysics the articulation of social institutions, legal and political bodies are subordinate to the good and dignity of the person while their unsubstitutable roles are fully acknowledged. Parliamentary democracy plays a key function in this personalism. Here the difference between the Maritain approach and that of Mournier becomes clear.

4. Qualities of the person

While personalism is not a philosophical system, it does emphasise the irreducible value of personal experience and give a stimulus to speculative reflection on what constitutes genuinely human values as well as motivating to action. This comes about when older ways of thought are confronted with the social, political and mental ways in which they alienate persons from their own identity, from their role in society and from their rightful relationship with God. Personalism is therefore a protest against any ideological way of organising social existence so that persons are not left the proper space for the expression of personal dignity and interpersonal relations. It was born out of the economic, political and moral collapse of the thirties. For Mournier the person was spirit, and the impersonal betokens matter and endless division in material particles. Rather than being a being, a person was more a presence than an illumined consciousness. A presence of course means that a person is not found in aggressivity or hostility and dispersion, but in recollection that is not just the awareness of self in itself nor in its psychological and subjective manifestations of its own power. European authors point out that this was the characteristic of Fascist regimes and of the *Übermensch*. Recollection, where the persons come to themselves, arouses, as it were, an awareness of a secret guest. The person is at once immanent to the subject and simultaneously transcends it. That presence is the mysterious appeal of another. The response to this appeal brings about both an incarnation and a deeper interiority.

Through this incarnation one becomes present to the other and this opens the door to communion. Mournier pointed to the person as "the total volume of the human". This metaphor of volume images the tension between the three dimensions of height, width and depth that are held in dynamic equilibrium in the one unique subject. Body is the dimension of length. Our stretching out and growing as a body-person provides the measure of our concrete incarnated being. What is directed to the heights arises in the depths and arouses the universal or transcendental side of our nature. What gives breadth to our existence is communion with others. Vocation, incarnation and communion are the three dimensions of the person. The three exercises necessary to arrive at personhood are: meditation as a search for one's unique vocation; engagement with history, and commitment to give oneself to others. The person who lacks any one of these remains essentially incomplete. Mournier wanted a spiritual revolution against bourgeois values and a culture with the person as the centre of all as a point for communion between persons. This was only possible by way of an interior renewal of spirit and a living faith that would sustain an élite who would witness this truth to the whole society. A Christian is involved in the "tragic optimism" of death and resurrection, a tension that can only be resolved eschatologically. A Christian is not one to renounce human values, but to witness to them even to heroism, that is, if necessary, martyrdom. We need to repropose sanctity as an ideal, as the moral structure of life and the ethical architecture that was known and tested by the Fathers and the great saints of the Middle Ages. In that architecture Christian experience was an adventure, a radical position taken before the challenge of life because abandonment to God is the hardest and most difficult human attitude to attain. Such a spirituality that will lay down its life for the goodness of human values is the Christian answer to Nietzsche, Freud and Marx. A Christianity that is forever inventing new ways to realise the fullness of humanity, that genuinely promotes human values, is the answer to Nietzsche's charge that Christianity is the religion of the weak and downtrodden. As regards Marx, it is obvious, as we have

seen with the fall of the Berlin Wall and the crash of the
Communist empire, that progress without transcendence does
not truly satisfy human aspiration at any level. As regards
Freud, the dynamics of personality should be discovered not
in instinct but in the person who can bring instinct and emotion to fullness in an integrated personality. The goal of any
psychological process, especially psychoanalysis, should be
an entering into the mystery of the person.

5. "A civilisation of love"

Personalism has a programme of moral and cultural re-
construction in mind, what Paul VI named "a civilisation of
love". This is the antidote to the sickening fear of dissolution
and even complete destruction by nuclear holocaust that haunts
our century. It has been pointed out that the preaching of the
end of the world was precisely what brought about a moral
reawakening in the Middle Ages. The fear for the future of
our world and its civilisation can be just as strong a motive to
incarnate Christian values anew, especially in a personalist
culture. One of the advantages the personalist movement has
brought to theology is an awareness of earthly realities and
how they point to the value of the person as it is to be
realised now. Theology has of course linked this to the idea
of unity with the divine persons through grace in the Trinity,
and with a communion with Christ by sharing both his humanity with which we identify and also his divinity through grace.

6. Ontology of the person

So far I have presented a phenomenological analysis of
Christian experience as sanctity in the midst of worldly realities, consecrating them to what God designed them for. This
type of personalism pays little attention to the basic structures
and metaphysics of the person. When the Greeks speculated
on the nature of humanity they emphasised rationality as the
distinguishing characteristic without attending to the person in

which the flame of reason was lighted. It was the idea of a mask through which a person sounded as a part in a play, that is, as a role to be performed. It also meant the mask of a god that one glanced at as one approached a temple. Its purpose was to shadow but not reveal the true personality of the divinity. In law a person was a subject of rights, that is, a free man and not a slave who could not participate in civic deliberations. A slave was literally a nothing, a thing with a price for his usefulness. Christianity saw that the mask definition reduced the person to a function without substance necessarily. By taking over the Latin "substance" or "subsistence", the Greeks could define the person behind the mask as having value *in se* as a *hypostasis*. It was thus that Trinitarian theology and christology put philosophy on the track of the person in itself. The human mind was understood as an image of the Trinity, with the generation of the Son being taken as a model for thought or intellectualism.

Personalism understands thought as an activity of mediation, firstly of personal being with itself and then with the other it encounters around itself which is perceived or intuited as an immediate object of perception or intellectual vision. From this object taken into the mind as its object one can proceed logically by deduction without taking the person into account. But a deduction that is not educed by the person ends in mere tautology without contact with extra-mental reality. We do not have innate ideas, but when the person recognises the object as mediating reality then the person is truly alive in the real world. It is thus thought which links and unites people together as surely as thought unites thinking with the person as subject and agent. It is thought based in personal existence that leads one to the universal aspects of reality and so establishes communication between persons. If the personal principle of thought is lost, thought loses its concrete, existential character and becomes a flight into impersonal abstractions. If the person that exists outside the mind is considered as a mirror of the self, then it follows that there can be actions that are quite inhuman because the thought behind them is impersonal or because the love that motivates them is somehow wrong.

7. A definition

Person may be defined as the being that expresses itself to
itself in the act of intending, wishing and loving. This definition
summarises a long history of speculation that underwent great
doubts and difficulties in coming to this insight. The Fathers of
the Church were spurred on to philosophise about the nature of
the person after the christological and Trinitarian disputes.
Gregory Nazianzen went beyond the image of a voice sounding
through a dramatic mask to emphasise the characteristics of
totality, independence and intelligence which led to St John
Damascene clarifying the situation with this definition: "a
person is a subject that expressing itself through its operations
and properties places such a manifestation of itself as distinguishes it from all others of the same nature".[1] It is necessary to
advert to the profound humanity of Augustine's thought to see
how he connected unity and singularity in an insight which led
him to define the human person as "Singulus quisque homo,
qui... secundum solam mentem imago Dei dicitur, una persona
est et imago Trinitatis in mente".[2] Each singular person is called
God's image because in his or her mind there is an image of the
Trinity. Boethius propounded what became the classic definition in the Middle Ages: "persona est naturae rationalis
individua substantia",[3] a person is the individual substance
possessing a rational nature. This resounds in St Thomas,
"omne individuum rationalis naturae dicitur persona",[4] every
individual with a rational nature is called a person. Rational
nature, therefore, is the specific difference that distinguishes a
person from every other existing individual. To possess its
existence in itself (ens in se), and through or because of itself
(ens per se), singularity, subsistence also called substantiality,
integrity, perfection, incommunicability and uniqueness are all
qualities attributed to the person by the medieval doctors.
Incommunicability was precisely described as meaning that the
existence of a person could never be divided into parts, nor
could the one same existence be united to others as their own.
The etymological play on the word person as per se una seems
to be mistaken even though the distinctive constitutive for the
person seems to be its substantiality or subsistence.

Contemporary personalism has added nuances that enrich this tradition. Mournier, not wanting to overemphasise the intellectual dimension, spoke of the person as, "une activité vécue d'auto-création, de communication, et d'adhésion, qui se saisit et connait dans son acte".[5] Romano Guardini defined the person as formed and founded on interiority so as to be spiritually fruitful.

8. Qualities following this definition

The qualities of the person that become clear as we look over this history are:

1. *Rationality*. This means the individual's capacity to be a source of light and understanding for one's own life and existence by illuminating from oneself the circumstances that condition them and with which they are in rapport. A personal subject has a presence of or from itself to itself in its own act while being at the same time open to another's presence to itself. This is what is undeniable in the concept of person. In the very moment one is open to another, one is present to oneself, as St Thomas notes, "eadem operatione intelligo intelligibile et intelligo me intelligere".[6] The presence of the person to itself, far from being exclusive, is actually necessary for being open to the totality of reality as being or *esse*. It has more kinship with being than with any other entity. Many modern personalists hold that personalism is based on the irrational or the non-rational, on instinctive drives or passions that reason will never penetrate. This is mistaken since it is the person who is rational. The person was created to reach out to the totality of the real in all its aspects – physical, psychic, spiritual and godly – so as to grasp its truth. The person is the point of departure for all knowing and it is the person itself that is known along with whatever object is grasped by thought.

2. *Unity and identity*. When the person throws light on its own operation of knowing, it recognises itself as a unity, not an abstract unit but a living unitary principle. It is at the source

of a world of experience that is unified by it and for itself as an identity. It is not just a formal unity that like an empty space or vacuum has to be filled with content. It rather forms the content by its own agency as an expression of its identity. This identity is projected into the passing stream of time and variations of place without being dissolved in that flux. Thus, while the person is inconceivable without time, it is not to be confounded with time as the passing instant. Identity therefore does not disappear in the passing instants of memory, but memory is the verification of the person identified over a spell of time. The person, as is well known, cannot be exhausted by its empiric manifestations, nor can it be caught up into a sum of experiences, but the person is precisely the subject needed to rightly interpret all empirical data about itself. The person is not the result of linking up phenomena of memory in experience, but is precisely the agent that does the linking through the luminosity of reason and the attractive force of good communicated to the will. Just as light is not the result of linking objects in a visual field but is the real cause of our experience of seeing, so practical reason unites various human acts and aspects of personality and identifies them with the person as their subject. Here is the possibility of the person penetrating to the universal intelligibility borne by the universe. In this knowing process the person recognises its own identity. But this process can lead to tensions and even splits, so that fractures between the person and the conception of its identity may develop as well as between the person and the world. These phenomena have been well studied by psychology without perhaps giving sufficient weight to their ontological and ethical manifestations and repercussions. The identity of the person should grow with experience, but this process may be cut short by the inner splits between person, self, act and world. Growth therefore occurs not as an automatic or deterministic evolution, but through overcoming doubts, quieting and balancing the rebellious drives of instinct, resolving tensions and experiencing suffering. Such is the reality or dialectic at the base of personal existence which we call salvation through healing grace. But if these tensions take over and dominate the personality it may develop a double identity as

in schizophrenia or as psychic disconnection of the person
from what it is identified with and owns as its action. Normality is what confirms the same identity throughout all these
struggles. It is the personality itself that draws out and makes
this identity emerge above the forces of disintegration. The
person is at the centre and source of the drive to overcome not
only contradictions, but the inconsistencies that arise from
error, remorse about mistakes made, and misdirected energy.
The person thus represents the centre and force of integration
for the identity of the person in its metaphysical consistency.
In the return to oneself in consciousness the self can divide
into the judge and the guilty one, or the legislator and the
subject under the law, or it can become triple as a division
between the umpire and two contending sides as in a game or
a court of law. In abnormal cases we see split personalities and
other psychic disorders. Normality, however, is the strongest
proof there is of the unity and identity that a person enjoys. It is
only normality that lets one become aware of the contradictions
and the guilt attached to such disassociations and the power of the
self to draw all the forces toward the centre that is the person
that allows them to be overcome and thus united in the self.

    3. *Subsistence*, or to hold one's existence in oneself. That
a person has being in itself means that it cannot have being in
another or as a mode of being or an attribute or as it were the
fetish of another. Whatever relation the person may establish
with another person or thing or whatever influence these may
exercise on the person, the only relationship that founds a
person's very existence is a metaphysical one with God. The
person always maintains the link with itself first, no matter
how intimate its relations with others may be. The Christian
idea of creation therefore ensures that the person has an absolute foundation in its relationship with God and that in this
relationship God always remains other, so that the person is
not identified with him without whom it could not exist. Ideas
such as reincarnation, the dissolution of the person into a
mystical nirvana, or pantheistic doctrines according to which
the person is a mode of infinite substance as in Spinoza or a
historic empirical determination of absolute spirit as in Hegel

contradict the *in se* subsistence of the person which is a
fundamental philosophical truth of human experience. In
classical metaphysics the *in se* character of the person is
conceived as the subsistence which maintains its identity in
the contingent acts it performs.

The idea of substance has been strongly criticised by Hume,
who showed there is no passage from the *cogito* to the *res
cogitans*, as well as the inadmissibility of the transcendental
deduction of a real self that is more than a phenomenon given
to subjectivity. The "io" or self is never caught in its state of
"pure self" but in the actuality of its activity as "I am alive."
Philosophers have recognised for centuries that the self never
comprehends itself as a pure essence in an intuition of the
immediate coincidence of essence and existence in the person.
As St Thomas says, "ex hoc enim ipso quod percipit se agere,
percipit se essere... De anima scimus quia est seipsam, in
quantum eius actus percipimus".[7] If there is no intuition into
our essence then we must enquire into its nature through the
acts we perform and the objects of our experience. These are
the mediations that reveal to us what we are at the centre of
our being as persons. It should be noted that the "io" as
phenomenon or as transcendental subject has never been able
to account for the singularity of the person as it is present to
itself. It is not reducible to sensible experience nor an *a priori*
form of experience. The critique of subsistence as a thing to be
perceived by the senses is valid. It is necessary to think of the
person as a "who", one who continues in existence as the
principle of his or her acts and irreducible to the single moments
of experience. Through our experiencing the contingency of
our activity we come to the logical and ontological primacy of
the person. If we deny the subsistence of the person then we
contradict the basis for the person's having value *in se* and
everything that flows from it as regards the rights and destiny
of the person.

4. *To be for itself, finality* and *automediation.* To exist *per
se* means that everything in the cosmic, political and social
orders can be a means or instrument for the realisation of the
good of the person. Again St Thomas says, "quod creaturae

rationales gubernantur propter seipsas, aliae vero in ordine ad eas... Sola igitur intellectualis natura est propter se quaesita in universo, alia autem propter omnia propter ipsam".[8] This ultimacy of value residing in the person demands that the person finds in God as Absolute its only reason and purpose to be known and loved. This is the reason for that "great respect" that God has as he looks on us, for, as the Book of Wisdom says, he disposed our existence with "great reverence". In modern philosophy the respect owed the person is consequent on his dignity and that follows from its uniqueness in existence. This dignity has no price and there is no equivalent for it, as Kant says. This dignity springs from human rationality and its autonomy so that the person is always to be treated as an end and never merely as a means, as is expressed in the categorical imperative. For Kant as for St Thomas the person exists as an end *in se* in as far as rationality implies dominion over one's acts and liberty in acting which establishes the specific difference from irrational nature which is passively determined to action. It is a distinctive characteristic of the human person to return to itself by its own act internally mediated by a process of self-realisation. The person does not exist for us except as the subject with which it is identified. But if the person were made or produced then it would be degraded to being merely another physical thing or object. The *per se* quality of the person has explained excess and defect in the history of philosophy. When the act of thought or of will by which I return to myself is seen as the radical constitutive of the self it becomes an autocracy, as in G. Gentile's philosophy. When, however, the act in its interior reality is seen as dividing the self from its activation, then this objectification becomes an alienation because the subject in its *in se* quality has been lost or annihilated as in Sartre's thought. By distancing the *in se* from the *per se* we turn the self-realisation of our existence into a lie that deepens the abyss separating us from ourselves. Neither should the human act be understood as self-creation in an absolute instance or over the duration of a lifetime. The solution is not found in any compromise between the two extremes, but in the fact that there is an excess of being and value which stands at the base and cause of every act as an expression of the identity of the person. The person precedes its act and gives it its value as personal. The *in se* and *per se* are irreparably split if the person does not recognise that it is *ab alio*, that its existence is an absolute gift from God to whom by nature it is made to respond with its whole self.

5. *Finitude*. But existentialism has recognised that *in se* and *per se* are not identical, because a person's act is never a perfect grasp of its being, because what we know is never perfectly adequate to what exists in fact. Here we see the finitude, the limits of our nature and existence. We just are not absolute, because with our own act we cannot bring about a perfect mediation between being and intention to close that hermeneutic circle. Philosophy in this century has outgrown the immanentist excesses of idealism and should not be allowed to fall into the utter pessimism suggested by many existentialists. We should rather be aware of the full horizon that our rationality arrives at by integrating rationality with finitude. By expressing itself rationally to itself the person flowers within the cosmic, social, metaphysical, psychological dimensions which it discovers by knowing itself as part of the universe, of the human *convivium*, and as related to God. These relationships pertain to the person in its fullness and integrity, for by becoming aware of them the person expands beyond its limits and so enriches its identity. The body, society and religion thus define the person as a bodily, social and God-related being and are essential constitutives in its definition. All of being touches the person and the person has to respond to being to be its self. Being, then, as it were, concentrates itself in and passes through each person. Hence we have images of the cosmos in the microcosm of the person. Here the person is not identified with being in every dimension but is open to being as otherness and so to become rationally aware of being in all its dimensions. Rationality then disengages the person from the empirically particular and without alienation penetrates what is universally significant. This personalised rationality becomes the measure of our freedom and responsibility.

6. *Freedom* and *responsibility*. Personal freedom follows the *per se* quality of the person and is the prerogative of the person to mediate its own existence with its own act. The person has dominion and control over its act as personal. "Quod dominium sui actus habet, liberum est in agendo"[9]. Freedom is so free that it can exhaust itself in itself, willing itself negatively by becoming the spirit of pure independence. From this basic liberty derives what St Augustine calls *libertas minor* or free choice, which expresses the liberty of free choice. Berdyaev called it formal liberty and it can adhere to evil as well as good thus becoming the source, the only source, of sin and tragedy in the world. This liberty has to be articulated by our rationality. It is the act by which the person chooses him or herself and energetically confirms this choice with the co-ordinates of the great field of being as already described. By this exercise of one's liberty the value of the human grows along history's path. Responsibility is the debit, the account-ability one experiences to being in the exercise of liberty. By being called to respond to the real being of persons, events and God we become responsible in each of these spheres of being. The person cannot dispose of itself totally in such a way that it could annihilate its complete being, even in suicide, by turning freedom against its very self. Responsibility is always of the person to itself, and mediately toward the other with which it is in relation; toward society, history and God. There is absolute responsibility only before the Absolute on whom our exist-ence, our freedom and its exercise are totally dependent and in whom they are radically founded.

7. *Person* and *individual*. As the concept of person be-came clearer over time it became necessary to distinguish it from that of the individual, with which it was often confused in the past. Jacques Maritain thought of the individual as the material pole of the person so that the individual was only a fragment of matter in the great web of relationships and forces between things, plants and animals in all their species. The person was conceived as the spiritual pole of our entity, superexisting and transcending by its intellect and will all physical conditions in which it may be seen as in continual

struggle for its liberation and purification. For L. Lavelle, however, the person is the individual in whom spirituality and interiority are concentrated. It is the crossways of all the forces and energies, spiritual and material, in the world. The person is the secret sanctuary where liberty finds itself alone with itself. Gabriel Marcel saw in the person the authenticity of the self so that it could open itself to another and so share and participate in the mystery of being. The inauthentic self, on the other hand, was precisely the self that closed in on itself in a part of just being an anonymous "one", and so becoming lost in the banality of life in a technical world. "One" here has no other reality than that of being a mere statistic and nothing else. This distinction, although supported by many Thomists, has been heavily criticised as compromising the personality of the person in its physical bodily existence and reducing the person to reflexive self-consciousness. They see a split introduced into the ontology of the person. Individual material and bodily individuality have a constitutive role in constituting the essence of the person. It needs to be pointed out that the distinction between rationality and corporality, or between person and individual, was never meant to be a separation but was meant to describe the human person as incarnate spirit, even though emphasising the priority of the spiritual over the empirical individual. It is indeed the person who appropriates its individuality, drawing it away from the play of particular interests and the pressure of the instincts and stamping its own unique mark on it. One's liberty must therefore be exercised to form instincts, inclinations and emotions into a personality with a determined character. This liberty means that life is always the overcoming of fate and the deterministic running forward of events without our control or intervention.

8. *Ramifications for morality.* The concept of the person runs in the face of certain epistemological conceptions in vogue in the social sciences. If one assumes a functionalist view it is impossible to distinguish a personal agent from a computer. In other words, a computer can perform the functions that we have come to associate with consciousness since the seventeenth century. Thus at the level of knowledge the

computer can form representations of objects, it can fabricate images that reproduce our fantasy life and even far outstrip it. Above all, the computer can calculate and we even say it can be a planner. Yet we know it is a machine. We do attribute to it qualities that belong to persons or at least higher animals. What makes the difference then? Consciousness. It is relevant but it does not explain all satisfactorily. Animals all have consciousness and display a certain intelligence, at least in the higher species. They can also follow certain laws and standards. There are very precise laws of animal behaviour and hierarchy in flocks, herds and other groupings.

In the case of the computer, although we say it is an agent and describe it as acting by performing certain functions, these are all human uses of the machine to achieve human purposes. A computer can perform mathematical calculations of the most complicated kinds so that we humans can understand what is the conclusion of such operations. What is most characteristic of the human is purpose as in making a life plan and following it out. A person is not only conscious and purposeful but can reflexively grasp and understand the meaning of these conscious purposes that it can represent to itself. In a computer there is no centre such as the self but there is a mechanical principle that governs its operation. Even in comparison with animals there are ends that are uniquely human, which when they inform emotion transform its meaning. As Charles Taylor, reflecting on the person, asserts, "There are matters of significance for human beings which are peculiarly human, and have no analogue with animals. These are... matters of pride, shame, moral goodness, evil, dignity, the sense of worth, the various human forms of love, and so on. If we look at survival and reproduction, we can perhaps convince ourselves that the difference between men and animals lies in a strategic superiority of the former: we can pursue the same ends much more effectively than our dumb cousins. But when we consider these human emotions, we can see that the ends that make up a human life are *sui generis*. And then even the ends of survival and reproduction will appear in a new light. What it is to maintain and hand on a human form of life, that is, a given culture, is also a peculiarly human affair."[10]

9. The import of consciousness

Consciousness is relevant to the description of an agent
which can be aware not only of self-chosen goals but of
goals that are nature given toward which it can guide itself
consciously by choice. "Morality requires some recognition
that there are higher standards on one, and hence the recognition of some kind of goal... Moral agency, in other words,
requires some kind of reflexive awareness of the standards
one is living by."[11] We therefore define persons through the
potentialities we know them to have. Thus, a person is an
agency who has a sense of self, of his or her own life, who
can evaluate it, and make choices about it. This is the basis
of the respect we owe persons. Even those who through
some accident or misfortune are deprived of the ability to
exercise these capacities are still understood as belonging to
the species defined by this potentiality.[12] These are the very
qualities we should reverence and nourish in human beings
whatever their condition. A person is one with the capability
of asking the vital questions: how are we to explain human
behaviour? And what is the good life? As Taylor points out,
scientific explanations in psychology and sociology based
on performance criteria that can be reduced to simpler elements and radically to matter in motion organised by an
engineering principle do not explain the uniqueness of these
questions, while at the same time providing some of the
reasons that condition or go toward a full explanation. In
other words, they do not grasp the situation or context of the
agent in its fullness. The only adequate descriptive terms
have to be at the level of the unique value of the person
itself. To catch the uniqueness of the context and goal of the
person means that we have to transcend the objectivity usual
in science that puts the uniqueness of the person as agent out
of account. It means that we cannot but consider the person
as engaged and even incarnated into its action. It is not enough
to give the physical, chemical, physiological parameters of
the action as its adequate description, for they never can
name what is the very centre and core of the action.

10. Science, freedom and human goods

Sociobiological explanations are currently strongly in fashion. They set out to explain human practices and values in terms of the goals of survival and reproduction which can then be conceived in absolutist terms. These are goals that can be predicated of animals and applied by analogy even to machines as we do in much computer talk. The variability and relativity of cultural practices is thus reduced to mechanistic laws that disallow all anthropocentric terms or expressions in their formulation. It is obvious from experience that this natural science model breaks down when applied in the social sciences. Such an absolutist account is not only value-free; it is culture-free as well. We cannot avoid, therefore, considering the person in terms of the ends that it naturally wants to achieve. What follows is that when we sit down to deliberate about realising these goals, the process is not what we understand as scientific in that it is not deterministic but is performed as a strategic manoeuvre. It also follows that persons have the power and capacity to form life-plans for themselves as their very own. And it is only by personally engaging themselves in that plan through choices along life's way in a contingent world that it will be realised. Freedom, therefore, does not flow from the instrumental reason we have already identified in natural science, but from strategic or personalised reason that grasps what are truly human goals and perceives how they may be achieved in practice. Taylor is very perceptive when he writes, "My claim is that the ideal of the modern free subject, capable of objectifying the world, and reasoning about it in a detached, instrumental way, is a novel variant of this very old aspiration to spiritual freedom. I want to say, that is, that the motive force that draws us to it is closely akin to the traditional drive to spiritual purity."[13] But there is a self-delusion here, because as person-bodies we cannot stand outside our emotional existence totally and completely, just as we cannot find a place outside tradition from which to view tradition. This does not mean there are no universal qualities we can invoke in defining the person, nor does it mean that emotion must so intervene as to ruin the objectivity of all

knowledge, scientific or otherwise. What freedom means here
is the rejection of paternalism as the imposition of outside or
heteronomous authority above our reason. Freedom means
that emotion is integrated to reason in the realisation of the
person. Scientism is essentially a flight from the human and
ultimately turns on freedom to destroy it.

The person is neither purely matter, as would please a
purely natural science view of the universe; nor is it purely
spirit, for then it would cease to be incarnate as a fragment of
the great material universe. The person is the principle of
union between spirit and matter that explains how it has a
unique vocation, an end beyond the world where it will be at
home with God.

NOTES

1. *Dialectica*, ch. 43, Migne, PG 94, col. 613.
2. *De Trinitate*, XV, 7, 11.
3. *De duabus naturis et una persona Christi*, ch. 3, Migne, PL 64, col. 1345.
4. *Summa Theologiae*, I, 29. a. 3 ad 2.um.
5. *Le personalisme*, Presses Universitaires de France, Paris 1950, 8.
6. *In I Sententia*, d. 1, q. 2, a. 1 ad 2.
7. *Summa contra Gentiles*, III, 46.
8. Ibid., III, 112.
9. Ibid., III, 112.
10. "The Concept of Person", in *Human Agency and Language*, Cambridge University Press, Cambridge 1985, 102.
11. Ibid., 102-103.
12. As Charles Taylor points out: "A person is a being who has a sense of self, has a notion of the future and the past, can hold values, make choices; in short, can adopt life-plans. At least, a person must be the kind of being who is capable of all this, however damaged these capacities may be in practice" op. cit., 97.
13. Ibid., 113.

SECTION II

Sources of a
Christian vision of action

4

Scripture, "the soul of moral theology"

Scripture was the substance of the great sermons and moral guidance preached by the Fathers of the Church; it was the subject that the monks contemplated in the *lectio divina*; it was the textbook that the great scholastic doctors Thomas and Bonaventure expounded; it is the manual of instruction for saints and the rule for a life according to the Gospel. It is so deeply rooted in tradition that the Church's highest teaching authority from Leo XIII to the Second Vatican Council proposed its study as the sure way to effect a renewal of theology overburdened by outworn distinctions and tired out by polemics and internal disputes. It is the essential return to the source, for, as St Jerome proclaims, "Ignorance of Scripture is ignorance of Christ." Indeed, summing up the Council Fathers' attitude, they named it "the soul of theology".

1. Specialisation in Scripture

As part of this renewal scholars have progressively developed specialisations in their study of Scripture. It is now customary to distinguish the ethics of the Old and New Testaments from the use of Scripture in moral theology. This chapter will but scratch the surface of the vast discussion about what were the ethics of the biblical world and what is the ethical message of the Scriptures. A word of warning is in order in so far as from World War II till a little after the Council it was felt that Scripture could easily be reduced to a number of themes running through the text from beginning to end. This was the golden period of biblical theology as a set of themes. This approach was found to be naïve in so far as it did not pay sufficient attention to the history and layers of meaning in a text, and the differences of times, mentality, motives and historical backgrounds of various authors. Various literary genres were fused without their unique characteristics having been recognised. Today Scripture scholars treat the Bible more as literature and so focus on its historical and cultural anthropological background. Recent studies are uncovering the sociology of Palestine and the Mediterranean world at the time of Jesus and Paul. These findings both enrich and complicate a moralist's approach to the Scriptures. It will be best to consider Old Testament ethical assertions against the history of the Old Testament and particularly its religious understanding.

2. The patriarchs

The oldest strata is that of the patriarchs whose oral tradition is essentially that of nomadic desert people. Their religion consisted essentially in a pact with their God who watched over them, guaranteeing them not only survival but prosperity. The identity of the individual was fused with that of the tribe by ties of blood and loyalty; to harm the individual was to put the whole group in danger of extinction, so great were the dangers of the desert. The tribe, as it were, moved as one person, its destiny summed up in the power and position of the patriarch. The key idea of their morality is that of "corporate personality". In and through this individual's covenant with their God the future of the tribe was assured. Abraham, Isaac and Jacob reflected the "morality of the desert" in their practices of extraordinary hospitality to the stranger, in their ruthlessness toward their enemies, destroying and killing all at the end of a feud. Women were treated more or less as objects necessary for the continuance of the tribe, and the practices of polygamy, concubinage and levirate marriage were the norm. The amazingly wonderful thing about the Old Testament is that God walked with these people, conversed face to face with the patriarchs and accepted them as they were to achieve his purposes through them. There is no hint of Victorian scandal-taking or condemnation of the people for being this way.

The patriarchs had a direct, immediate relationship with God, who walked, talked, argued, quarrelled and even struggled with them physically. Theirs is a simple morality of following the inclinations and inspirations that God stirred up in their minds and hearts. They were directed by God who appeared and spoke to them. Their direct contact with God predates the covenant of Sinai. Many theologians have seen in their experience the true condition of those who live by natural law where God speaks to the heart.

3. Covenant

But it is obvious that Old Testament ethics did not start out as a finished whole but evolved along with Old Testament religion and was finally purified through and through by Christ. And here the principle of corporate personality achieves a new and final sense, for we are all "one in Christ", the extension of his personality into the mystic body. Christian tradition likes to see Christ as pedagogue or teacher and the Old Testament as his progressive teaching and graded instruction leading to the Messiah. Eichrodt sought to organise the Old Testament around one theme, that of covenant. There is a *prima facie* case to be made for this argument and it has had a tremendous influence as the main paradigm for moral theology. The idea is that God intervenes in favour of his people, he saves them from slavery in Egypt or exile in Mesopotamia and they make a sacrifice of praise in response to his initiative. Thus they become his people, chosen by him. "I will be your God, and you shall be my people." The fundamental paradigm for all moral living is formed by the religious reality of the covenant, an unbreakable pact between God and his people. The condition of the pact is that the people follow the command or stipulation of their Lord; they are bound to obey his word. In this sense the ten commandments are the "ten words" of the covenant that make God's will known. The standard of judgement for ethical behaviour was therefore what, of all the customs and practices of the peoples surrounding God's chosen flock of Israel, could be taken over by and used as befitting a community dedicated to the worship of the Lord. Old Testament morality is inseparably connected with religion so that some customs could be adapted to his worship and others had to be rejected as inconsistent with faith in him. The Hebrew term *torah* originally meant teaching, instruction and direction, and not simply "law" as it was translated in English. It refers both to the teaching and the content of God's revelation to humankind. What is revealed is a total way of living in harmony with the will of God, and not observance of a set of rules largely of a ritual character. Thus the statutes, precepts and ordinances of the Torah were to act as guides to how Israel was to mould its ritual, cultic, moral, social, legal and economic life so as to achieve God's purposes in the world. These ordinances were strictly enforced and so we came to think of them falsely as coercive law. The Israelites believed that God created the world with a divine purpose and that he disclosed his will by electing them as his chosen instruments, making a covenant with them at Sinai. Underlying the theme of covenant is the more basic idea of election; that God had chosen this people as his very own, loving them above all others, that they owed their very existence to his creative predilection. Another notion that mitigates against the theme of covenant as the key to all Old Testament ethical terms is that of creation; that we owe all to God and are therefore responsible to him for what we make of our existence, for how we act before him. The idea of God as judge, as desert *goel* who vindicates his blood relative, comes to the fore here. Creation from nothing is a conception that only emerges at the close of the Old Testament when the prophets had firmly established monotheistic faith with its unique worship and morality. The multiple names and conceptions of God had to be purified to their depths to recognise the incomprehensible reality of the one true God. Following in the way of this Lord would mean that this God must fulfil his promises to his people. Faith in him meant that one followed his Word communicated by the covenant.

The model of biblical covenant comes from the common practice of the nations of the ancient Near East to make compacts with each other. The Hittite treaty formula illuminates the covenants which God struck with Noah (Gen 9:9-17), with Abraham (Gen 15:1-21), with Israel at Sinai (Ex 20:20-23), and with David (2 Sam 7:1-16). Hittite-style treaties were of two types: (1) a parity treaty between monarchs of equal status; or (2) a suzerainty treaty generously offered by a superior monarch to an inferior. In the latter the superior stipulated his conditions to his vassal, who was expected to give loyalty and tribute so that the suzerain would protect him from enemy attack. However, in the covenant between Jahweh and Israel, Jahweh graciously and without the above conditions made a covenant with the Israelites, freely adopting them as his own people (Ex 19:4-5). The covenant code which God commanded the Israelites to observe involved two specific kinds of relationships. The vertical relationship required that Israel remain faithful to God and obey his law (Ex 20:3). The horizontal relationship was intended to promote peace, *shalom*, among the Israelites by removing causes of discord from among them. The worship of God would be rendered worthless if the Israelites failed to live in harmony with one another (Amos 5:21-24). They were expected to show justice to the powerless, the poor, widows, orphans, slaves and resident aliens. Although Jahweh as Creator was in no way bound to make a covenant with Israel, once he made it he was obliged by it in the same way a Hittite suzerain was bound to his vassals. So Jahweh would bless the Israelites if they observed his laws summarised in the Decalogue, but a curse of retribution and punishment would come upon them if they transgressed them.

The Israelites could trust God because he alone could work great signs and wonders (Deut 4:34) and other gods were nothing (Is 41:29; 44:9). His might was demonstrated by his victory over Pharaoh and by his leading the Israelites from Egyptian bondage to freedom in Canaan. He was the one who not only initiated their liberation; he freed them with his outstretched arm; he was the doer, the one who performed their release from slavery. And therefore the Exodus became the model for God as Liberator from all evil when the poor called to him. And God continued to protect the people of Israel if only they remained loyal to him (Lev 20-22). It should be realised that the covenant was of no gain to Jahweh but it was of the greatest profit to the Israelites. This is what makes the covenant between God and Israel unique in human history. This people was holy because it was set apart for the worship of the true God. The divine injunction was, "You shall be holy, for I the LORD your God am holy" (Lev 19:2 and Mt 5:48). This command clarifies the rationale of the Holiness Code (Lev 17-26). The Israelites are to have the highest standards of holiness and justice; the emphasis on the worship of God is laid on actions not words. Other gods, the idols of the nations, were believed to be motivated by appeasement and an outward show of piety. Old Testament ethics aimed at changing the heart, that is, the inner intention, by teaching them to observe the covenant. God required not sacrifice but a broken, contrite heart (Ps 51:17), the essence of true holiness.

4. Kingdom and prophets

According to the Deuteronomist, God's blessings were thought to relate directly to Israel's obedience or disobedience to the stipulations of the covenant (Deut 28:1). God administered justice in historical events. The books of Joshua, Judges, Samuel, and Kings were formulated to illustrate how God judged Israel and the nations in historical events. The cycle begins with God's loving initiative in the covenant, followed by the people's infidelity, consequent punishment and disaster that leads them to repent and return to the Lord. For God alone directs and controls the course of history. The cultural anthropological background to the war of conquest and settlement of the land with the struggle for supremacy among the Israelite tribes, the coming of the judges and finally the establishment and division of the kingdom is that of an agricultural, sedentary community living in towns, villages and a few cities. Business and trade became more important and the king began to assume for the nation decisions previously made by the tribal elders. Religion shifts its focus from God's wandering desert existence in a tent to the great temple as the centre of the nation and its worship. The close-knit tribe is left behind for the immensely greater national kingdom and the expanding ideology surrounding the king. Contact with foreign gods and religions tempted Israel not only to lukewarm service but to outright infidelity and apostasy. Israel began to accept the pagan kings of the nations as their ideal, setting out to rival them in power and might. In this new situation the prophets were "the conscience of Israel" and their call to repentance meant a radical purification of Israel's moral sense. They cried out against idolatry and cultic prostitution as infidelity to God. They called for a return to Israel's first love in the desert experience of being the uniquely chosen lover of Jahweh, her jealous husband. For the prophet, Jahweh alone is king and he alone will be the faithful shepherd of his oppressed flock, Israel. The more the nation's leaders connived with foreign powers and ignored Jahweh as the master of Israel's destiny, the more the prophets realised that the future of God's chosen people did not lie in great success and empire building. War and its associated virtues are no longer a sacred duty as previously, but are removed to the secular sphere and are often perceived as running against God's will. Instead they emphasise building up the nation internally through care and concern for the needy and oppressed.

In the mentality of the ancient Near East the gods appointed kings to act as their representative in the administration of justice. Among their important responsibilities was to act as guardians of justice for the poor, the widow, the orphan, the alien and the oppressed. It was the king's duty to rescind social and economic laws or constraints that harmed the common people and drove them into poverty. There was in Israel a general amnesty every seven years, when debt and obligations were dropped. Debtors and slaves were freed and had a new lease of life. The land that had been tilled for six years was left fallow, reverting back to God who repossessed it for the common good of the whole people. King Solomon prayed to God for wisdom to rule the nation of Israel (1 Kings 3:9). God remained the judge to whom the oppressed people could directly call whenever they were confronted with injustice (Judg 11:27; Ps 82:8; Gen 16:5). God the compassionate king of Israel would listen and mete out retribution to the oppressors. The prophets were God's agents in bringing about an egalitarian and compassionate society because God took the part of the poor. In Psalm 88 God is portrayed as taking the radical step of deposing the gods, that is, the rulers, from their divine and immortal status to that of humans because of their dereliction of their judicial duty as it applied to the poor, the widow and the orphan. When there was a complete breakdown of justice, the prophets proclaimed and the people expected that God would intervene to establish equity and peace.

The prophets rekindled the people's waning faith by calling them back to the one God who not only led them out of slavery in Egypt but who created them out of pure love. God is the Creator of the world, and his rule is universal. His statutes were relevant to Israel as well as to the people of other nations. It was the prophets who saw the relevance of the goodness of creation, of monotheism, of God's universal justice and the fact his will and law applied to all nations through what he had done for Israel in the Exodus. They saw that the God who had saved them had decreed a universal moral law which all the nations were expected to obey in holiness. God had chosen Israel for a special mission: to be a light to the nations (Is 49:6).

5. Wisdom

The awareness of an order inherent in the world which God had willed so that it might make sense to us was the mainspring of the search for wisdom by the Israelite sages. These were concerned with the problems of everyday living and their wisdom grew out of reflection on the events of life and the enigmas they proposed. "Older wisdom", as von Rad calls it, served to educate young officials to the demands of court life. After the exile, when these same maxims had often been discovered outside Israel, they were explicitly made to serve her faith. Avoidance of greed, selfishness or opportunism are important for a young man if he would succeed in life, but motivated by Israel's faith they become expressions of the value of justice, respect for one's neighbour and trust in

Jahweh who guides human destiny. Wisdom begins in an immediate experience of awful wonder at the personal God of the patriarchs and the covenant who is now confessed as the Creator of Israel and her Redeemer. Creation is perceived as the continuous and unobtrusive blessing of God who sustains all by his saving actions. The beginning of wisdom is in the numinous experience of God's presence and action in the world. There is an unmistakable religious quality in the "fear of the Lord" which is the basic human reaction before the divine mystery. In effect Karl Rahner's "mysticism of every-day things" provides a model for living or "way of life" such as we find in the wisdom literature. This approach to morality is very broad, since it takes account of a full range of human emotion and motivation. It is truly existential, pragmatic and even self-interested. But this confident approach to creation and hope in divine recompense for righteousness trips up on the facts of the human condition: the good and the bad both suffer, they die equally. How can this be explained as divine justice? Here is the "crisis" of wisdom, evidenced at first hand in the books of Job and Ecclesiastes. This brutal state of human affairs issues for the later wisdom writers in a scepticism that acknowledges that we simply do not know and understand the ways of God. "His ways are not our ways." Wisdom thereby gains the boldness to confront the divine mystery. This leads to the Hebrew insight into the meaning of immortality, not in the Greek sense of the soul living forever, but in the sense that those who have loved God in righteousness are his children for eternity. This is a truth of salvation that brought forth at the time of the Maccabean martyrs a firm belief in the resurrection of the body.

6. Images of Old Testament morality

The Old Testament yields three potent images of moral living embodied in three personages belonging to three different social settings: the desert patriarch who walked in face-to-face conversation with God, the prophet driven by God's Word to establish his will and his justice in Israel above royal power and political ideology, and the seeker of wisdom in the land of exile who discovered the Lord's presence and purpose in the midst and enigmatic depth of life's experience.

7. New Testament morality

All biblical morality is religious. New Testament morality centres its message on salvation won for us by Christ. By living a life of love and service that leads to the Father we enter through faith into the Kingdom of God and enjoy eternal life. New Testament morality belongs to its times and their literary genre of expression. It does not, however, conform to the Stoic and Epicurean philosophies which claimed that one only developed a good character through the practice of their ideas: these philosophies wanted to convert individuals by their own efforts from lives dominated by passions and false desires to lives of self-mastery. Nor did the Torah's definition of how persons should conduct themselves as members of a people living in covenant with God fulfil this aim. The Christian lives "in Christ", who is God's last and eschatological Word transforming both natural religious morality and the covenant of Sinai into the new covenant in his blood. The Christian was more than the "wise person" or "universal citizen", living in harmony with the universal law of nature, whose freedom consisted in the control of mind and passions. Christians could claim that their lifestyle embodied the best ethical insights of Greek thought. They could not accept the élitism of the Essenes at Qumran nor their apocalyptic vision of the world torn apart by the twin powers of good and evil. Christians believed that God had saved the world and that redemption was offered to all in Christ. Therefore the New Testament had no need to create new legal or ethical structures to guide the lives of believers. Jesus is no interpreter of the law, nor a founder of community like the Essene Teacher of Righteousness. He is not like other rabbis who gather disciples for the study of the Torah till they in turn became masters in Israel. He calls for total, lifelong commitment and discipleship even unto death.

7.1 The originality of New Testament morality

The leading question in New Testament ethics today is how the scriptural sources can be shown to establish the distinctiveness and originality of Christian morality. It is the same merciful God who judges human conduct and speaks through the Scriptures in the community of Christ's disciples, the Church. The Scriptures remain the record of how human conduct is evaluated by God even though the Christian community is not devoted to Torah observance (Mt 5:17-20; Jas 2:8-13). Everything is now measured by Christ as the pivot, centre and goal of history. The early Church used Old Testament stories as examples for moral exhortation, e.g., Moses in 1 Corinthians 10:1-13. The Synoptic Gospels present Jesus' debates with the Pharisees over the interpretation of the law as claiming a higher standard of obedience to God's will. Unlike the scribes and Pharisees who gathered disciples around the study of the law, Jesus summons disciples from the populace at large and directs his preaching to the people as a whole rather than to Torah specialists. He uses parables and proverbial sayings much in the manner of the wisdom literature to upturn the people's false presuppositions about how they stood in God's eyes. "The first will be last, the last first." He also adopted the style of apocalyptic warning common in his age but purified it with a message of mercy in God's universal judgement on human evil. Divine judgement plays a role in ethical exhortation in the New Testament. Faithful Christians are assured of reward or vindication when the Lord comes (1 Thess 4:13-18). They are exhorted to continue lives of virtue, to worship of God and mutual love in view of the coming judgement (1 Cor 7:25-31). Those who remain under the dominion of sin and are enemies of the Gospel will be condemned at the judgement (Rom 1:18-2:16). Apocalyptic warning therefore leads to the conviction that the righteous could not persevere without God's help, that grace is necessary for salvation, and that the earth could not be cleansed of injustice against the hopeless and oppressed without divine intervention.

Pheme Perkins has succinctly summarised the issue of moral sources in the New Testament. "When the NT adopts

the rhetorical forms and content of Greco-Roman philosophical ethic, it does so within the framework of biblical and
apocalyptical images of salvation which negate a central claim
of the philosopher-preacher. Human reason properly schooled
by philosophic conversion is not the source of happiness,
justice or truth. The 'renewal of mind' (Rom 12:2) which
makes Christian ethical exhortation possible comes through
God's saving activity."[1] In this way Jesus and Paul are quite
distinct from the wandering Cynic preachers, and the early
Christian community from the closely knit and familial household gatherings of the Epicureans. Paul used the epistle, the
diatribe, household codes and the *chreia* not as a "self-taught"
Epicurean philosopher would but, in his original expression,
as "taught by God" (1 Thess 4:9).

The New Testament approach to ethics is not, therefore,
simply to establish its normative distinctness. Discussions on
normative ethics have focused on the fact that New Testament
ethical rules concentrate on the views commonly accepted for
ethical rightness in their culture: e.g., the Stoic view of reason
operative in nature or the Jewish view of all creation existing
under the sovereignty of God. There does seem to have been a
general cultural agreement about the norms of ethical behaviour accepted in the ancient world. Conscience could then
enforce common moral norms by castigating the wicked with
inward pain (Wis 17:11). At the same time the specific Christian element cannot be easily reduced to *paraenesis*, exhortation, inspiration and motivation. It does have a definite
substantial content. The New Testament does not engage in
extensive moral arguments, nor is it a moral system as such. It
is the good news of salvation that must be lived out morally if
one is to belong in God's Kingdom. A descriptive approach
traces sources, particular themes and perspectives, and respects the characteristics of individual writers and schools.

7.2 Approaches to New Testament morality

New Testament authors presume that God's salvation in
Christ makes it possible for those called to faith to lead lives

worthy of the Lord. Salvation comes as a gift of God-given liberation and freedom that is lived out in moral choices. This is not a logic that falls foul of the is-ought distinction, rather it is based in the gift of new liberty before God and humanity worked out in free human decisions. These authors also presume that Christian communities are places of mutual exhortation. Ethics is not pursued as a separate topic independent of the conviction that the decisive salvation humans expect from God has already been realised in Jesus. Because of this conviction they believed that the apocalyptic dominion of the evil powers over the cosmos had already been shattered by the exaltation of the risen Lord to God's throne (Phil 2:6-11). The Gospel of Matthew invokes the authority of the risen Lord as the basis for a universal preaching of his teaching. The New Testament claims general applicability of its ethical teaching on the basis of what God has done in Christ, and not on the basis of applying some events of Christ's life as universalisable examples of "walking in the Spirit" or "entering the Kingdom of God".

The New Testament is essentially optimistic, not predicating its morality on the "corrupt human nature" of this "present evil age", but on the premise that forgiveness of sin has already put human beings into a new relationship with God. Christians are expected to lead a life that expresses that reality. It is also realistic because the ongoing process of communal exhortation, forgiveness and reconciliation shows that the transformation of persons is truly a continuous permanent process of conversion. We can conclude that while New Testament ethics incorporates moral prescriptions, e.g., to honour one's parents, to reject marital infidelity etc., the authors do not interpret these prescriptions as a self-contained legal code but live from a standard that exceeds anything that could be formulated in legal terms (Mt 5:20; Gal 5:22-23). Nor can it be analysed as a set of universal ethical principles. It is true that all that is required by the law is mercy and love (Mt 5:43-48; 22:34-40) and that all persons are equal as children of God; he loves all equally (Mt 18:10-14), and Jesus' fellowship with sinners and other marginal persons demonstrated the universality of God's love. The various attempts at a "universal principles" approach assume that these assertions illustrate the universal principle. Only these specific assertions translate into binding obligations for Christian action today. It is insufficient merely to invoke "the motivating power" of an appeal to God. Otherwise its principles are indistinguishable from a philosophic humanism or liberation praxis based on critical theory. Christian ethics starts in a fact, not an idea. Nor is the idea of encounter with the living God sufficient to explain it. This preserves the reality of God's forgiving Word being prior to the moral efforts of human beings, all of whom stand in need of being justified in Christ (Rom 3:9-21). But it negates the need of Christian communities for a clear and concrete expression of the Lord's will in their regard such as St Paul never tired of giving his converts. Another idea of the New Testament is that it is a contextualised response in love, i.e., it is primarily concerned with relationship between persons in terms of love, reconciliation, humility, placing the needs of others above one's own interests (Phil 2:1-5). These are all exhortations to follow what God's love in Christ requires in specific situations. Such relationships become the norm of Christian living because they effect the building up of Christian communities. This conception challenges the individualism of modern life, i.e., one individual asserting his or her rights in competition with other individuals. It emphasises communal concerns and the self-sacrificing quality of love. However, if the New Testament renders only tactical examples of love's application, love itself remains indeterminate and hence is not a genuine norm, nor could it effectively help settle disputes in the community. Attempts to separate New Testament ethics from the person of Jesus and his preaching have always failed. His message is not some gnosis but the power of God for our salvation.

7.3 Focus on Jesus

The content of New Testament morality as it is revealed in the authors and text of the New Testament has been well presented in two major works: *The Moral Teaching of the*

New Testament by Rudolf Schnackenburg (Herder, New York 1965) and W. Schrage, *The Ethics of the New Testament* (T & T Clark, Edinburgh 1988). They both seek to follow the schema of: (1) the ethics of Jesus; (2) the ethics of the apostolic preaching; and (3) the ethics of the early Church.

The ethics of Jesus is focused on the preaching of the Kingdom. He proclaimed that the power of God's reign was already breaking through into human existence (Mt 12:28; Lk 17:20). His exorcisms are manifestations of the power of God overthrowing Satan (Mk 3:27; Lk 10:18). The parables of sowing the seed announce the time of joy because of an unexpected harvest. Unlike Jewish apocalypse there is no hiatus between Jesus' ministry and the manifestation of God's rule. The gift of salvation brings joy and gratitude more than the drive to strive against the evil of a world doomed to destruction. His disciples are to live as persons who experience the renewing power of his rule. Forgiveness and mercy characterise God's power and are expressed in Jesus' ministry to the marginalised and oppressed. Forgiveness becomes a standard for the disciples standing before God (Mt 6:14-15; 7:1-2; 18:21-34).

Jesus criticised the current Torah interpretation of the Sabbath observance, of valid grounds for divorce, of pure and impure foods, of tithing and the provision for ageing parents as diversions from radical conversion of heart that issues in reception of the Kingdom. Jesus does not attack the Torah as God's expression of justice. He restores it to God's original intention as a bearer of holiness by condemning its manipulation to make it fit the conditions of a world marred by sin. Discipleship means breaking with the customs that all societies hold sacrosanct such as burial of parents (Lk 9:59-60), family ties (Mk 3:31-35) and hospitality to a guest (Lk 10:38-42). These can be suspended in light of the reign of God so that the believer may put aside all day-to-day anxieties and rely on God's providence (Mt 6:11, 25-34; 10:16-31). To lead this life depends on God's power and not upon the calculation of human potential (Mt 19:10-11, 16-30).

7.4 Apostolic kerygma

The moral message of the apostolic kerygma is most strongly evidenced in St Paul's moral exhortation. For him the moral life of Christians expresses their new identity as persons "in Christ", empowered to walk in the Spirit (Gal 5:25; Rom 8:1–14). The motive for all his pastoral action and concern is "to form Christ in you", that is, to shape Christian communities exhorting them to be holy, blameless and pleasing to God. The same purpose is evident in 1 Peter and James. All these authors presume that conversion to Christianity implied adopting a style of moral life in contrast with their past life as pagans. This life requires holiness, freedom from sexual immorality and mutual love. This type of behaviour should commend the respect of nonbelievers.

St Paul holds first place in formulating the ethics of the apostolic Church because he grasped better than anyone else the intrinsic connection between salvation by grace and the obligations of the moral life. We are reconciled with God through Christ, but we have still to reconcile ourselves with God (2 Cor 5:18f.). Our old sinful self has been destroyed in baptism, being crucified and buried with Christ (Rom 6:6), but we are also to divest ourselves of our old self and its deeds and put on a new identity (Eph 4:22f.; Col 3:9f.). We live in the Spirit but we are also to make the Spirit the rule of our conduct (Gal 5:25). Thus the moral imperative is grounded in the indicative of salvation. Moral action is impossible without the divine life of grace; but this life is there to be realised in moral action. The driving force of this new life is the Spirit who is given in baptism and now impels the Christian to abandon the works of the "flesh", to root out evil passions and lust, and to produce the fruits of the Spirit (Gal 5:16; Rom 8:12f.). The weakness of the "natural man" is overcome, the empire of sin is broken and the slavery imposed by practice of the old law done away with (Rom 7:14-24). The Christian gains true moral freedom (Rom 8:2; Gal 5:1, 13) which means to serve God by doing good (Rom 6:16f.). "The law of Christ" (Gal 6:2) integrates Christian morality into the reality of redemption in Christ.

Paul recognised that conscience plays a decisive role in moral matters. As the innate sense of moral values it holds the same place for the pagan as the Mosaic law for the Jew; it goes back to creation and God's proclaiming the natural law in the covenant with Noah. For Christians too it functions as the ultimate court of appeal in case of doubt (1 Cor 8:7, 10; Rom 14:20, 23). As a capacity for right judgement it needs to be formed and educated, especially through love and concern for the weak (1 Cor 8:9-13; Rom 14:15f., 19f.). The principles of "life in Christ" are then applied to worship and the sacraments, to relationships within the community, to the sharing of wealth and well-being, to sexual morality and relationships with the world. The supreme rule in the law of Christ is always the demand of charity in imitation of Christ who laid down his life for us.

7.5 Morality and the Gospels

The Gospels record "the words and deeds" of Christ as preached in the primitive Christian communities. The earliest part of the kerygma was the recounting of the passion, death and resurrection of the Lord. The essential facts of salvation history are identified as the life-history of Jesus the Christ. Mark emphasises Jesus' call to discipleship. Jesus was an authoritative teacher and healer who came to suffer and to serve. Discipleship requires that his followers show the same willingness to suffer and to serve, to endure persecution and to go to the Cross with Jesus. Matthew's Gospel includes the epitome of Jesus' teaching, the Sermon on the Mount which sets out the "blessings" that form Jesus' "greater righteousness" (Mt 5:20), the character traits of his true disciples. "Poor in spirit" suggests the anawim, the little ones of Jewish piety. Mourning, hungering and thirsting for justice describe those who seek God's will in an evil age. Mercy, meekness, purity of heart are active qualities demonstrating the effects of salvation. Thus the Beatitudes are not just ethical qualities that anyone might cultivate. Bernard Häring has called them goal-commandments of the Kingdom and they represent a new

community of discipleship that comes into being through
Jesus and is to be proclaimed among the nations. Luke emphasises forgiveness and compassion. His Gospel announces that
the time of God's salvation is already present and is spreading
from Jerusalem to the nations. The stories in the Acts of the
Apostles provide a model for the type of Christian community
Luke envisaged, in terms of authority and sharing of goods as
service. John presents Jesus as the Messiah, he who in himself
is the truth, the way and the life. He is the one descended from
heaven in order to return to his Father, manifesting his glory.
Jesus thus becomes the model of Christian living; he is
the standard set for Christian discipleship, he who is to be
imitated by doing the will of the heavenly Father.

Christian morality is inseparable from the teaching of
Christ. Jesus is no classroom teacher who can deliver his
message and then disappear behind it. In principle any human
teacher we have ever had is dispensable and interchangeable
with someone else. The content of an algebra or a language
course is not uniquely tied to the person teaching it. Jesus is
the teacher of morality in a uniquely eschatological way, as
God's final word on how to please the Father. John P. Meir
summarises his view of Matthew's Gospel under five headings that relate to morality.[2] These are: (1) Christ is the teacher
of Christian morality; (2) Christ not only teaches Christian
morality, he grounds and embodies the life he exemplifies; his
death and resurrection make this new existence possible; (3)
this christology is inextricably bound to ecclesiology as Christ
is inextricably bound to the people; (4) the Church's mission
as regards morality is to teach and interpret all that he commanded during his earthly ministry; (5) this commission will
only be fulfilled when Christ returns as glorious judge at the
end of time so that all morality has this final scope and
eschatological dimension. Christian morality is summed up in
salvific directives that characterise the new covenant. "It was
said of old... do not murder... do not commit adultery... do not
swear falsely... but I say to you... do not bear hatred... or
lustful thoughts... do not swear but let your yes be yes and
your no be no." In this way Christ has not only interiorised the
law, he has created a new force, a new divine life of son and

daughtership in the Spirit. It is this Spirit that makes Christianity distinctive beyond formalism and casuistry. "I have come that you may have life and have it to the full" (Jn 10:10).

7.6 Principles for the use of Scripture

The fundamental principles for the use of Scripture by the people of God was laid out by the Dogmatic Constitution on Divine Revelation of the Second Vatican Council. This document binds Scripture interpreted by tradition and taught authentically by the successor of Peter in union with the apostolic college to the dogmatic statements of the Church. As the enlivening force behind scholarly reflection on morality Scripture is "the soul of theology". It is above all the inspiration and driving force for the Church's life of praise and thanks in liturgy, of meditation and spirituality for the mystic, as the standard of service and justice for the saint. The Church has witnessed a revival of the *lectio divina* since the Council. This is a slow, meditative immersion in the Word of God by lay people, religious and those in ministry. It bears fruit in the renewal of the life of the Church as a liturgy and praise, as administration and service, as proclamation and prophetism. Scripture is normative for the moral teaching of the Church, for her activity of education and formation of conscience, for her ministry to the poor, for ecumenical dialogue and service of the world. "This cultivation of Scripture is required lest any of them become 'an empty preacher of the word outwardly, who is not a listener to it inwardly'."[3]

NOTES

1. "Ethics (NT)", in *The Anchor Bible Dictionary*, Vol. II, Doubleday, New York and London 1992, 655.
2. *The Vision of Matthew: Christ, Church and Morality in the First Gospel*, Paulist Press, New York 1978, 43-44.
3. The Second Vatican Council, Dogmatic Constitution on Divine Revelation, *Dei Verbum*, 18 November 1965, n. 25.

5

Tradition: the getting of wisdom

Cicero has left us the great saying that "History is the teacher of life." The communication of Christ as "the way, the truth, and the life" occurs from generation to generation down the centuries and it is the work of tradition. Tradition here is more than the digging up of the past, the study of tomes in long dead languages; tradition has a doctrinal sense for Christians as the continuing living presence of Christ among us in the Church and world. By tradition we are in contact with him as the one who has the power to gather up the wisdom of the past, and instils the strength to face the challenge of the future and the wisdom to decide rightly in the present moment. For the Church it means that she may decide prudently how to conduct her life in the present epoch. Karl Rahner considers the Pastoral Constitution *Gaudium et Spes* nothing other than a prudent decision on how the Church should live the Gospel in the present moment.

1. The Fathers' contribution

Moral theology has benefited from the biblical and liturgical movements that have renewed the Church's life this century. The patristic renewal has also restored the moralist's awareness of the Fathers of the Church. Born only after World War II, the history of moral theology is today a discipline in its own right. Its aim is the study of the sources of our moral tradition so as to enrich and renew our moral awareness. It is a truism that those who are ignorant of history are destined to repeat its mistakes. Many of the conflicts in contemporary moral theology have their roots in ancient debates, e.g., disputes between laxism and rigorism recur as do tensions between situation and principles, absolutes and exceptions to moral rules. F.X. Murphy notes that there is considerable development in patristic thought from the first post-apostolic catechesis in the *Didache* to the properly moral treatises of St Ambrose and St Augustine in the West, and the homiletic exhortations of St John Chrystostom and St Maximus the Confessor in the East. This pattern "consists in a fusing of the Judaic concept of divine Wisdom (*hokmah*) and the Holiness Code of Leviticus and Deuteronomy into a Christocentric moral way of life."[1] This evolution was stimulated by the assumption of Greek philosophy into the faith vision of the early Church.

Nearest in time to the New Testament are the *Apostolic Fathers* who apply the Christian message for converts from the Hellenic world. Their writings are mostly ethical treatises whose substance is moral catechesis. They include the *Didache*, the *Letter of Pseudo-Barnabas*, the *Letter of Clement of Rome*, the *Shepherd of Hermas*, the *Letters of Ignatius* and the *Letter of Polycarp*. The catechetical practices of the early Church shine through the *Didache* as it emphasises the doctrine of the "two ways" of good or evil, as "life and death". It repeats the fundamental principle of Judeo-Christian morality, love of God and love of neighbour, adding the axiom of the golden rule. It then interweaves the prescriptions of the Decalogue with these principles of life in Christ and uses them to resolve the practical difficulties of existence. Pseudo-Barnabas symbolises the "two ways" as those of light and darkness where Christ sheds the light of true *gnosis*. Ignatius of Antioch sees Christ as the immediate and absolute foundation of moral living. His martyrdom in imitation of Christ set the standard for all believers. The Christian is the one who imitates Christ in his passion; this is the motivation of his daily life. The Christian demonstrates his or her love through care for "the widow and orphan, the oppressed, the prisoner as well as the freeman, the hungry and the thirsty" (*Smyr* 6: 2). The Christian ethic is based on the Word of God as revealed in the Scriptures, and has as its end obedience to and union with the heavenly Father. It is not self-justifying or self-contained as is the Platonic ideal of contemplation or the Stoic achievement of the good or *honestum*. We have here a good insight into moral instruction in the early Church as "the law of the Spirit". The Decalogue spells out "the way of God" and so integrates traditional moral teaching in Israel into the new covenant in Christ's blood. The early Church also witnessed disputes over penance and excommunication from the flock of the holy as a sign of her purity before God. The *Shepherd of Hermas* is a treatise on penance and conversion which is anchored to the law of God as represented by his Son. Church order is seen forming and the ideals of being one with Christ in life and death are strongly projected to following generations.

With the *apologists* of the second century the atmosphere changes. They witness to the revolution introduced by the new religion. They use new cultured ways to defend their fellow Christians from the criminal calumnies levelled against them by their pagan or Jewish enemies. At the same time they begin to assess the moral and philosophical thought of their contemporaries, attacking the idolatry and superstition of their religious ideas. They use the literary fashions of the day to claim a hearing for the divine truth of which they were heralds. Justin Martyr is typical of their claim that Christianity alone is conformable with what is noble and right in the human soul; it alone can realise what the pagans aspire to. There is thus a true *rapprochement* between the Christian moral message and human reason, because, as Justin saw, both flow from the same divine Logos. Irenaeus of Lyons gave the first systematic treatment of Christian morality. He began by refuting the gnostic doctrine of evil as a primary principle of reality, co-equal with goodness. He insists on the unity of the human composite in Pauline terms of flesh-soul-spirit. His anthropology has its roots in the incarnation. In Christ we encounter the perfect man, who has a true earthly body and soul, yet is a spirit because he is also God. In creating us according to his image and likeness we are truly *imago Dei* on the model of Christ, his only begotten Son. As Christ entered creation, becoming human and enduring the same struggle with evil that we undergo – but instead of suffering defeat by temptation he actually triumphed over sin and death in the resurrection – so we are destined for final glory and deathlessness with Christ. This transformation is worked out in the Church which is the body of Christ. It will be accomplished only in the final resurrection, in the "recapitulation" of all in Christ, a fulfilment that had its start in God's decision to "make man in our image".

Eric Osborn in his masterful *Ethical Patterns in Early Christian Thought* observed how in the second century the problems of converted intellectuals, pagan ridicule and philosophic attack combined to make Christians feel insecure and hastened the Hellenisation of Christian thought. "The process is most rapid in Clement" (of Alexandria).[2] He viewed pagan wisdom as "so many seeds strewn by the Logos". His three main writings, *Protrepicus* (Exhortation), *Paedagogus* (The Instructor) and *Stromateis* (Miscellanies), form a progressive account of Christian knowledge. He describes a typical day in the life of a Christian with its temptations, challenges and duties. He defends marriage as "the perfection of the world"[3] against the gnostics who denied its natural necessity for the future of society. He also entered into the dispute over the possession of wealth by Christians. He saw that the problem was not so much in the possession of wealth as in the desire for it and in its misuse. Even a rich man could be saved if he used his riches to succour others. The Word of God is ever present to Christians to bring them into union with the Father with whom they share immortality through deification, a theme dear to the Oriental Church. His successor Origen gave an essentially Platonist interpretation of Christian praxis in which moral life is an *askesis* through which the believer is led, under the tutelage of the Word and Spirit, to fulfilment by centring his or her all in the divine mystery. He also wrote in praise of martyrdom. Tertullian in Africa saw Christian life primarily as *disciplina*, that way of life involving continence, purity and simplicity as obedience to God's will in contradiction to the world's idolatry that must expect the impending judgement. He is responsible for fashioning much of the West's Latin formulas in dogma and morals.

The peace of Constantine in 313 AD brought a completely new orientation; the desert Fathers and monks tried to continue a morality of "white martyrdom" by "flight from the world" and dedicating themselves completely to "the search for God", as St Benedict expressed it in his Rule. The religious or monastic life became the ideal for living Gospel values and theology was done as *lectio divina*. In Athanasius of Alexandria, Basil of Caesarea and his brother Gregory of Nyssa the *monastic movement* found interpreters who set its practices within the framework of an ascetical and mystic theology.

The *Fathers of the Church* were great bishop-preachers and teachers of Christian faith and practice through their pastoral leadership of the Christian community. They are referred to as Church Fathers not only because they were so close to the apostles, but more because out of that contact they generated the teaching, leadership and institutions that have been a normative reference-point for subsequent history. They gave the Church's moral teaching a shape that has endured down the centuries. St Thomas Aquinas called the Fathers "Saints" because their lives and preaching set the standard for the Church. He says, "The goal of Scripture is the instruction of men. But this instruction of men from Scripture cannot take place except through the expositions of the Saints."[4] The model pastor was St John Chrysostom, who heroically withstood the corruption of the imperial power in Constantinople and was a reformer of clerical laxity and luxury. His homilies remain the great statement of concern for love and justice in personal and public life. John saw ethics as a pastor. He preached with the aim of turning his hearers from conventional Christianity to an inward and outward dedication of life. He attacked the scandalous neglect of the poor and denounced the double standards of men and women in sexual behaviour. His preaching was always the power of Christ's love for his flock. "Love is the great teacher. She is the power to free men from error, to form their minds, to take them by the hand and to lead them on to wisdom."[5] His teaching forms the key to moral doctrine in the East.

St Ambrose prepared a manual of pastoral practice and moral instruction for the clergy, *De Officiis*, that took over from Cicero's work the title, plan and leading ideas such as the cardinal virtues. St Augustine is acknowledged as the Doctor of Divine Charity whose life and theology dominated

Catholic thought through the Middle Ages into the present. Cardinal Newman asserts that St Augustine, as it were, gave "a new edition of Christianity" and "though no infallible teacher formed the mind of Christian Europe".[6] He wrote his *Confessions* to give an account of himself before God to humanity: "Apud te, haec narro, generi meo, generi humano".[7] The incommunicable experience of his conversion and way to God has been of inexhaustible value to everyone who has sought for meaning in life and could settle for nothing less than the truth of the redeeming God. By entering his or her soul the believer sets out in search of wisdom as that ultimate truth whose possession alone can render it happy. God is this final end, the absolute good whose presence is revealed only by yielding in faith to the movement of his love in the depth of the human heart. The modern psyche too has come to recognise itself in this spiritual odyssey toward wisdom. Although at first Augustine was in error about the nature of the truth he sought and was so inwardly confused by lust as to be unable to follow the light, he never abandoned trust in the name of Christ who led him through Manichaeism, neo-Platonism and the ethics of the Stoics to the truth of the Scriptures. He found reason must yield to the reasonableness of faith. "Unless you believe you shall not understand." His acceptance into the Catholic Church transformed his understanding of moral obligation and the function it played in conscience. He saw that authority was necessary because, re-echoing his dilemma from Romans 7, "we approve one thing by our reason and pursue another in our vanity" (*De ver. rel.*, 24.45). Authority is the "medicine of the soul" that will bring it back to health. And what does authority stipulate? The way of life enjoined by belief in the scriptural laws, precepts and commandments. "A way of life agreeable to these divine commandments will purge the mind and make it fit for higher understanding" (*De ver. rel.*, 7.13). For Augustine morality is ultimately founded in the *rationes aeternae* of the eternal law that we perceive through contemplation in the interior Master's illumination. In this way moral law became binding in conscience, for, as Roland-Gosselin observes most accurately, pagan morality while searching for God "did not succeed in effectively establishing the concept of duty in the inner conscience".[8] The unity of our will with the will of God is a work of personal love. For St Augustine this relationship is spelt out by St Paul and St John. "We cannot even have an effective will to love Him if He does not first come, by His grace, to arouse our love, to strengthen it, increase it, and raise it to Himself."[9] We depend on prayer to live in love and grace. "Give me what you ask, and ask what you will."[10] In the end all depends on love and grace, as became obvious in his defence of free will against Pelagian determinism. "Neither knowledge of the divine law, nor nature, nor the mere remission of sin constitute grace. Grace is given us by Jesus Christ, our Lord, that through it the law may be fulfilled, nature liberated and sin over-come."[11] Augustine's idea of morality becomes fully evident in his treatise *The Sermon on the Mount*. It is an ethics of beatitude that unites the moral virtues with the gifts of the Spirit in the new law. This conception was expanded by his defining love as the centre of Christian life; in his conviction that the powerful, pervasive force of evil must yield to grace in the progress of history; in an understanding of sexuality that provided the base both for the monastic tradition and for Christian marriage; in a theory of politics that linked order, justice and peace so as to define both good rule and good citizenship; in establishing moral parameters for the justification and the limitation of war. Embedded in the culture of the late classical world he formed the tradition that has guided religious thought, Catholic and Protestant, ever since. His approach was continued by Pope St Gregory the Great but in a simpler fashion, particularly in his commentary on Job and his *Moralia*, which became the bishop's manual right through the Middle Ages.

2. The Middle Ages

The *Dark Ages* are usually considered a *nul point* in the history of moral theology. They were, however, of paramount import for the formation of *popular religion* and religious practices in Western Europe. It was in this period that the cult of the martyrs took hold and particularly the veneration of relics. Saints were seen as intercessors with an unapproachable divinity. In fact, in superstitious religion they seemed to substitute for the pagan pantheon, each saint having a particular clientele whose work and welfare had to be protected. This is the period when the feudal structure of society passed over into the religious ideology as the idea of heavenly patronage. The myths and stories of the martyrs and saints set the pattern of heroic living and striving that guaranteed heavenly protection. Nowhere was this mentality more evident than in the expiation and remission of sin. With the collapse of public penance in the late Roman empire the Celtic monks spread the practice of private confession from the British Isles across Europe to Germany, France, Switzerland and Italy. Set penances were fixed for set sins so that the system became known as tariff penance. The books to which the monks resorted to determine the fine or penance to be done by the penitent after confession were called *Penitentials*. These lists of sin remained in vogue up till the sacramental reform of Innocent III introduced the paschal duty in the Fourth Lateran Council in 1215. Afterwards they still continued to form the base for the *summas* and manuals used by priests in their confessional work. It may be said they represent a privatisation and clericalisation of sin, penance, forgiveness and reconciliation in the Church. Associated with penance was the practice of indulgences to remit the effects of sin from the treasury of the Church. The Middle Ages progressively projected a very physical image of hell as perdition, perdition not so much as loss of God but as punishment by way of mental and corporeal torment. The idea of mortal sin as requiring eternal punishment became strongly rooted in popular preaching and belief, while the mercy of God was communicated through the compassion of Christ and the intercession of Our Lady. One must look to the decrees and canons to find documentary evidence of how the Church leadership faced the crisis of the Dark Ages.

Intellectual life began to revive with the School of Chartres in the eleventh century and with it the renewed study of dialectic and the reading of the ancient authors. St Anselm gave an original account of St Augustine's moral thought, reflecting on the source of moral goodness and how it relates to liberty. The tensions inherent in his thought come to a climax with the dispute between Abelard and St Bernard. For Abelard the principal determinant of good and evil in actions was the intention of the agent. Conscience is good or bad in so far as the agent consents to and acts from a good or bad intention. This line of thought which seems to cut conscience loose from the objective moral order was balanced by the condition that the intention should seek the objective good. Sin in this way of thinking is deeper than an objective bad action and touches one's intimate relationship with God. St Bernard as a spiritual master could not but see the validity of purity of intention, but he feared that without an objective standard the agent would become a law *a se*. There were notable developments in ethics in the twelfth century as regards logic, the theory of virtue and of education. These developments combined with the new translations of Aristotle's works that were spreading through the universities. Peter Lombard's *Sententiarum Libri Quattuor* is the classic monument to twelfth-century theology and became the approved text for students of theology for nearly four hundred years. Moral questions were treated especially in book 2, on the fall of Adam, under the titles of freedom and sin; book 3 asks if Christ possessed all the virtues and goes on to the theological and cardinal virtues along with the gifts of the Holy Spirit; in book 4 on the sacraments the moral problems connected with them are expounded.

The *thirteenth century* saw the reception of *Aristotle's great philosophical works* on metaphysics and ethics as well as the coming of the mendicants to the great universities, particularly Paris. It was the masters of the Faculty of Arts of the University of Paris who especially elaborated a scientific exposition of ethics that St Thomas would integrate into his theology. The *Franciscan school* from Alexander of Hales (d. 1245) to John Duns Scotus (d. 1308), including St Bonaventure, produced a theological and moral synthesis — centred on the person of Christ. They believed that moral theology should serve not just for contemplation but to make us better by instilling goodness. Bonaventure is remembered as the Seraphic Doctor, the Devout Teacher, by reason of the spiritual unction manifested in his writings and sermons. To grow in the things of the Spirit, he would say, love must go hand in hand with learning. At a certain point it must let study dally behind while it runs ahead with interior joy toward the gift who is God himself. The greatest of Bonaventure's works is the *Itinerarium Mentis in Deum*, the journey of the inner person inwards and upwards to God. It is a deeply theological and mystical study of how the human person soars toward God. God speaks to the loving believer as the one and only Master of knowledge, illuminating his or her mind. The whole of creation speaks to him or her as a world of signs and traces in which every being is a word of God. Starting from the humble and suppliant prayer of a Friar Minor, keeping the eyes of body and spirit open to the contemplation of the Infinite and the infinitude of beings, Bonaventure reaches up to the highest speculation. Indeed, he may be said to have synthesised the vision of Pseudo-Dionysius with the most authentic insights of Augustine. Although he benefited from Aristotle's philosophy, he remained sceptical of its rationalism, never allowing it to overshadow faith and a will rightly directed to God.

Albert the Great led the way in coping in a Christian manner with the pagan Greek and Arabic learning just then being discovered. He was the first scholastic to comment on Aristotle's *Nicomachean Ethics* and his researches and teaching pointed the way for Thomas Aquinas. The principal problem facing any effort to synthesise Christian tradition and Aristotelian learning was how to reconcile the history of salvation with the philosophic idea of science. This problem was implicit in all the medieval *summas*. St Thomas brought both ideas together in the *exitus-reditus* pattern that could be used to explain how creation and redemption flowed from God and returned to him in a circular movement of which God was the cause, the alpha and omega. Theology is therefore a rational development of faith, a science subalternated to God's own knowledge of himself. The moral theology of the Angelic Doctor is a theology of the person as the image of God, created by God, returning to God, through Christ. The *Summa*

Theologiae is elaborated in three phases: (1) God in himself as one and Trinity, and his creation and the providence he exercises over it; (2) the return of the human agent to God, "motus in Deum", which sets the foundations of morality; and (3) Christ as the way back to the Father through the Church and sacraments. The second part is subdivided into general moral theology, which treats God as our final good and beatitude; human action as the way of reaching him through deliberation, will and the passions; virtue and vice fashion the agent in goodness according to grace and reason, or in sin by deviation from God; law sets our path to God whether as fixed by God himself in eternal law, as shared with us in natural law, as determined and fitted to the human situation by reason in human law, or as revealed in the old or now in the new covenant, the new law where we are led by the Spirit to the fullness of charity; finally, grace enables us to live the new life of the liberty of God's children through justification and co-operation with God's providence. The second subdivision counts as particular moral theology, which may rightly be characterised as a theology of the virtues. It surveys theological life in faith, hope and charity, and human morality under the power of grace in the cardinal virtues of prudence, justice, fortitude and temperance. All the virtues are analysed according to the virtue itself, the gift of the Spirit that completes it, the sin opposed to it and the precepts that govern its activity. He adds the charisms of prophecy and inspiration, and of episcopal leadership in the Church, and the vocations of the active and contemplative lifestyles. This picture is part of a total theological synthesis so that moral theology is theology properly so called as knowledge of how God moves in human life and history to lead us to himself, our final happiness. For the first time the moral parts of theology were systematically grouped together, not as an autonomous discipline but as an integral part of theology. St Thomas' thought has become a necessary pivot or centre-point and criterion of judgement in the intellectual history of the Catholic Church. It has had two great revivals; in the sixteenth-century school of Salamanca and in the neo-scholastic renewal promulgated by Leo XIII with *Aeterni Patris* in 1879.

3. Nominalism

Hardly had Thomas produced his synthesis when it came under attack and began to disintegrate as a cultural force. A number of propositions held by St Thomas were included in the condemnations at Paris and Oxford in 1270 and 1277. These had the effect of turning theologians' attention from the intrinsic necessary reasons of things to considerations of the contingencies of divine and human freedom.

John Duns Scotus reacted against philosophic rationalism by making the love of God the supreme and absolute norm of ethics.

Following on the Franciscan position that it was always God's will to incorporate humanity into his Son, it follows logically that the precept of loving God in obedience to his will is the one and only norm indispensable and immutable in moral theology. God is infinite goodness and the supreme object of love. The first three precepts of the Decalogue are therefore absolute and indispensable, while the others depend on a positive will of God. To disobey them is evil not intrinsically, but because the action has been forbidden or prohibited.

Scotus, however, says that adultery, for example, is against the natural law. This means that all in all it is recognised as doing evil in society, but could in case of necessity, e.g., if the human race were in danger of decimation by underpopulation, be dispensed by God. Thus the Franciscan school emphasised the primacy of charity and the primacy of the will.

William of Ockham, whose nominalism denied the existence of essences and who held that words were nothing more than names for collections of things without any real reference, changed the direction and understanding of Christian morality by his treatment of moral obligation.

Ockham looked to theology for what he could not prove in philosophy. Proofs were to be established not from *a priori* principles but by studying concrete existents. By giving first place to intuitive knowledge of the concrete individual, Ockham prepared the way for the experimental method in science and casuistry in moral theology. As free beings humans are subject to obligation. The ontological foundation of obligation is the dependence of the creature on the omnipotent, holy will of God. Obligation arises in the encounter between a created free will and the divine will. "By the very fact God wills something, it is right for it to be done."[12] If God as conceived by faith is good, it follows that whatever God wills is good, and whatever God commands is right. But God is in no way determined. "Obligation does not fall on God since he is in no way under any obligation to do anything."[13]

Ockham's idea of God goes outside the range of philosophical proof and fits into a Christian conception of doing the will of God above seeking one's self-fulfilment. If one does seek happiness it is because one has been commanded to do so by God. The divine will is thus the ultimate norm for the Christian.

This does not mean, however, that humans are absolutely dependent on revelation to distinguish between right and wrong. Ockham also appeals to "right reason" as a norm of morality. If a person is ignorant of a moral law through no fault of their own, then it becomes a matter of conscience. "A created will which follows an invincibly erroneous conscience is a right will." This stance justified for later moralists an action as good that St Thomas could only excuse from sin. Since Ockham sees no contradiction in God ordering one man to kill another or to commit fornication, he maintains that God by his absolute power, *potentia absoluta*, could command what in fact is forbidden. Such an act, he says, would be good and meritorious. But God has so created humanity that certain acts are harmful to human nature and society. This makes a rational ethics possible, since God wills by his *potentia ordinata*, his power in relation to his actual creative activity, that humans are to follow the dictates of right reason. Reason through experience can discern something of the moral order that God has established. Morality thereby becomes a legal contest between untrammelled freedom and divinely imposed obligation. By identifying all philosophy with necessity of the will, obligation became a matter solely of God's will that divorced faith and reason for future centuries. Philippe Delhaye notes quite astutely that "It was no accident that Ockham's followers tended to confuse law and morality, turning their backs on an ethics of charity and the virtues."[14] The University of Paris became the centre of nominalist thought, as may be seen by such exponents as Jean Buridan, Pierre d'Ailly, and Jean Gerson. Gabriel Biel gave Ockhamism the scholarly form in which it influenced Martin Luther.

Martin Luther's entire religious life as an Augustinian friar and as professor at Wittenberg was overshadowed by a preoccupation about how to stand right before God in full peace of mind. He had an illumination, an experience of God's justification inspired by his studies of St Paul's Epistle to the Romans, and "the gates of paradise were opened". This was probably in 1512. In his explanation of how this occurred Luther rejected the logic in the traditional teaching of the Church. He held that justification was not an ontological transformation of the sinner into a friend of God. By grace he or she ceased to be identified as a sinner. According to Luther the Gospel reinstates the sinner *qua* sinner in the sight of God. Grace then acts to cover the state of sinner which remains. As God's gift it makes the sinner acceptable to God. These ideas gradually formed between 1513 and 1518 and led to his breaking with the Church. His theology of "homo simul justus et peccator" grew out of a very personal experience, a preoccupation with personal salvation that was to occupy Catholics and Protestants with questions of grace, freedom, predestination and damnation over the coming centuries. He went on to condemn what he saw as the works-righteousness inherent in Catholic philosophical theology. He thus emphasised the tension between Gospel and Law, speaking of "grace alone", "Christ alone", "Scripture alone", and "faith alone" as aspects of the saving event. Luther emphasised the importance of everyday life and particularly of the marriage vocation for salvation. Today there is a *rapprochement* between Lutherans and Catholics, particularly on the question of justification as a basis for further dialogue in Christian ethics and moral theology. Reformed theology in the Calvinist tradition emphasises God's transcendence as the "utterly Other" whose commands are to be followed in faith.

4. The Tridentine reform

The sixteenth century saw the growth of reform movements among Catholics as well. The *Thomistic renewal*
appeared simultaneously in Germany with Conrad Köllin,
with Cardinal Cajetan in Italy and Pierre Crockaert O.P. in
France, who replaced Lombard's *Sentences* with Thomas'
Summa as a classroom text. This move considerably influenced the evolution of moral theology since Pars II was the
most widely taught and commented upon.

The reform spread to Spain and especially Salamanca,
where Francisco de Vitoria O.P. introduced the new methods
of the Parisian masters. The school of Salamanca was before
all else a school of moral theology and Pars II was studied
with an eye to contemporary problems. Francisco de Vitoria is
famous as the founder of international law which arose from
his reflections on the Spanish conquests in America and his
defence of the rights of the Indians from the charge of natural
slavery and that they had ceded their dominion to property by
sin. Vitoria reinterpreted St Thomas in his *De Indiis et de Iure
Belli Relectiones*: "Dominion is founded on the image of God;
but man is God's image by nature, that is, by his reasoning
powers; therefore dominion is not lost by mortal sin" (I. 320).

Melchior Cano renewed theological method with his *De
Locis Theologicis*. Dominic Soto's *De Justitia* became the
model for future tracts on justice in its individual and social
aspects. Bartholomeo de Medina propounded the formula of
probabilism in order to find moral solutions for a society in a
ferment of cultural and economic change. Dominic Bañez
continued the same tradition but in a more speculative way.

Toward the end of the sixteenth century the two *Jesuits*,
Gabriel Vásquez and Francisco Suarez, came to Salamanca.
They adopted the *Summa* for their teaching but they approached
it with a new freedom, much in the spirit of the Renaissance.
They both accentuated the roles of law and philosophy in
moral theology, particularly as regards the theory of natural
law. For Vásquez natural law is identical with human nature.
Nature forms the foundation of morality; natural law receives
its obligatory character from rational human nature. An act is

good when it conforms to human nature and evil when it defects from it. Suarez, in his *De Legibus et Legislatore Deo*, makes obligation the central feature of law. Law then is "An act of a just and right will by which a superior wills to oblige his inferior to do this or that." Command is no longer primarily an act of intellect as in St Thomas, but of a superior's will binding a subject. Therefore the obligation to follow the divine law comes immediately from God; the obligation to obey human laws derives proximately from the will of the superior, although ultimately it comes totally from the will of God. Suarez managed to balance an ethic of intrinsic goods and evils with an idea of obligation that inevitably led back into the divine will and power.

The *Summas of practical cases*, usually arranged in alphabetical order as dictionaries of casuistry, were popular from the fourteenth to the sixteenth century. The best known were the *Summa de Casibus Paenitentiae* of St Raymond of Peñafort (1275), the *Summa Pisana* (1338) of Bartolomeo of San Concordia O.P., the *Summa Angelica* of Angelo di Chivasso O.F.M., the *Summa Sylvestrina* of Sylvestre de Prierias and the very successful *Enchiridion Confessariorum* of Navarrus, which went through eighty-one editions between 1549 and 1619. St Antoninus of Florence's *Summa Theologica* is much more extensive and reflects the economic and moral condition of Renaissance Florence. His work pointed the way to the Tridentine reforms. There were also *Confessionalia* which were vademecums for priests as confessors.

The end of the sixteenth century witnessed the invention of a new way of doing moral theology that fitted somewhere between the commentaries on the *Summa* and the alphabetical lists used by priests as confessional manuals. The *Institutiones Morales* were really a consequence of the Council of Trent. It had called for a renewal of pastoral practice, particularly of the sacrament of penance and of the study of moral theology. The seminary was a new way of preparing future priests for their ministry with a cycle of studies much shorter than the universities. Two years were given over to the study of cases of conscience. This led to the writing of a new manual for the study of cases of conscience as the professional knowledge required of priests as ministers of reconciliation in the Church. Its ground plan derives from the *Ratio Studiorum* of the Society of Jesus. With a view to the administration of the sacrament of penance it culled whatever seemed useful on human acts, law, conscience and sin from Pars II of the *Summa*. Particular cases were then studied in the following order: the ten commandments and the commandments of the Church, the sacraments and ecclesiastical censures.

Beginning with the practice in the Roman College introduced by the Jesuits, a separate professor was assigned to the exposition of this new discipline. This is the origin of the separation of moral theology from dogmatics, spirituality and ascetic theology. When Juan Azor published his *Institutiones Morales* in 1600 it was an instant success because of its immense practicality. This plan was used by many Jesuits in the seventeenth century including Thomas Sanchez in his *Opus Morale in Praecepta Decalogi,* Paul Layman, Fernando de Castro Palao, Juan de Lugo and Hermann Busenbaum, whose *Medulla Theologiae Moralis* became the model of this genre of theological writing. The plan advocated in the *Institutiones* held sway into the twentieth century, even up till the Second Vatican Council. The other great achievement of the seventeenth century was the *Cursus Theologiae Moralis* by the Carmelites of Salamanca. It fortunately escaped the ferocious controversy of the schools that century.

5. The Jesuits and Jansenism

The Jesuit manualists assimilated the *system of probabilism* as it had been formulated by Bartholomeo de Medina O.P.: "if an opinion is probable, it is permissible to adopt it, even if the opposite be more probable".[15] A probable opinion was therefore "one that is put forward by wise men and confirmed by very good arguments".[16] It proved to be a most useful instrument for a society in rapid change and for a Church caught in the confusion of the age and striving to reform its own internal life.

Once the theory was well articulated it spread through the

universities and stimulated case studies as already noted. The purpose of the system was to give a person sufficient certainty to act morally by overcoming or resolving doubts that could paralyse action. It was meant to issue in tranquillity of conscience. It strongly advocated the principle advanced by Suarez that a doubtful law does not oblige in conscience. It privileged the position of the one in possession. Tensions associated with late Renaissance culture, disputes over Church reform and the *de auxiliis* controversy between Jesuits and Dominicans on the question of grace and free will easily overflowed into quarrels on how to weigh moral opinions and on the meaning of probabilism itself.

It is true that some moralists did extend probabilism beyond all reason with opinions too favourable to novelty or indulgence. Among those numbered as *laxists* are Diana whose *Resolutiones Morales* examined over 20,000 cases, Antonio de Escobar, Tommaso Tamburini and Juan Caramuel y Lobkowitz, called "the prince of laxists".

In reaction the benign optimism of the Jesuits in the sacrament of penance was called into question by the rigorists. Unfortunately this reaction got mixed up with the Jansenist movement for reform. Saint-Cyran and Cornelius Jansenius "professed a desire to save the Catholic Church from what they considered the corrupt morals of the Jesuits by installing their nightmare creed which closed the gates of God's mercy to all but a select coterie".[17]

Blaise Pascal delivered a withering attack on the Jesuits' moral theology and spirituality with his *Lettres Provinciales*, which had a tremendous success as a literary effort and turned public opinion against probabilism. Their effect is felt even today in the popular prejudice against casuistry as nothing more than equivocation. Jansenists wanted a delay of absolution where a penitent's conversion was not perfect and a return to the rigorism of the penitential practice of the ancient Church.

Here we reach the nub of the seventeenth- and eighteenth-century crisis in moral theology. In 1656 the Dominicans, who had been moderate probabilists, began to change their position, espousing *probabiliorism*. This meant that in a conflict of conscience between a law and personal freedom of action the law was to be given greater weight. By the end of the century severity ruled in France and spread from there to Louvain and to nearly every Catholic country. The magisterium intervened only to limit or cut off the extreme opinions. Alexander VII (1665-66) and Innocent XI (1679) condemned more than 100 laxist propositions. Alexander VIII (1690) condemned both laxist and rigorist theses. The Holy See, however, refrained from intervening in the dispute between probabilists and probabiliorists as such.

6. St Alphonsus

The consequence of this crisis in moral thought was a wave of alienation of ordinary people from the Church because they found her unapproachable, particularly in the sacrament of penance. The debate raged fiercely in Italy when two Dominicans, D. Concina and G.V. Patuzzi, attacked a number of Jesuit moralists and Alphonsus Liguori.

Alphonsus had been trained in the rigorist school but was converted to probabilism by his pastoral experience on parish missions. He strove his whole life to unravel the problems set by probabilism. He always had a *pastoral aim* in view, *the salvation and sanctity of the people.*

In his *Theologia Moralis*, as well as in the *Homo Apostolicus* and in his many dissertations, he strove to develop an original system that would remove the tensions caused by both rigorism and laxism. This he called equiprobabilism. Where there is a law in possession of conscience it must be respected as the truth. Where the law does not bind, the person remains free. Where, however, law and freedom seem to balance, freedom is in possession since the law is doubtful.

Alphonsus thus became the apostle of freedom through a search for truth in the depth of conscience. His genius is also evident in his spiritual writings and his pastoral innovations that aimed "to leave the soul firmly bound to Christ".[18] He proposed a full Christian programme of life that instilled sound moral reasoning and a deep devotional life of prayer.

Father Labourdette O.P. summed up his contribution as his setting out moral decisions "weighed in the conscience of a saint".[19]

His approach set the tone for the Church over the last two centuries. In 1831 the Sacred Penitentiary issued a decree stating that all the moral opinions set forth by Alphonsus could safely be followed in the confessional. In 1839 he was canonised and in 1871 declared a Doctor of the Church by Pius IX for his moral and spiritual teaching. Pius XII declared him patron of confessors and moral theologians in 1950.

The manual tradition was continued in the nineteenth century by J.P. Gury S.J. and A. Ballerini S.J., who revived the question of the character of probabilism in St Alphonsus. The Redemptorists Wouters, Konings, Marc-Gestermann, Aertnys-Damen and Visser continued the thought of their founder, updating it from changes in canon law, dogmatics and society itself. St Alphonsus' opinion, if not his system, became the common doctrine of Catholic moralists about the time of the First Vatican Council.

7. The fate of casuistry

Paralleling the development of probabilism was the practice of casuistry among some Protestants and particularly in the Anglican Communion. The *Caroline divines*, especially Robert Sanderson and Jeremy Taylor, were great casuists of a probabiliorist kind. The English Civil War was a religious war that led to a loss of power and prestige for these divines.

What should not be passed over in silence is how casuistry was transformed by the *secularisation of thought* beginning in the seventeenth century. The key figure in this process is John Locke. He borrowed the ideas and techniques of the Catholic casuists and planted them in the practice of the law. There was, as Edmund Leites notes, a deep antagonism between lawyers and casuists. They both understood themselves to be vying for control over conscience.

The same applied to political theorists. Lawyers thought that clerics should not meddle in the lives of the people by determining what was permissible and what forbidden in matters that should be the sole concern of the common law. With this mentality went a new awareness of the penal power of the law as an instrument of a government's control over society. Clerics should not be judges of conscience relying on the punitive power of the law. They were to be teachers, spiritual and moral formators. Both Grotius and Locke envisaged an entirely educative role for the divines. The function of the clergy was to encourage people to form their characters on the basis of the love of God and neighbour. "Law, Locke wrote, works by force, but the task of religion is to make men true Christians in their hearts."[20] A wedge is here placed between the teaching authority of the Church and the conscience of the believer.

This process of laicising the moral direction of conscience and placing it in the hands of governments whose instrument was the civil law became a principal platform of the Enlightenment. It spread to Catholic countries particularly after the French Revolution and eventually became the principal reason for the disappearance of casuistry in Catholic institutions of higher learning.

8. Renewal in Germany

John Michael Sailer and *John Baptist Hirscher* were pioneers in a vital renewal of moral theology in nineteenth-century Germany. They saw that casuistry was overconcerned with setting down limits to the positive law and had forgotten grace and the divine law written in the human heart. They wanted a moral theology that would project the ideal of the Christian life. Their technique moved from jurisprudence to a language nearer to life and the Gospel.

Sailer's first attempts to present moral theology in a new mould bear the marks of Enlightenment rationalism. At the height of his intellectual and moral maturity he wrote his *Handbuch der christlichen Moral* ("Handbook of Christian Morality", 1817), whose subtitle indicates that it is for the formation of priests as directors of souls and for the educated layman. Bernard Häring's *The Law of Christ* in 1954 took up the same practical programme of presenting the ideal of Christian living for priests and laity.

In contrast with his earlier work, Sailer moved away from the coldness of rationalism to a theology of the heart well suited to the high tide of Romanticism. The title of Hirscher's classic opus also reveals his intent, *Die christliche Moral als Lehre von der Verwirklichung des Reiches Gottes* ("Christian Moral Teaching as the Realisation of the Kingdom of God").

Later the *school of Tübingen*, following the lead toward studying the development of doctrine set by Adam Möhler, produced several important moralists who underlined the dynamic character of the Christian life. They do not look upon Christian life as the application of static norms but as the living out of grace. F.X. Linsenmann saw that as life in God grows the believer becomes ever more aware of the divine call as vocation and that this is the source of his or her God-given liberty. His *Lehrbuch der Moraltheologie* is a fine balance between the practical and the speculative, between inspiration and casuistry. K. Werner, B. Fuchs and M. Jocham were also famous names in the Tübingen school. These theologians strove to enrich moral teaching from Scripture and the Fathers and to meet the intellectual demands whether of the Enlightenment or of Romanticism. Worthy of note are Martin, Simar, Pruner and Schilling, who remained in more traditional lines.

9. Wider attempts at renewal

Leo XIII's encyclical *Aeterni Patris* (1879) strove "to restore the golden wisdom of St Thomas, and to spread it far and wide in the defense and beauty of the Catholic faith".[21] As a consequence neo-Thomism emerged as the dominant strand in Catholic theology. Manuals were composed "according to the mind of St Thomas", and Dominicans in particular, Merkelbach and Prümmer for example, tried to organise their matter according to the virtues in preference to the commandments, and to go beyond casuistry to set down a firm theoretical base for morality in nature and grace.

Some authors such as Otto Schiller tried to reconcile the Tübingen school with Thomistic principles by organising their matter on the principle of charity as a threefold cycle of duty toward God, toward self and toward one's neighbour.

The manuals which were composed or revised after 1917 can be further distinguished by their attempt to assimilate the new code of *canon law* promulgated under Benedict XV. This, of course, deepened the juridicisation of Catholic morality and brought on criticisms of the manuals as being legalistic and far too narrowly conceived. The textbooks of the Jesuits Genicot, Tanquery and Noldin remain casuist in the mould of probabilism. Arthur Vermeersch S.J. and M. Zalba S.J. tried to give their casuistry a solid foundation in doctrine.

Joseph Mausbach (d. 1931) had paved the way for a more systematic moral theology. He was well aware of the tensions between Catholics and Lutherans in Germany, and strived to present Catholic doctrine in an appealing way. He was also aware of the difficulties that arose from Kant's charge that Catholic morality was heteronomous because it sprang from the imposition of external law. Mausbach is the author of the widely quoted *Die Ethik des Hl. Augustinus*. His *Katholische Moraltheologie* ("Catholic Moral Theology") was not primarily intended as a pastoral aid for priests and confessors but as an explanation of how Christian morality is perfected through love, whether in the private life of the individual or in society at large. He preserved only those treatises that concern morality as such, that is, the general principles of moral theology, divine virtues and the commandments. He leaves questions about sacraments, censures, indulgences and the three canonical states to liturgy and canon law. His manual was continued by Gustav Ermecke whose tenth edition appeared in 1961.

Franz Tillmann, the Tübingen exegete, broke with the scholastic method altogether and based himself entirely on the inspired word in *Der Meister Ruft* ("The Master Calls", 1937), and expounded Christian moral teaching as the realisation of the imitation of Christ. In 1940 the Louvain theologian Gustav Thils called for a radical reshaping of moral theology which "ought to become more fully Christian in all its perspectives and universal in its extension to all that is human, ontological in its ultimate foundation and sacramental in its concrete base and finally theological in the soul which vivifies it".[22] In 1949 another Louvain moralist, Jacques Leclerq, proposed a christocentric morality that would replace the wooden and alienating methods of the neo-Thomists.

These aspirations were met by Bernard Häring's *The Law of Christ: Moral Theology for Priests and Laity*. He centred morality in worship, as our response in Christ to the call of the Father. Religion and morality are inseparably bound, and moral theology is founded on the Word of God. Häring opened moral theology up to the biblical, patristic and liturgical movements. He was also acutely aware of the contribution of history and the social sciences to moral understanding. One of his great strengths was that he could bring all this to bear on his Alphonsian heritage and rich pastoral experience during the Second World War, which gave his writing a ring of truth and authenticity. His book pointed the way to the Council. Another figure, but from the nineteenth century and who fits no recognised category of Catholic theology, was John Henry Newman. His moral teaching was at once in touch with the modern mind while critical of the excesses of liberalism. A great exponent of the place of Scripture and the Fathers in the development of doctrine, he advocated consulting the laity in what concerned the welfare of the Church. A convert from Anglicanism, he gave experience a place in his reflection much as did St Augustine. He believed that a sincere and faithful conscience, however mistaken, must in the end lead to a loving God.

10. The Second Vatican Council and after

The Council itself, in *Gaudium et Spes*, evoked a whole new programme and presentation of Catholic morality open to the whole of humanity with all its riches and problems. As a discipline for future priests, moral theology was to (1) be nourished by Christ speaking in the Scriptures; (2) be elaborated systematically; (3) bear fruit for the salvation of the world (*Optatum Totius* n. 16).

The period since the Council has been one of furious events and unexpected developments. *Humanae Vitae* will rate as a watershed in the relationship between the magisterium and theologians because of the opposition and open dissent to the encyclical that led to widespread doubt about Catholic moral teaching among the public at large. The question of the uniqueness and specificity of Christian ethics came to the fore. Questions about the foundations of morality itself and the justification of moral norms were also widely discussed. At the same time the study of the Church's social teaching and the whole range of social justice issues in the modern world were consigned as a challenge to moral theology for the twenty-first century. More than ever moral theologians need to be conscious of the history of their discipline so as to discover the resources with which to answer the questions of our age. The need that I.T. Ramsey, the editor of an important study of *Christian Ethics and Contemporary Philosophy*, perceived just one year after the Council closed is even more urgent today. At the end of the book he asserts that we need "such a thorough biblical and patristic study, including a study of Christian moral theology down the ages, as enables us both to formulate the most reliable Christian principles and the moral obligations they express, relating this understanding to some key phrase in terms of which the full Christian Commitment is given".[23]

Karl Rahner has written forcefully about bad argumentation in moral theology. For it is often difficult to discern what stands behind a moral stance or a Church teaching. Reasons for moral teachings can be discovered only by sorting the tradition as communicated in the experience of the Church. We need to distinguish "between a tradition that really carries on an indubitable divine revelation and one that is merely 'human' and possesses no guarantee of its correctness and supratemporal validity".[24]

NOTES

1. "The Background to a History of Patristic Moral Thought", *Studia Moralia* I (1962), 53.
2. Cambridge University Press, Cambridge 1976, 50.
3. *Stromateis*, 2.23.141.
4. Quoted by Walter H. Principe C.S.B. in "Thomas Aquinas' Principles for Interpretation of Patristic Texts", in *Studies in Medieval Culture*, VIII and IX, The Medieval Institute, Western Michigan University 1976, 111.
5. Cited by E. Osborn, op. cit., 139.
6. Cited from Jean Guitton, *The Modernity of St Augustine*, Helicon Press, Baltimore 1959, 7.
7. *Confessionum libri tredecim*, lib. 2, cap. 3.
8. "St Augustine's System of Morals", in *A Monument to St Augustine* by M.C. D'Arcy et al., Sheed and Ward, London 1930, 234.
9. Ibid., 239-240.
10. *Confessions*, X, 29, 40.
11. *De Gratia et Libero Arbitrio,* 14, 27; *PL* 44, 897.
12. *Reportata*, Bk IV, Q. 9. E-F.
13. *I Sent.*, q. 1N. See also *IV Sent.* q. 14D
14. *Medieval Christian Philosophy*, Hawthorn Books, New York 1960, 120.
15. In his commentary on St Thomas' tract on Prudence in the *Summa Theologiae*, II-II, 47-54.
16. See John Mahoney, *The Making of Moral Theology*, Clarendon Press, Oxford 1987, 136-137. For Jansenism see 89-96 and for probabilism 135-143.
17. Edward A. Ryan and Robert H. Springer, "Jesuits, the Moral Theology of", in *Encyclopedia of Morals,* (ed.) Vergilius Fern, Philosophical Library, New York 1956, 250.
18. My rendition from the *Opere Ascetiche*, Vol. III, *Selva di Materie Predicabili*, Marietti, Torino 1867, 288.
19. Quoted by L. Vereecke in "History of Moral Theology", in *New Catholic Encyclopedia*, Publishers Guild Inc., Washington D.C., Vol. 9, 1122.
20. *Conscience and Casuistry in Early Modern Europe* (ed.) Edmund Leites, Cambridge University Press, Cambridge 1988, 3.
21. See John A. Gallagher, *Time Past, Time Future*, Paulist Press, New York 1990, 123.
22. See Gallagher, 142.
23. See Osborn, op. cit., Preface vii.
24. "On Bad Argumentation in Moral Theology", *Theological Investigations* XVIII, Crossroad, New York 1983, 80.

A Christian vision
of action

6.

The meaning in human action

Humans have always tried to make sense of their lives by telling them in narrative detail, that is, they have made sense of their experience by focusing on their actions. We from childhood have been haunted by the questions of who, what, where, when, and why: and the answers that we give in adulthood are ways of finding meaning in our actions.

1. A phenomenology of action

Paul Ricoeur believes that such explanatory stories are elicited by and supported by the narrative character of human action itself. He enquires into what makes a human action different from a physical event. He answers that a human action brings into play a conceptual framework with the following features.

1. *Goals*. Actions are directed to goals that are usually events or states of affairs we wish to realise. They may be fixed so that we consciously form a conception of them prior to acting. Often they are ill-defined and not completely conscious and only become determined through action. In this case we gradually become aware of our goals by realising that our action is moving in a certain direction. An end may emerge slowly over the course of a sequence of actions. Goals are thus values for us. They are important or valuable because we are willing to summon our resources to realise them. They depend on our conscious and unconscious interests. They have implications for our lives and for those around us in society.

141

2. *Motives*. Actions are motivated in the sense that we can give reasons why they are performed. Motives do not have to be conscious or explicit for us to act, but there can neither be action nor explanation of action without reference to them. The very notion of action implies that we can give an account of what we have done and why we did it. This does not mean that we can always fully plumb the depths and meaning of our own motivation. It is not possible always or even most of the time to be aware of what is happening in our unconscious. There are aspects that are hidden or fragmented or repressed that can hardly be grasped reflectively.

3. *Agents*. Both the motivation and the goal that charac-terise an action are those of the agent, the person whose action it is. The action is his or her deed, so that he or she becomes responsible for it and for its effects on others in as far as these can be willed and foreseen. The agent's identity emerges in and through his or her action, but is not identical with them. It is rather that which gives these actions a measure of unity and an identity as his, hers, mine, theirs or ours. There are accounts of agency that go beyond the individual person, as when we talk of a moral person in law or of a nation through its parliament or leaders being committed to a particular project. In all these cases this is an extension of personal agency.

4. *Context and circumstances*. Actions are embedded in morally significant contexts that determine their character. The idea of a "basic action" as a morally neutral atom of behaviour is not only suspect but unreal and never realisable. Of course, there is something fundamental about our bodily movements, since these are the locus of our presence and action in the world. We do identify these actions by physical descriptions such as "turning on the light switch". There are thousands of such terms that we use every day that allow us to identify what we are talking about as a human activity.

Bodily movements when taken by themselves are seldom actions. They are typically identified as actions in some con-text that gives them their specific character. Even the small-est, most insignificant movements or mechanical acts get their meaning and relevant description from the larger frames in which they are embedded. This can be broken down into constituent parts and even neural firings and muscle contractions. We understand these supposedly simple acts only because we presuppose a much larger context in which they get their point, purpose and meaning. Thus turning on a light may mean the initiation of a study project, a way of surprising a thief, a way of demonstrating a principle in a physics lesson.

5. *Interaction with others.* Our actions frequently involve others with whom we either cooperate or struggle. Love and hate, attraction and repulsion are essential qualities of human activity. We become allies or antagonists in courses of action that have significant moral consequences. Scandal, cooperation and so-called occasions of sin that were treated in the moral manuals fit into this framework.

6. *Meaningful existence.* No matter how trivial or routine an action is, it is always a part of a larger project, namely the agent's attempt to live a meaningful, fulfilling life. Even acts of drudgery and extreme toil are done against a background of an ideal; life that is worth living. Every action is part of a life that involves misfortune, luck, happiness, suffering and fulfilment as these are embraced by God's providence in a personal destiny.

7. *Responsibility.* Because an agent's action is his or hers, the person is held responsible for it and its immediate consequences and even its long-term effects when it can be foreseen that this action is a proper cause of such effects. Agents are thus said to be answerable for what they do. We hold ourselves and others responsible because we recognise moral agency and its consequences, and because we feel our interrelatedness and interdependence in performing actions.

These seven features that form the conceptual framework for action, tradition and virtue are intrinsically narrative. It is out of the stories that form a society that we can understand how we act and what type of character results. Given this

implicit framework to moral action we now pass to its detailed
analysis as rational or prudent action.

1.1 Prudence and right reason

Aquinas defined prudence as "recta ratio agibilium", or
right reason in dealing with actions or right practical reason.
Prudence in this sense had been set aside, and there are many
reasons for this. In casuistry it had become a sort of native
shrewdness, especially in money matters. Kant identified it
unabashedly with self-interest. The reaction came when
moralists tried to break from the old casuistry. There were
four possibilities: (1) to identify conscience with prudence.
This made conscience much more actual, less wooden and
faced it into the situation; (2) a return to St Thomas that said
prudence was more than a good conscience judgement because it guided execution through the act of command of the
intellect called "imperium". Thomas Deman O.P. was its main
advocate. He, however, did not understand the relationship of
intellect and will correctly and believed prudence could make
up for a wrongly formed conscience; (3) there was a reversion
to seeing prudence as conscience but conscience in a wider
context than ever before. Here St Thomas was left behind and
conscience was given a Kantian twist as in G. Grisez's modes
of responsibility. It began to be seen as a wise "valuative
faculty" under the guidance of the Holy Spirit. This has been
Father Häring's approach, developing St Augustine's conception of discernment; (4) a rebellion against rational accounts
of prudence which is now treated less as practical knowledge
and more as affectivity.
    What is needed is an integrated view that brings together a
metaphysics that shows how to relate will and reason or intellect, a psychology of agency that shows how these two faculties work together to produce an act, and a theology of the
virtue from which this act results. The key used to unlock this
treasure-safe is the moral or practical syllogism beginning
with Aristotle.
    Aristotle's account of practical reason is much debated.

Setting human activity off from that of animals, he shows how animals are moved by desire (instinct) to seek its satisfaction through an action to which their nature is determined. Humans are not so tied down to determined actions, because by thought they can deliberate rationally about what is to be done and how to do it. This opens up a space of freedom. There is a sequence of desire-deliberation-perception-choice-action as typically characteristic of human voluntary striving. He begins then to treat practical reason as a means-end process that issues in action in this form: (1) telos (an end or purpose); (2) the means (which may involve more than one step) leading to that end; and (3) the action to be taken first.

In the *Nicomachean Ethics* VI and VII Aristotle adds a new dimension because a person may deliberate well, that is, logically, for a bad end. He therefore wanted to establish a strong link between choice and character and therefore set out to show that a particular case fell under or was to be assumed under a universal rule. We then have a syllogism in this form: first premise: universal rule; second premise: particular case; conclusion: action.

Some authors argue that the two syllogisms are in fact identical. However, it seems better to divide them as two different cases of how desire leads rationally to action. The first is the reasoning involved in deliberation, and explores the range of possibility before one. The conclusion of this syllogism then becomes the first premise or rule under which a particular case is judged in a syllogism issuing in a decision. The action itself results from another syllogism when this decision is applied in the execution of the action. Aristotle paid little attention to the aspect of actual realisation and its rationality. If one follows the first type of reasoning a strongly teleological morality results, based on the search for purpose, the achievement of an end. If the second is emphasised a legalist morality results, since morality becomes a process of deducing more particular rules from more general ones. If, however, the application of rules falls under the search for an end, it becomes a case of giving life meaning through a value to be realised. If there is no such subsumption a conflict between a morality of purpose and a morality of rules

inevitably occurs. There is no doubt that Aristotle saw life as
the progressive achievement of the human good by virtue, and
that rules of conduct had to fit that purpose in service of the
person in community as the point not only of moral reasoning
but of moral living itself.

1.2 St Thomas on right reason

St Thomas Aquinas' account of practical reason, according to Daniel Westberg, has been dogged by inadequate and
mistaken understandings of his thought.[1] Firstly, many authors
believe that Aquinas perverted biblical morality by introducing
Aristotle into its interpretation. This charge can be set aside
because Aquinas never departs from revelation as the supreme
rule of his reasoning. He never compromises with Aristotle
about God as the beatitude and happiness sought by human
persons. Yet the form of reasoning established by Aristotle
works well to exploit the Christian meaning of beatitude.
Aquinas has been charged with introducing concepts such as
will and *synderesis* that are foreign to Aristotle. Will explains
how the execution of action was seen in a way impossible for
Aristotle to visualise. And *synderesis* is at the origin of mistakenly seeing natural law as a geometric system of rules
logically ordered among themselves to render a complete
account of human action. What results is in fact a split between intellect and will. Intellect is seen by itself to supply the
rules and their justification as a rational system. Will then
applies them autonomously to action in complete freedom.
The doing of an act is then solely a matter of the will which is
restrained to this act by an obligation joined to the law as a
sanction imposed on the will. Westberg and other authors
have rightly seen here that morality becomes a system of laws,
a legalism, reinforced by voluntarism as a sanction or threat of
punishment attached to the application of the law.

What did Aristotle say about the relationship of intellect or
reason and will? And what did St Thomas assimilate from him
in this matter? In the *Eudemian Ethics* Aristotle says, "choice
is not either opinion (*doxa*) or wish (*boulēsis*), neither one of

them nor both... it must result from both of these; for both of them occur in one who chooses." While Aristotle did not have a developed theory of the will he did postulate the premise that reason and desire or will both collaborate at each stage of practical reason. In this he and Thomas Aquinas are thousands of miles from legalistic or Kantian accounts of practical reason.

2. The metaphysics of agency

St Thomas developed his philosophy of action not from a system of law but from the doctrine of being. Being which exists as substance is dynamic. This is the basis for the assertion that being and good are convertible, the both of them being transcendentals with truth. The potency of being is for the actuality of its action. A thing must exist before it can move or be changed. A thing can only move and be moved because it already has being or perfection. "Everything which is moved is moved by another."[2] This movement to perfection is a progress from potency to act. Movement requires another being already in act. And the movement from potency to act can be described as perfection. The metaphysics of agency is expressed in terms of good as in *S.T.*, I, q. 5.

The good is a function of something being desirable. Because it is good it exercises attraction and so stands at the head of a causal series. A thing thus desires or is instinctively inclined to its own completion and perfection. Agency is thus explained through final causality that puts a cause into motion, changing the matter in question by evoking a new form. In the order of execution this order is reversed, since the good in question is only arrived at after the form is implanted by the action of the agent. Now a thing only exists through its form and it has a natural desire for that form. For Aquinas the desire for perfection becomes the force of love in the intelligent agent who is a first-person agent and conscious source of action. This type of agent is characterised as a self-mover in the sense of being the source of its own movement. An animal depends on sensitive knowledge that activates its instincts. In the human the end is set by the agent who can understand and choose it freely. By deliberation a human agent is able or not able to move toward an end. He or she is a mixture of actuality and potentiality: their essence is not their activity as in God. To act they must have faculties or potentialities of action. We have a variety of activities, for example, sensing, choosing, deliberating, deciding etc. These cannot simply be reduced to the soul as their immediate principle, since they are various and can be grouped under multiple heads. In fact, they are specified by the objects they attain. Thus the object of the understanding is the truth (*verum*) and the object of the will is the good (*bonum*). Each of these powers is interchangeable with being, which means that they can relate to the whole of reality. The faculty that is inclined to universal good itself is called the will. Unlike sense appetite that is awakened by an individual good, its object is the good as such, that is, as recognised by the intellect. This means that the good to which the will is inclined need not be actually good but must be perceived by the intellect as apparently good.

Intellect and will are natural powers that combine wide-ranging freedom with natural necessity. The will is not determined to any particular object but to the ultimate end, the universal good, just as the intellect must adhere to the first principles. The will participates in the metaphysics of being through its necessary ordination to beatitude. Only those things that have a necessary link to the beatific vision have necessarily to be chosen. Ordination to any particular good in this life, even God, is not necessary therefore. Unless something is presented to the will as perfectly good it is not necessitated, and this is the reason why the intellect must enter to determine the will. No single object will necessarily draw the will except God himself, but he is not always recognised by reason clearly and plainly as our beatitude despite our desire and ordination from creation toward him. The relationship between intellect and will is complex. Truth and falsity are in the mind, but goodness as the object of will is in real existence outside the mind. On this basis, since God is above the mind it is better to love him than just to know him. Objects below the mind are of more value in the mind as truth than as objects to be really sought. There is also a relationship of potency and act. The will is moved not just by the good but by the good as known, that is, by the intellect. While it is true that the intellect moves the will *per modum finis,* it is just as true that the will moves the intellect *per modum agentis.*[3] The will moves the intellect and all the other powers of the soul to their particular ends. The intellect is ordained to universal truth, but its determination to any particular truth happens through the will. How is it possible to escape a regress to infinity here? St Thomas posits God as first cause in both orders, i.e., as moving or specifying the intellect to its first movement, and also as moving the will to its first motion as final cause. Could it be that he subscribed to a Platonic "sovereignty of the good"? But since being is the transcendental embracing both truth and goodness, and being as such is the object of the intellect, it must be given priority. Things are knowable to the extent they are participants in being, and on that basis are lovable. In the order of causality, therefore, the will is the efficient cause, the intellect the formal cause, and the object itself the final cause. This is the solution to the problem of the priority of the will as self-mover in seeking the good. The problem was raised by Dom Odo Lottin, and a number of other commentators have developed it into a modern form of Thomistic voluntarism. It follows that in the order of execution we find the sequence of love-desire-delight, so that love sets desire alight till it is satisfied by delight. In the order of intention the sequence is reversed so that delight acts as an end that inspires desire which evokes love that moves the person into action.

2.1 The will's part

Since the will can never choose the universal good as its direct and immediate object, it chooses particular goods under the heading of being good. This means that the will is dependent on the intellect's certitude which is gained from reflecting on how its light abstracted a universal from the phantasm. This reflection shows how there is a correspondence between mind and reality that we call truth which has the quality of certitude. The will needs to be determined at two levels: (1) to act or not to act: this depends on the subject and belongs to the execution of the act set in motion by the final cause. Ultimately this is God as all goodness and the cause of all good; (2) to this object or not to this object: there are many objects that may determine the will's act: specification thereby depends on an external object. The passional part of human life comes under the dominion of intellect and will and is determined in the same way.

2.2 The structure of human action.

The account and structure of a human act has been the cause of ferocious debate among ethicists and moralists. Students familiar with the *Nicomachean Ethics* will notice the addition of several stages in the usually accepted scheme among moralists. From desire-deliberation-choice-action we move to the twelve-step account evenly divided between acts of intellect and will. The mind was understood to set the terms in which the will acted effectively. Thus there were twelve acts in this sequence:

About the end	About means	Execution
1. apprehension	5. deliberation	9. command
2. wish	6. consent	10. application
3. judgement about the end	7. practical judgement	11. performance
4. intention	8. choice	12. enjoyment

This schema dates from Cajetan through Billuart who understood it as a general account of good living. It shows how the will becomes habituated to goodness through grace. The human act for St Thomas was not a general account of morality, but the explanation of how I managed to do this act rightly. He therefore wanted to show the structure of the individual act in its ontological constituents. There was not a long tradition of analysing the human act previous to St Thomas. St Augustine had not tried to see the relationships of intellect and will as they applied to the whole sequence of human action. The tradition came from John Damascene's assimilation of Maximus the Confessor, who in turn was dependent on Nemesius and the Stoics. St Albert the Great had treated the human act as that of practical reason and so emphasised the intellectual element.

The key to understanding the human act in St Thomas is his way of analysing *liberum arbitrium* which, following Aristotle, he sees as decision, that is, a judgement of the mind incorporating the power of the will and leading to choice or *electio* which is an act of the will incorporating a judgement of the mind. He is insistent that there is not a temporal sequence between intellect and will but they are complementary causes mutually incorporating the other at each stage. His first principle is therefore the collaboration of intellect and will. He then sees that an act must be specified or determined before it can be chosen. This determination is the result of deliberation where the possible choices are multiple. If one applies the basic Aristotelian insights of mutual collaboration between intellect and will and between deliberation (reasoning) and decision (judgement) to the multiple acts described by St John Damascene, then the following schema results:

	Intention	*Decision*	*Execution*	*Deliberation*
cognition:	apprehension	judgement	command	counsel
volition :	intention	decision	application	consent

This schema shows the fundamental structure of intention-decision-execution. Deliberation is only needed when a judgement on what to do is not easily, clearly and simply forthcoming. Then we must reason to a judgement. It will be seen that each of these stages has an intellectual and a volitional element as described. This schema of course presumes a knowledge of the *voluntarium* as the inner source of action among rational agents, and a consideration of what are the circumstances of a moral act, not just physically but as influencing the moral character of the act. The Augustinian scheme of desire-love-fulfilment or enjoyment also helps relate will, mind and emotion in human action.

Intention means to tend toward something. It is more than desire. For instance, one may desire to be physically fit but one cannot intend to become so without wanting to take the means involved. For an intention it is not only necessary to have an ideal, but the will must be directed to an object in which or through which the end or ideal can be realised. A person may of course have several intentions even for the one action. Thus studying may lead to entry into a profession such as medicine or the law, as well as on the one hand, being very lucrative, or being a vocation to the service of the poor, on the other hand. These purposes may be ordered by the intention itself to their final end. Sometimes the ends or purposes have a natural order that does not depend on our decision. Thus it is impossible to become proficient in the knowledge needed for a profession without study, or love grows in a marriage through the appropriate acts of mutual love. An act may have multiple effects. Those which are intended are those to which the will turns as wanting to effect them, while others may be foreseen but are not those to which the will was directed as intending them even though they result from its action. In an operation to amputate a gangrenous leg the surgeon intends to save the life of the person and not do the patient harm.

Decision means that when we know what is the best course of action that action must still be chosen to make it a truly human action. All human actions involve reason in reaching a decision. Decision is about where one stands with the conclusions of deliberation from which it is distinct. It involves one's commitment or not to what deliberation has delivered. All human action involves decision. Deliberation and decision are two different ways of practical reasoning for which Aristotle has two distinct syllogisms. These differ in the process of the overall act, their style and function. Deliberation is used to identify the means needed to achieve an end, whereas decision reasons "yes" or "no" to being committed to using those means. For example, a sick person has a choice of taking the medicine prescribed by his or her doctor or not. Decision is about alternate courses of action where the means are already clear. He or she does not have to deliberate and discern the relative value of different medicines. The thinking behind the decision may be swift and easy or long and even tormented, but it is always present in a decision as its rational element.

We have actually to decide to do an action we have deliberated about. We have to apply our mind to the action by committing ourselves to do it.

For example, one has to consider whether an act is sinful or not. Once it is seen as sinful, one makes a concrete choice to avoid it. While deliberation considers means to an end, choice considers how a particular means is to be put into action. I want to get into good physical form. I think that I should jog for thirty minutes per day. I therefore choose to get up an hour earlier each morning. The choice unites the judgement of reason on the act to be effected and the movement of the will connected to that commitment. The syllogism involved here is not just proving that this is a particular case of a general rule, or that this is the means to this end. It is rather an act of recognition by the agent that the general rule applies to the act proposed. "I am the person to whom this rule applies." This is more than just a case of a general rule; it is personalised knowing that makes a decision. Since a particular judgement is involved, it is fruit of a perception not such as senses the hardness and colour of objects but an "interior sense" such as perceives a geometric figure to be a triangle. The particular reasoning involved here belongs to prudence, "by which particular reason is perfected for judging rightly about the particular tendencies of action."[4] The mind therefore connects the general principle with the particular occasion in what St Thomas called "the operative syllogism".[5] The agent thereby perceives the singular case in its universal principle. Thus, when doctors, with their medical knowledge, see a patient before them with certain symptoms, they recognise that the patient has a determined disease. In decision that knowledge is applied to action. Choice follows the conclusion of the operative syllogism.[6] "The nature of prudence is to stop at the particular action to be done, to which it applies general knowledge. The particular conclusion is deduced from a general and a particular proposition. Thus the nature of prudence derives from a twofold understanding."[7] This is the type of syllogism we use when dealing with the contingent matters of life. It is a true syllogism productive of truth and certainty as far as its matter allows. Intellect and will function together in harmony, not in series as has so often been believed in the twelve-stage schema of the human act that springs from Billuart in the eighteenth century.

Intellect and will are so coordinated that they combine to form one principle of choice. They are in fact related in choice as form and matter, reason giving to the will's energy and exertion its characteristic shape and determination and direction. The complete union of intellect and will is represented by the first principle of practical reason: do good and avoid evil. It specifies all activity in its goodness and attractiveness, and thus the generativity of the will is in complete agreement with it in so far as it is true and good. This principle is the basic ground of all voluntary action, and all other practical principles are specifications of it. In the operative syllogism the will is involved in the selection of the minor premise as being relevant and beneficial to my life. The person assesses the act proposed in the circumstances in a setting of responsibility and not just the individual pleasure it might bring. Decision is thus a test of character for the agent and forges the link between intention and execution.

Deliberation is necessary only in uncertain or dubious situations where the judgement as to what to do does not come forth spontaneously. Here there is need of enquiry or investigation or what is called "counsel". Routine actions that make up the normal rhythm of the day are rational but do not require deliberation. Where there are set means to an end, deliberation does not feature. So many virtuous acts, because we have learnt to do them pleasantly and spontaneously, call for no long consideration. Deliberation considers the variety of means to an end not because of their necessity but for their usefulness in action. Train and bus are both good means of travel, but can be distinguished because of price, convenience, time taken on the trip etc. The conclusion of deliberation is a particular action or actions that one may then choose to do. *Consensus* as the part played by the will is a pleasure or complacency in the means, a preference that precedes and leads to choice.

The principles of human action are knowledge of the truth and desire for the good. Desire is the motivation; reason interprets and specifies the activity. There is no need to add obligation as an extra motivating force, and often rules are not needed to instruct us how to act. Since we can often judge that this action is an instantiation of the good, it is not necessary to invoke a rule or law in that case. Most of our actions of forming friendships, carrying out work etc. are judged to be right and executed as such. But when it is not clear what is good and right to do, the way to truth and goodness must be investigated and searched out. Even before the fall Adam needed summaries of experience and practical rules to guide him. If our insight into the human condition is lessened and the power of decision weakened by sin, then it becomes obvious that law as the rule or plan of action has a much greater role now. It is grace that ultimately heals this condition not only by enlightening us but by actually empowering us in God's goodness through Christ. Law as we know it enlightens us about the right relationship of means and end in human action. It enters into practical reasoning precisely at the stage of counsel or deliberation. It filters out bad or ineffectual means, thereby securing our true good. We are often enough ignorant of some danger, but the civil law will require us to take precautionary measures, e.g., speed limits on the road, safety fences when putting up a swimming pool. In these cases a person is expected to know the law, and ignorance is not a reason for excuse or clemency where it is violated. It is precisely at this stage of counsel that a person is open to suggestion and so can be moved by the Spirit through the gift of counsel. The Spirit moves through our practical reason when a person is searching to discern his or her way or life or to resolve the conflict over which vocation to follow.

Execution is the last psychological stage in an action. It has intellective and volitional aspects called *imperium* or command and *usus* or the actual application and doing of the action. This stage has been keenly disputed and greatly misunderstood. Suarez transferred command from reason to the will. This deprived action of its rational content or rationality in planning. In practice, for example, it meant that obedience in religious life was a line of action imposed by the will of a superior, and not a rational plan or line of action communicated by a superior. There was a much needed reaction to this voluntarism when Thomas Deman O.P. recognised that

command was the essential act of the virtue of prudence. He
even went as far as saying that a truly prudent command
would right an incorrect conscience. This is impossible, since
no command can ever right a bad decision. In other words he
had confused command and decision. Command does not
specify the act. That occurs prior to decision as already explained. Aquinas understood *usus* here not in its Augustinian
sense as distinguished from *fruitio*, but in an Aristotelian
manner as "the execution of that which is ordered to an end".[8]
To move into action is to apply the interior principles of
acting, the psychological powers, to the bodily members. In
this way the interior intention becomes embodied in the exterior activity which completes and perfects it. Execution translates the decision into bodily movements. The *imperium* or
command directs by putting or setting the action into order.
This requires awareness, firmness and flexibility in performing the action. It is easy enough to see how the focus of
the virtue of prudence falls here. Even such a simple act as
walking demands both reason and freedom so that we keep
walking, that we are aware of the persons we encounter and
that we recognise dangers that may threaten.

Daniel Westberg highlights how the whole human act has
an end-means structure.

> The agent in deliberation formulates this structure and
> identifies the particular actions when there is uncertainty:
> then he comes to a decision by choosing on the basis both
> of its correctness and of its attractiveness, and carries out
> the action under the guidance of both intellect and will.
> Because circumstances may change the validity of a
> particular means-end structuring, both intellect and will
> are constantly involved in the formulation, choice, and
> execution of all actions.[9]

2.3 Sources of moral goodness

We see now what St Thomas intended by calling man the
image of God in the prologue of his moral theology in the

Summa Theologiae. It means that he is intelligent so as to be able to deliberate, he has freedom being blessed with free choice and has dominion or control of his free actions as their agent and executor. This means that there is a certain subjectivity in human action because the person is the fount and source of all doing. Personal being is at the source of action. It is reason that coordinates and connects the person in so far as it is the image of God and thereby the source of action as its agent and its situated character in so far as it needs to be oriented in its search for the good or happiness. The moral value of an act is that established by reason which reaches out and embraces the good as a person's fulfilment. There are according to St Thomas four sources or founts of action that make it morally good or evil:

1. generic goodness, *secundum genus,* that the act as such is good;
2. specific goodness, *secundum speciem,* that is according to the object proportioned or right for that act;
3. circumstances, *secundum circumstantias,* as if they were accidents;
4. the end, *secundum finem,* as in relation to the goodness of the act.

(1) The first thing that he indicates is the subject in so far as the act gives it or enriches it in being, makes it exist in its *ontological fullness.* A parallel with the natural world may help. Occasionally animals give birth not to normal offspring but to monsters. What is meant here is that an act does not come out morally as it should. We need to be sure that it is not morally misformed even before we enter into any other consideration. Thus the act should achieve the intent and type of act it is meant to be without being warped or misshapen so as no longer to be a moral act and thereby lack the being due it. It must therefore be a rational, free act, an *actus humanus,* and not, like sleepwalking or stroking one's beard, an *actus hominis* that does not properly engage the person as its subject. An act may occur under such psychological pressure, or because of shock resulting from a war experience, that it fails to be truly

human but may be judged as done from compulsion. Reason is at the origin of every human act. Where it is missing or lacking the act falls short of what it should be. As St Thomas says, acts are called good or bad in relation to reason because human goodness consists in being conformed to reason and evil in being contrary to reason.[10] An act is judged by moral standards by the fact that reason enters in to constitute it as reasonable. The difference between a good and a bad object stands in their relationship to reason.

Action as moral is an overflow of our being as existence. It is an expression of the person but as such can never fully express the being of the person. It is precisely growth in personal being and has its own type of autonomy. *Actio sequitur esse*. Since reason measures or determines the basic character of an act, a good person can produce a bad act and a bad person a good act, but there is a radical tension and inconsistency in practical reason itself in these cases. The person is the fount of moral goodness by acting according to reason which distinguishes good from bad in human acts.

(2) The second feature determining the goodness of an act is the *object*. It is what sets up the right proportion between what one wants and the act one does, what makes the act fitting or *conveniens*. This is the feature that a certain tradition isolated and almost absolutised so that the act became so objectified as to lose its dynamic quality already described. The act is here considered in itself, as a fact, even as a reality *secundum objectum conveniens*.

The object of the act is that which the act as moral and therefore as determined by reason attains to. In ordinary English we would say what it aims at immediately, or what we arrive at just by the performance of this act. It is not just an external object in its materiality, but that object as it is presented to the will by reason as what one is doing. We need to distinguish an act as a physical event in the world from its immediate essential moral meaning, that is, its object. For example, the difference between an act of killing which may be capital punishment, an act of war, a crime of murder; it may be manslaughter or it could be self-defence. The problems opened up by the principle of double effect are implicit here. A surgeon may amputate a gangrenous leg. This is not mutilation as a moral object but a life-saving act.

(3) *Circumstances* are what add variety and colour to human action. They are concerns such as time, place, manner, amount, relationship, active and passive aspects of an act, its context, and even its purpose and why. These are of traditional interest to rhetoric, to lawyers pleading cases, to preachers who communicate the Christian message to an audience as hearers of the faith. In morality, when a circumstance qualifies an act it is thought to remain external to the core of the act, its formal description as an act. Thus the fact that a boy has red hair does not cause either intelligence or that he may become extremely angry when provoked. It may, however, make him a handsome man and a striking figure. In classic rhetoric, circumstances were all those features that adorned or stood around an act so as to make it known to us in a way that it could be judged and rightly assessed. A circumstance is not a volitional element in an act; it does not change at will but it is cognitive in so far as it helps us understand the act in context. The early Church availed itself of rhetoric and the medievals joined this to Aristotle's moral evaluation of circumstances. Thus penance is adjusted to the seriousness of the sin and the condition of the person. It is the work of reason to discern how a person's circumstances or condition change the moral judgement on an act or a person. For St Thomas a circumstance may cease to stand around or near an act and may enter its very definition, so changing its essential moral character. For example, to steal is wrong, but to steal sacred objects from a church is sacrilege. In this way such an act cannot be defined without that circumstance which penetrates into its very meaning being an integral part that constitutes the species of its definition. One must therefore be very attentive to see whether a circumstance is peripheral or essential to the description of an act where "cirumstantia transit in conditionem objecti". A circumstance may manifest the fitness or convenience of an act, it will reveal to reason that it is worthy of being done or should be avoided. A whole cultural setting may be taken as

the setting in which a person must act. This set or complex of circumstances that can define a period or an age in history are today often treated as the historicity of human action. There is no such thing as a theory of action or any act that can occur outside history. In this way the growth of technology, urbanisation on a global scale, the application of science to living conditions, social planning and social engineering, mass communication, sport as public entertainment and many other conditions are defining elements of the human condition today and enter into our concept of what is moral and not moral. Morality as a true and right way of living is cultural and cannot be otherwise. This does not open a spectre of endless relativism and cultural conditioning, because acts still have their essential definitions and characteristics that can be universally appreciated and valid. The moral evaluation of new cultural circumstances, e.g., the new medical technologies, are necessary for their humanisation, for their assimilation into a fuller, better and more human life for the person in society.

(4) In morality *the end* or *remote purpose* or *finis remotus* is of prime importance as a circumstance. It is the most important defining characteristic of an act, giving it direction, purpose and its final meaning. "Finis est causa bonitatis, est causa principalissima," says St Thomas in *S.T.*, I-II, 18. 4. This end, which observed from outside appears as a circumstance, added to the act presented to reason, e.g., giving money to the poor (external act), may be either real charity and love of the poor or vainglory and status seeking. What is an adjunct to an external observer is the real moral determinant for the person as agent. This end is the object of the interior act of the will. The act itself that is willed must be in a right proportion to this end. This means that the morality of the external act, what is usually called the object, must be taken into account when assessing the morality of an act. There are acts that are such that no good end and no circumstances may ever justify their being performed. These acts are what we call *intrinsically evil* and are always in contradiction with the moral law. We may say that these are the acts prohibited outright by the ten commandments. The morality of an act consists in having

a valid end and an act that as a means and in itself is right and has a proportioned and correct relation to the end desired.

2.4 The interior and exterior act

A vital distinction that follows on these four goodness-causing qualities of the human act is that between interior and exterior act. The interior act is the act of the will itself, while the exterior act is that act which arises through powers other than the will. It is the difference between choosing and doing, or the elicited act of the will and the acts of the other powers that are moved by the will and commanded by the intellect. The external act is the agent's doing an action and the object is what is done in that action. If we look at an action from the point of view of what is done or achieved in the world, we have what St Thomas calls the object of the action. If we ask why one act is done rather than another, the answer is found not in the external act but in the internal act and intention of the will. This brings into high relief the conviction that an act is good not only because of the good it produces in the world, but more importantly because of the good or perfection it causes in the acting person. This means it is directed to its proper end and this arises in the will. But the interior act must be directed or related not only to the end but to the object itself of the act. Thus the interior act of the will has two objects, the end and the object. In any moral act an agent wills both what he does and why he does it and the goodness of the act depends on both of these. If an act fails in any aspect to have the goodness it should possess, the act itself is deemed bad. The exterior act can have a goodness or badness independent of the interior act and so can determine the goodness or badness of the interior act which is directed to it. In another way, however, the interior act can determine the goodness or badness of the exterior act because the moral quality of the end of the interior act is transferred to the exterior act and thereby bestows upon it a goodness or badness it did not have itself. For St Thomas the relation of interior to exterior act is that of form to matter that is shaped and determined by that form.

3. Other views on action and normativity

This view of human action can be contrasted with that of Kant and John Stuart Mill. For Kant moral goodness is placed in the will alone. He postulates that moral goodness consists in the conformity to the moral law and the moral norm arises out of duty or inner moral obligation. It is respect for the moral law above any inclination or interest or desire for happiness that implants goodness in the will. St Thomas agrees the will can have a goodness independent of the object of the act. A good act can become evil because of a corrupting intention, as in the case of Kant's shopkeeper who refuses to cheat his client only in order to retain his business. Moral goodness then depends on the will but not on the will alone.

For Mill and the utilitarian school the source of goodness is placed solely in what is to be done. The goodness of an action is assessed in terms of what the agent is proposing to do. Motive, says Mill, may reveal something of the agent's character but it does not enter into determining the moral quality of the act. But, as we have seen, moral goodness depends on the motive or end as well as on the intrinsic value of the action.

The view of the human act outlined here is an integration of two fundamental insights. On the one side the morality of the act arises from the person in the intention it infuses into the act and the end it wants to realise. On the other side the goodness of the act depends on what the agent does when he or she acts. One cannot ignore the goodness or badness that the act produces in the world. At the same time, on the other hand, no act should be considered morally good unless it reflects, and indeed effects, the moral goodness of the person acting.

What is conspicuous in both Kant and Mill is that God has faded from consciousness, and human action follows in a completely Pelagian fashion. In this sense some forms of moral autonomy are not far removed from ancient heresy. The factor that has disappeared is an awareness of providence, that is, that our action really does work toward the good that God has prepared for us, and that hence we should work out our lives in collaboration with him. This means bringing my will into line with his since he has first willed me all the good I could wish or hope or need. He will be my good, "my inheritance", says the psalm, for ever. The goodness of the will depends on the end it seeks to realise. The only end that will satisfy man is the greatest good itself. So St Thomas draws this conclusion about the goodness of the will in *S.T.*, I-II, 19.9:

> For an act of the will to be good, then, it must be ordered to this highest good. This good fundamentally and directly relates to the divine will as its proper object. Because each particular thing is right and good to the extent that it attains its proper measure, therefore the human will, if it is to be good, needs to be conformed to God's will.

It will now be obvious why both deontological and teleological theories of the moral norm are judged not just inadequate but mistaken. The encyclical *Veritatis Splendor* in fact criticised both theories for distorting human agency in the relations they set up between human freedom and moral truth. The encyclical's point of reference was the human act and its intrinsic finality to happiness. Deontological theories have freedom imposing its own law on itself without regard to any other reference to reality. This puts such theories firmly in the Kantian camp. The fact that consequentialist theories with a number of their derivatives explained an action without maintaining the proportion right reason establishes between means and ends shows how kindred they are to utilitarianism. These theories fall broadly in the zone outlined in Mill's way of thinking. Modern theories are committed to taking the norm either as a construction of freedom or as a calculation of values in play but not as moral truth. After the great debates following the introduction of teleological and deontological theories into moral theology, it has to be acknowledged that these theories have made moralists much more aware of various currents of contemporary ethics but that as general theories of action for the justification of moral norms they have not been at all successful, as hoped.

It is only God who can embrace the good of the whole universe and human destiny, and so by seeking good in human action, even though we do not know it or advert to it, we are acting in union with him and fulfilling his providence as our own good and advantage.

4. The epistemology of action as achievement

Human action is dialogical; it is the meeting-point of the person and the world he or she inhabits. Action is precisely what integrates the acting person into the universe at all its levels. Michael Polanyi studied the action of living beings from the most primitive up to the personal. He illustrated how there is a hierarchy of actions corresponding to the capacities of the agent and to the structures of the real world. His particular concern was to rebut the influence of reductionism in a positivist account of the sciences, whether natural or social. Reductionism explains everything at one level, that is, as mass in motion. For him the highest level of action is that of the person who incorporates into him or herself all the lower levels of reality in the universe. By action a person indwells the universe and makes it his or her home. This means that we are really involved in the world at every level and that whatever we know or do is a commitment to reality.

In Part Four of his insightful study of modern science, *Personal Knowledge*,[11] Michael Polanyi bases his analysis of the relation of "Knowing and Being"[12] precisely on this logic of achievement. Our comprehension of a living being implies awareness of subsidiary particulars, e.g., organs, as parts of a whole not specifiable in these more particular terms. To comprehend a coherent whole is to conceive a being at a higher order of existence, e.g., a machine cannot be explained completely in terms of physics or chemistry, but by its functional principles in engineering. In animals there is an active centre operating in an unspecified manner sustaining vital functions and organic striving. "We start from the fact that no material process governed by the laws of matter can conceivably account for the presence of consciousness in material bodies." Thinking and human action have features of originality and responsibility that must be conceived of as another level of reality. From an entity's total performance the scientist takes the system apart to discover how each part functions in conjunction with the others. This idea of "perceived organisation" is Aristotelian rather than Democritean, for we cannot have complete knowledge without relying on our personal knowledge of these comprehensive features. Polanyi formulated his findings thus: "Commitment may be graded by steps of increasing consciousness; namely from *primordial*, vegetative commitment of a center of being, function and growth, to *primitive* commitment of the active-perceptive center, and hence further again, to *responsible* commitments of the consciously deliberating person."[13] At the highest level, he argues, where the person lives under a firmament of values that guide human life, moral ideals are only known by following them. Polanyi concludes his *magnum opus* with a meditation on evolution as a "*heuristic field*" that gathers together clues from creation pointing to the Christian God.

Polanyi elaborated this insight into "a structural kinship" between what we know and our way of knowing it. Since concepts arise from the integration of a multitude of details into a focal unity or meaning, the dynamic of knowing follows reality's contours into its inner depth. And action as orientated and guided by such knowledge not only unites us with the real but actually integrates us into its very structures, for action makes us present by impinging upon the very nature and existence of a reality. In all cases of tacit knowing there is a "correspondence between the structure of comprehension and the structure of the comprehensive entity which is its object". The conditions needing to be organised by a higher principle Polanyi, following Einstein, calls "boundary conditions". Thus each level remains open to a higher level which in turn is open to a more fully developed level. "The vegetative system which sustains life at rest leaves open the possibility of bodily movement by means of muscular action. This level leaves open the possibility of integration into innate patterns of behaviour. This leaves open the sharing of intelligence."[14] The highest level in our world of the hierarchy of being is "the responsible person". The person is the pinnacle of all progress, material, cultural and spiritual. Thus these levels of reality and understanding are open upwards but not reducible downwards. The more our knowledge of the universe increases, the more we are convinced that we are following "the gradient of meaning" that reveals the objective rationality of nature.

Polanyi fashioned his intuitions from the stuff of scientific experience. Objectivism and positivism were disasters for science because they denied spiritual values intrinsic to thought and human action. His writings are important for relating theory and practice and for proposing an image of the human agent that respects both moral values and the complex hierarchical structure of the universe. It is precisely the execution, that is, the completion and full achievement, of the human act that integrates personal intention into the structures of the world. St Thomas describes this as intention becoming real in those structures, as the form of intention fashioning a human home out of the matter supplied by the universe. It is the internal act informing and being realised in the external act. In that act the material elements of human nature, its physical and chemical composition, the physiology of the body and the working of the psyche are all combined by human intention to make sense of our world as we work out our destiny with God. It was Polanyi's great achievement to show what science could contribute to a personalist morality. He has understood how the acting person participates in the universe in all its dimensions.

NOTES

1. *Right Practical Reason: Aristotle, Action and Prudence in Aquinas,* Clarendon Press, Oxford 1994. The whole volume is dedicated to this argument.
2. *Summa Theologiae (S.T.)*, I, 2.3.
3. See *S.T.*, I, 82, 4.
4. St Thomas Aquinas, *In VI Ethic.* (1142a23), lect. 1215: "Et ad istum sensum, id est interiorem, magis pertinet prudentia, per quam perficitur ratio particularis ad recte aestimandum de singularibus intentionibus operabilium."

5. In *VI Ethic.* (1143a35) lect. 1247: "sed intellectus qui est in practicis est alterius modi estremi, scilicet singularis et contingentis et alterius propositionis, id est non universalis quae est quasi major, sed singularis quae est minor in syllogismo operativo."

6. *S.T.*, I-II, 13. 3.

7. *S.T.*, II-II, 49. 2 ad 1.

8. *In I Sent.*, I, 1. 2, "uti autem nominat executionem eius quod ad finem ordinandum est."

9. *Right Practical Reason*, Oxford University Press, 1994, 183.

10. *S.T.*, I-II, 18. 5 in c.

11. *Personal Knowledge: Toward a Post-Critical Philosophy*, Routledge and Kegan Paul, London 1958. This book records his Gifford Lectures 1951-52.

12. Ibid., 327-405.

13. Ibid., 339, 358, 363.

14. *The Tacit Dimension*, Doubleday, New York 1967, 33-34, 41.

7.

The heart of conscience

Conscience is the key term in moral theology for reflection on the morality of action. It has become identified with personal rights and even subjectivity. The word is often interchanged with authenticity. This chapter will first consider the existentialist view of conscience, and then a Christian advocate of many of the same values, John Henry Newman, who will introduce a discussion of how conscience has been understood in the Church's history. The claims of a mistaken conscience have always been a test case of how it is to be understood. Lastly, the teaching of the Council will be expounded.

1. The existential meaning of conscience

Conscience is the key word to describe existential morality; it unlocks the mysteries of personal decision, our inner grasp of right and wrong. Etymologically it springs from Greek popular usage more than from sophisticated philosophy. C.A. Pierce says, "it comes complete with its own connotation, as, basically, the pain suffered by man, a man, and therefore as a creature involved in the order of things, when, by his acts completed or initiated, he transgresses the limits of his nature".[1] It implies "to know in common with" and therefore "to know in oneself" as a witness to personal good and evil. The phenomenon of conscience was first elaborated by the Stoics as right decision in harmony with the *logos* which was the world-plan of human destiny. St Paul saw that only the blood of Christ could "purge our conscience of dead works to worship the living God" (Heb 9:14). Christians thereafter thought of conscience in biblical terms as the "heart" where God had written his law. St Augustine traced the authority of conscience back to God so that listening to God's voice was the act of conscience. For Thomas Aquinas conscience was "the application of science to an act" and was concentrated in the last practical judgement we place before acting. Bishop Joseph Butler, the great Anglican divine, thought of it as the "moral sense", the deepest sentiment for righteousness that can motivate us. Dissatisfied with an emotivism that isolated conscience abstractly in one or other of the faculties, Kierkegaard thought of it as the passion of subjectivity oriented to the objectively true. Heidegger sought its ontological ground in concern as the disclosure of the concerned self as total response or self-relatedness to one's existential situation. Kierkegaard says: "It is really the conscience which constitutes as personality... For the conscience may slumber, but the constitutive factor is its possibility."[2] The self is conscious of itself as finite freedom. Its possible concrete ways of existing and realising itself are revealed through conscience. There is a hiatus between what the self is, what it might have been and what it will in fact be. These three dimensions of conscience correspond to the three temporal ecstasies that relate us to our own being as what has passed into history, as what lies before us a pure possibility and as the summons to realise responsibly the demands of freedom in the present. For Heidegger then conscience is "the call of concern", and in this existential sense we speak of persons having a social, religious, ecological conscience as a concern issuing in deep personal convictions and values on these issues. The function of conscience is to lead one from inauthentic to authentic existence, from the suppression and "fallenness" of everyday existence to resolve and commitment. In this view everyday existence defines a person as an "anonymous one" and suppresses a person's unique possibilities which can only be regained by their courageous affirmation through conscience. "The anonymous one" voices conventional standards of behaviour, external legal sanctions that never penetrate to personal reflection and authentic existence. This is public conscience seen as retreat from subjectivity and freedom.

Kierkegaard noted how the courtroom analogy for conscience simply breaks down. Conscience has to do with inner counsels rather than external demands. But as Kierkegaard rejected heteronomy that leads to legalism, he also rejected Kant's ethical autonomy because it leads to lawlessness since it lacks the compelling element necessary to arouse the self to freedom. Heteronomy and autonomy are transcended in a third factor, namely, in the structure of self-relatedness. In a religious sense this implies a divine-human encounter where, he says, "God's power is in the conscience."[3] Kierkegaard thus rejects a heteronomous view of conscience in which the directives of conscience are rooted in a legalism of rules and laws; he also rejects ethical autonomy in which a human acts as his or her own lawgiver. Conscience is then rooted in an inward freedom which transcends both law and autonomous reason and is ultimately grounded in God. Heidegger also rebels against "public conscience" which seeks its norms and standards outside itself. "Conscience as a phenomenon of *Dasein* is not an external and passing-on factuality."[4] The call of conscience comes not through some external source but from the being which I myself am. It is characterised by personalness, and calls me contrary to my everyday expectations and wishes. It has something to say about me. It uncovers the universally human in the existence of the individual that transcends the external and inauthentic view of conscience, which Heidegger analyses phenomenologically under the fourfold heading of the "common" view of conscience: (1) it is based on the moral categories of good and evil as reinforced by censure and warning, i.e., moralistically; (2) it looks to an external judge; (3) it considers only the isolated acts of the individual without taking motives and intentions into account – personal being remains immune to the pronouncements of conscience; and (4) it is essentially critical and ignores anything positive in the phenomenon of conscience. Heidegger believes conscience should be transmoral because it goes beyond a moralistic understanding of right and wrong to the existential summons of *Dasein* to its authentic possibilities. Conscience as the call of concern then has a threefold structure: as "caller" it is *Dasein* or the self in its facticity or abandonment in the world (pastness); as "called to" or protended into the possibilities of being (futurity); as "called forth" to authentic possibility of being as finite concern. Corresponding to the call is the phenomenon of hearing. This does not mean that conscience is "merely subjective", but that it is an authentic understanding of the universal and obligatory voice of conscience; it touches the aspects of universal guilt and of universal possibility inseparable from the human. These are the ontological foundations of conscience for Heidegger. Kierkegaard has described guilt as "the most concrete expression of conscience".[5] Jaspers sees conscience as the running up against the "boundary conditions" which constitute the insurmountable limits of human existence. Conscience discloses guilt. Conscience speaks to us in our finite freedom and brings us to the reflective self-awareness that we have not become what we might and should have been. This finite freedom is constituted by the polar synthesis of possibility and necessity – or of freedom conditioned by the factor of destiny. Guilt is always present as a possibility of one's freedom, a possibility for which we must always take responsibility. Guilt then is both active and passive as acquired through one's actions and as suffered in the given situationality of one's destiny. There is thus an element of inevitability and universality attached to guilt. It is the unavoidable boundary condition of our existence. Thus in every choice I am "cutting off" other possibilities that are constitutive of my being. Like death, guilt is phenomenologically both a universal determinant and a principle of individuation for human existence. Conscience through guilt calls the individual back to its unique self with its unique responsibilities. Just as the death the self must die is uniquely its own death, so also the guilt in which the self is involved is uniquely its own. Guilt is to be understood as discontinuity of human experience in which the self experiences estrangement within itself as possibility of being. Guilt can be qualified in religious experience as estrangement of the self from God. In their original freedom human persons are free to sin (*posse peccare*) or not to sin (*posse non peccare*). But the first choice in which they chose to sin and every succeeding choice bears the marks of this original act of rebellion. Unauthentic guilt is that which is defined through externalised and objectified norms, a defect for which one must make amends that places guilt outside the person. Authentic guilt is a matter of personal responsibility and situational unavoidability given one's choice. According to Heidegger, the human subject does not just have guilt, it *is* *guilt*, and the role of conscience is to call the person to the possibility of being.

In our modern mentality it is the inevitability of having to lose so many of freedom's possibilities that renders us guilty and it is guilt that leads us to conscience as awareness of the self. This is a view that owes much to Nietzsche's view of a morality "beyond good and evil", a morality where we are forever doomed to be guilty not only because of our actions but because of our situation. This is an unredeemed conscience that does not acknowledge the power of God as Creator or Saviour. Guilt serves to reveal our alienation from God, our lack of grace, our eternal hopelessness left to ourselves.

2. John Henry Newman

Newman also took a personal, existential approach to conscience, but from a wholly faith perspective. The power of God's attraction magnetising our hearts reverses the charges attached to the atheistic or agnostic existential account of conscience. Newman believed that God has impressed his eternal law in our minds and that the reception on our part of this divine light is nothing other than conscience. Conscience in this first radical sense should then be our personal perception of the natural law, and of whom we are before God, our Creator. The divine law is our supreme rule of action. It is "the internal witness of both the existence and the law of God".[6] "It is a principle planted within us", he says, "before we have had any training, although training and experience are necessary for its strength, growth and due formation." He understands it in a thoroughly christological sense. It brings moral recognition that ministers to Christ's grace of salvation. "Conscience is the aboriginal Vicar of Christ, a prophet in its informations, a monarch in its peremptoriness, a priest in its blessings and anathemas, and, even though the eternal priesthood throughout the Church could cease to be, in it the sacerdotal principle would remain and have a sway."[7] Conscience does not serve selfishness, nor will it submit to force from any power. In the popular mind the notion of a "Moral Governor" has been lost so that conscience has now often become identified with following one's own arbitrary wish or opinion without regard to moral rule or the Creator. But, "Conscience has rights because it has duties; but in this age, with a large portion of the public, it is the very right and freedom of conscience to dispense with conscience, to ignore a Lawgiver and Judge, to be independent of unseen obligations."[8] Its counterfeit would encourage a person to follow any religion or none at will, without regard to its truth. "Conscience is a stern monitor." Newman in the aftermath of the definition of papal infallibility set out to refute the falsifying liberal idea of freedom of conscience upheld by Gladstone. While the Pope may scoff at such excesses as proposed by the liberals, he said, conscience has another value in the Catholic sense, for "there is no scoffing of any Pope, in formal documents addressed to the faithful at large, at that most serious doctrine, the right and the duty of following that Divine Authority, the voice of conscience, on which in truth the Church herself is built".[9] To speak against conscience would be suicidal for the Church, since the authority of her message of right and wrong rests on that foundation. Her mission is to supply the urgent demand "to elicit, protect and enforce those truths which the Lawgiver has sown in our very nature".[10] Revelation, although distinct from nature, is not independent of it but is "its complement, reassertion, issue, embodiment, and interpretation".[11] Papal authority would not have lasted down the centuries had it been in contradiction with humanity's deepest religious sense revealed through conscience. It is therefore, claims Newman, "a dutiful obedience to what claims to be a divine voice, speaking within us".[12] Conscience is not speculative knowledge but a judgement about what is to be done here and now. In this way it cannot come into conflict with Church authority whose teaching proposes general truth and condemns particular errors. A collision is possible only in case of particular commands or orders. "But a Pope is not infallible in his laws, nor in his commands, nor in his acts of state, nor in his administration, nor in his public policy."[13] Newman argues that obedience is due to the Pope as a religious authority acting as Vicar of Christ, and not from any temporal or political motive. "Since then infallibility alone could block the exercise of conscience, and the Pope is not infallible in that subject-matter in which conscience is of supreme authority, no dead-lock... can take place between conscience and the Pope."[14] However, before opposing the Pope these considerations must be borne in mind: obedience to the Pope must always be considered in possession; only after prayer, reflection and wise consultation may one proceed. Legitimate disagreement and refusal to follow the Pope's supreme authority can only happen after "serious thought, prayer, and all available means of arriving at a right judgement on the matter in question... Unless a man is able to say to himself, as in the presence of God, that he must not and dare not, act upon the Papal injunction, he is bound to obey it, and would commit a great sin in disobeying it."[15] Authority is to be presumed to be in the right, and this because of our faith and confidence in the Church as the communicator of revelation. This respect is our "bounded duty". Obedience is a duty for Newman. "If this necessary rule were observed, collisions between the Pope's authority and the authority of conscience would be very rare."[16]

3. Conscience as fundamental moral experience

Without conscience we should not know the difference between good and evil. It is fundamental to all moral experience and as such has become ever so controversial. It is conceived as the voice of liberty and authenticity of the person. By arriving at a position of conscience a person takes his or her life in hand and becomes master of his or her destiny. We understand this as the achievement of human autonomy and maturity which are the key to self-realisation. Psychologically and empirically conscience has assumed another meaning: that of Super-Ego, as opposed to Ego as the source of rational control and of Id as the instinctive, impulsive and drive level of personality. Super-Ego is what one learned from one's family and culture as the moral law in force. Often this was in deep conflict with one's best and deepest aspirations and impulses to develop one's own personality. Super-Ego requires conformity to the social order and law. In a sociological sense conscience has been understood as adjustment to social structures and forces. In this sense TV and the media form people's consciences. In a religious sense conscience has come to be thought of as part of our dialogue with God who reveals himself interiorly in word and action. It is hearing and listening to the voice of God within us. Psychologists often perceive in this religious conception nothing more than the mechanism of internalising parental authority, as Freud said.

Conscience has been recognised as a cultural force, for example, in the option for the poor or in advocacy as in the ecological movement, both of which are thought of as conscience stances. We should not be surprised that so often conscience becomes the shield for arbitrary opinions and even for outright subjectivism and emotivism. "What I do has nothing to do with other people. It's a matter for my conscience alone." This is the ultimate devaluation of conscience in an unauthentic ethic. All of the meanings of conscience in vogue today concur in attributing to it the faculty of awareness of the moral self that assumes responsibility for its actions in a mature personality. Conscience is thus identified as the very deepest level or centre of our personality. Here is the fount of human liberty on which the consciousness of self and all life's projects are constructed. It is the centre from which we discover our spiritual-physical unity as persons. This is where Freud wanted to arrive with psychoanalysis, and this has given rise to the idea of conscience as being able to be plumbed in depth psychology. Jung, of course, changed this schema to one of person and shadow as two aspects of self-consciousness. We can see then that conscience must be considered against the pluralism of opinions operative in contemporary society. In view of this it is necessary to understand the history of the idea of conscience and how it has developed in theology. This does not mean relativism but an awareness of how our conception has grown through historical reflection.

All authorities agree that the idea of conscience arose in the Western European world. The reflexive awareness of consciousness came to be in the cosmological-mythological world of the ancient Greeks. It was first thought of as taboo, as what was forbidden by custom, the doing of which turned a person against themselves. Conscience arose out of an awareness of offending against the order of the cosmos and so against the gods. It was felt as conflict, as an interior wounding because one was not in harmony with the world. The Stoics were the first to thematise conscience in a philosophical manner. For them conscience was experienced as bad conscience when one disobeyed the natural law as God's will establishing order in the cosmos. When man was created he was given conscience as the faculty of judging good and evil in human action. Conscience was thus a "fragment of God" (Cicero, *De Legibus*, 1, 24s 59), a divine spark in the human depths. Humanity thus learnt how to be moral in an innerly coherent way that we would describe as rational. The result of this emphasis was to focus on the inner and intimate values more than on exterior social conditioning. It is to the Stoics that we owe the concept of *syneidesis* as the fundamental capacity to distinguish right and wrong.

4. The Christian conception

Christian thinkers readily synthesised Greco-Roman wisdom with the history of salvation by interpreting *syneidesis* in terms of the Old Testament concept of *leb* or heart as the inner depth, the centre of motivation and sentiment. Here the conflict is not so much with divinely established cosmic order, leading to a split in wounded consciousness as for the Greeks, but the person focuses outward on God and is aware of guilt by falling short of his will and command. This conscience grew out of a relationship with God in covenant. A Christian is aware of God's closeness, of being united lovingly with him and therefore doing his will or of failing him. The wounding of sin is a wound in our relationship with God and thus narrows our awareness of his goodness by

diminishing our humanity. Psalm 51 summarises this understanding dramatically:

> Have mercy on me, O God,
> according to your steadfast love;
> according to your abundant mercy
> blot out my transgressions.

Heart means a trusting, open, and steadfast relationship
with God based on his previous love for us, a love that called
us into existence and calls us to exist and bloom humanly. The
very core of this relationship when reflected upon rationally
came to be recognised as conscience in Christian wisdom. In
the Old Testament there is no word nor explicit idea for
conscience, since the voice of God sounds in the human heart
and so morality was identified with attentiveness to God's
wishes. It was God-centred and not reflecting on self. The
prophets, by making morality reside in the human heart, can
rightly be called "the conscience of Israel".

Philippe Delhaye summarised the scriptural teaching on
the heart as: (1) the witness to the moral value of our acts; (2)
the sanctuary where the divine law is interiorised; (3) the
source of moral life, the fount of goodness, health and vitality;
and (4) God can convert it and bring it back should it stray
and lose him.[17] Prudence and wisdom are themes kindred to
conscience in the Bible and bring out other aspects of God's
action in our regard.

The fundamental distinction which is reflected in Scripture, the Fathers and all subsequent philosophy and theology
of conscience is that between habitual and actual conscience,
or, as some would say today, fundamental and situational
conscience, or between consciousness of the values by which
we live and the judgement that choice should follow. This
distinction is embodied in the two terms *synderesis* and conscience. Actual conscience is usually understood in a more
psychological way. It is the practical judgement *hic et nunc*
that such and such has to be done because it is good or omitted
because it is bad. It may also be applied to the moral rightness
of acts in the past. This act of conscience is an act of know-

ledge, while habitual conscience is the *habitus* or capacity from which the act emanates. Therefore the habitual conscience is the psychological capacity from which moral judgements proceed; it is a strength of the soul constantly qualified to form these judgements. In this sense St Paul indicates that the pagans have within them an inner law in relation to which they judge their acts.

The New Testament retains the Old Testament theocentric experience of conscience in Jesus' preaching of the Kingdom of God as an eschatological reality. For the Christian, good and evil are perceived in the horizon of salvation worked by God in Christ. The encounter with Christ thus becomes an encounter with the Messiah in a dialogue of salvation. The New Testament in general does not explicitly advert to conscience except in St Paul, who takes his lead from the common language of the people. He uses the term *syneidesis* as an anthropological term that underlines how Christian identity is worked out in relationship with God. In the letter to the Romans it can even substitute for *pistis* as faith. Philosophers and theologians have taken it in moral terms as good faith so as to signify the very centre of our self-awareness as moral agents who live out of the freedom gained through relationship with Christ, whether it is a question to do with the State (Rom 13:5) or to do with meat offered to idols that pits the liberty of those strong in the faith against the scandal aroused in the weak (1 Cor 10:23-33; Gal 2:4; 5:1-12).

"For freedom Christ has set us free. Stand firm, therefore, and do not submit again to the yoke of slavery" (Gal 5:1), says St Paul.

"But if someone says to you, 'This has been offered in sacrifice,' then do not eat it, out of consideration for the one who informed you, and for the sake of conscience (*syneidesis*) – I mean the other's conscience, not your own" (1 Cor 10:28-29). He recognises its function as that of a judge of an action and this not only in the sense of the tension and bad effects of an evil action but as a witness that approves or accuses us. It is a reflexive reality that accompanies all our actions.

Philippe Delhaye has isolated a number of themes from St Paul that are important in any philosophical consideration of conscience. Conscience is a judge and a norm. In Romans 2:14-15, he declares, "When Gentiles, who do not possess the law, do instinctively what the law requires, these, though not having the law, are a law to themselves. They show that what the law requires is written on their hearts, to which their own conscience also bears witness." To judge the rightness of an act the Jews refer to the law of Moses, but the Gentiles do not have that criterion. But they have within themselves a moral capacity that indicates to them what is good and to be done. What people do as it were by moral instinct is understood as being done by human nature and therefore has been understood by Church tradition as asserting natural law. In the Pelagian controversies this "by nature" was held to mean "not by grace". But St Paul was not eulogising Greeks or Jews, for he says, in Romans 3:9, "For we have already charged that all, both Jews and Greeks, are under the power of sin." Precisely in order to sin there must be knowledge. If the Greeks sinned it is because they did not follow the interior law that instructed them, even though at times they were good spouses, fathers, citizens etc. In these things they followed their moral instincts or inclinations, but if they failed to be inspired by charity these acts were not considered meritorious. Conscience had a precise role in all this by making a moral judgement upon an act. It compares behaviour with a moral imperative. This is a judgement that can also be made about others, as we see in Romans 2:15 and following. By reference to the law as found in conscience, the Greek has a moral index to the acts of other men, approving or disapproving them. Paul later says, "I am speaking the truth in Christ – I am not lying; my conscience confirms it by the Holy Spirit" (Rom 9:1 and 2 Cor 1:12-13). This conscience is inhabited by the Holy Spirit who guides and enlightens it. On one side there is the person, on the other the witness to the truth of its action. Conscience is a part of ourselves, a constitutive of nature that continues to function even for lapsed human nature. Conscience can also apply moral knowledge to the acts of others, as when one would refrain from eating meat offered in pagan sacrifice because another would thereby be led to sin. So far conscience has been referred to rather impersonally as pointing to God's sovereignty. But it is also a personal reality, identified with each individual. It can be subject to error and otherwise quali-fied, so that St Paul speaks of "good conscience", "bad con-science" and "weak conscience". Good conscience (Acts 24:16; Heb 13:18; 2 Tim 1:3; 3:9; 1 Tim 1:19) implies not only the absence of faults but the constant will to persevere in the good. A bad conscience is one that has been corrupted and deliberately remains committed to doing known evil. "To the corrupt and unbelieving nothing is pure. Their very minds and consciences are corrupted" (Tit 1:15). There is a stigma on the bad conscience (1 Tim 4:2) which causes the personality to wither; it is the complete opposite of the witness of the good conscience. Weakness of conscience occurred in the case of food offered to idols because these folk judged an objectively indifferent act to be bad. This reveals a further inconstancy of character and vulnerability to bad example. In St Paul conscience, as well as being an interior witness, is also sus-ceptible to outside influences for good or evil. It therefore is open to be formed in holiness or in malice.

St Paul clearly teaches the obligation to obey the judge-ment of conscience. The fact that conscience judges the acts of the past and issues imperatives shows that we have to follow it. When Paul teaches that we are to obey civil rulers he is simply teaching this. "Therefore whoever resists authority resists what God has appointed... one must be subject, not only because of wrath but also because of conscience" (Rom 13:2, 5). In the following chapter Paul treats of the same problem of the erroneous or simply doubtful conscience by using the term *pistis*, which here implies good faith or sincere and complete conviction. Certain Christians were not com-pletely free of their old pagan practices and convictions about sacrifices to idols, for example. Those whose lives were dominated by Christian faith were thereby freed from the old taboos. But the weak members still fell under their sway. "The faith that you have, have as your own conviction before God. Blessed are those who have no reason to condemn themselves because of what they approve. But those who have doubts are condemned if they eat, because they do not act from faith; for whatever does not proceed from faith is sin" (Rom 14:22-23).

The force of conscience is such that one must follow its judgements even when they are erroneous. If one swerves from it, one sins. He expands on this in 1 Corinthians 8, where he distinguishes enlightened Christians who know that such meat has no religious significance and their consciences are free. Some Christians, however, do not know this. What would happen if they did not follow their mistaken conscience? "They still think of the food they eat as food offered to an idol; and their conscience, being weak, is defiled" (1 Cor 8:7). They are obliged to act according to their convictions even though these are not objectively founded. It is not possible to give a better explanation of the distinction between the objective norm and the truth as perceived by conscience, and the obligatory force of the judgement of personal conscience. These people sinned because their act was against conscience when they mistakenly thought they were acting against the truth.

Some other principles referred to by Paul in solving this case are the radical freedom of Christian conscience and how it is prudent and foresightful in the situation. "All things are lawful", but "not all things are beneficial" (1 Cor 10:23). The rule that guides this foresight is charity, the genuine good of the neighbour which is spelled out at length in various ways and in various places. But it is not only a question of fraternal charity, for love of God also intervenes. "So, whether you eat or drink, or whatever you do, do everything for the glory of God" (1 Cor 10:31). This is a text often quoted with reference to good intention and correctly so. It means that whatever we do has to be able to be referred to God's glory. It means that any intrinsically evil act, whether directly against God as in blasphemy or indirectly through harming our neighbour, would be a contradiction of divine charity and against the fundamental intention of the Christian life itself. In indifferent things a person also has to consider what among all the things possible fits his or her state and condition. Here there are no prefabricated solutions, for they are all lawful so that one has to reason to what seems best in these circumstances.

St Paul's doctrine on conscience has been touched on all too briefly and partially here. He is important for showing how conscience works from natural law, how it is a process of knowing in which we apply our conscientiously held convictions to the situation at hand, and how this builds up the virtues, especially charity, till the Holy Spirit becomes the light and guide of our existence.

5. The Fathers

The patristic teaching on conscience is incredibly rich and multiform. It utilises to the full the biblical terms "heart" and "conscience" in accord with the cultural resources of the times.

What is most striking in the phenomenon of conscience is the affective reaction that accompanies or follows a good or bad action. It means unhappiness with one's self, inner discord and bitterness as the fruits of evil. St John Chrysostom's homilies are justly famous. "Even in this life the sinner finds punishment for his fault... Look at his conscience: there you will see the tumultuous agitation of his sins, in fear, tempest, discord. As a sort of tribunal the mind sits as it were as a judge on the royal throne of conscience, using the memory of what one has done as so many executioners, suspending the course of thought, cruelly causing the sins committed to be expiated. It is impossible to silence its accusing voice even when it is a question of things known only to God."[18] This is one of the moderate but felt descriptions of the remorse of conscience.

The joy of a good conscience is an encouragement to charity. "The greatest festival is a good conscience... For the man who lives and acts in a good way, even ordinary days are festivals", says the same John Chrysostom. The testimony of conscience is unimpeachable so that its testimony is the only motivation the good person requires (2 Cor 1:12; 1 Jn 3:20). Origen points out that there is a kind of primary intuition which no one lacks, since it is so close to a natural instinct. We must not do to others what we would not have them do to us (Tob 4:16, or in its positive form in Mt 7:12). Natural law also played a part in the thought of the Fathers, not so much as has become common over recent centuries as a superior law of human nature over the State and all institutions, but rather as an "unwritten law" that affirmed the primacy of conscience when one acknowledged beyond words right and wrong in one's heart. The Fathers, following St Paul, put the instinctive knowledge of conscience in contrast with the law of Sinai which was of divine origin. One is therefore responsible to the Creator for judging rightly according to conscience. They pointed out that conscience too was of divine origin, having been implanted into human nature at creation. The fundamental awareness of the most basic and undeniable values cannot be erased from the human heart, but where conscience falls into error we should try as far as possible to overcome our blindness. Many of the Fathers were influenced by the Stoic conception of the Divine Reason that penetrated all creation and was most intense in the spark of conscience. They christianised this philosophy as the presence of God to conscience. The Fathers displayed an optimism about human nature, believing that even in our fallen state people have the moral equipment for judging right from wrong even when they lack the grace to perform it. They believed firmly in the "natural seeds of the virtues". Jansenius cleverly rebelled against this notion centuries later, but it was the Christian humanism of the Fathers that authentically represented St Paul. They could not see how a just God could punish anyone for violating his law without knowing it. Nor could one approve, esteem and admire what is good to the point of condemning oneself for falling short of the mark, without having in one's being an inclination to the good. It is precisely the grace of Christ that liberates this will to achieve the good. St Augustine saw in conscience a way of discovering the image of the Trinity imprinted in the soul by which we live in the divine presence.

6. St Thomas Aquinas

It is precisely as *a return to oneself by reflection* on the act we have done or on the act we are about to do that St Thomas understands conscience. Conscience is therefore an aspect of our moral awareness when we reflect on the moral rightness or wrongness of our performed or proposed actions. In a more primary sense it can mean the reflexive awareness that we have performed this or that action. It is our assertion that this act is real, it exists, and I am its agent or author. It is the application of our moral knowledge to the act in view. It can be called our knowledge of how our act corresponds or is consonant with the moral law valid for everyone. In this sense conscience is always the same, and St Thomas says it does not vary over time. The judgement on a certain act as good or bad is an abiding evaluation when it is true. In conscience we assess our acts in view of our most basic values. This assessment covers reason's whole range, touching values directly relating to divine things as well as earthly realities or, as Augustine calls them, superior and inferior reason. "Through conscience the judgement of *synderesis* and of superior and inferior reason is applied to the examining of a particular action."[19]

This meaning also emerges from an examination of the common attributes of conscience in ordinary language. Conscience is said "to witness, to bind, to incite and also to accuse, to torment and to rebuke". All of these Aquinas considered the result of "the application of our thought or knowledge to what we do". As act he related conscience to actions in a twofold sense. On the one hand he viewed the conscience as the act of applying knowledge; on the other this act is directed toward an object, "that which we do". We must take into account the act of applying and what it is applied to. This means first of all analysing conscience ontologically as act and so as an element of human nature, and secondly locating this particular act in relation to human actions in general.

Since conscience is the application of knowledge to particular cases, he located it in the rational soul and then in the cognitive part which is practical by being action-directed. The conscience is therefore neither primarily volitional nor speculative. It is a special category of practical rationality. He posits a real distinction between the powers where the cognitive is superior to the appetitive, although the object sought may be superior to the soul so that "love of God is better than knowledge of God" (*S.T.*, I, 82, 3). Thus, however much St Thomas' reflection derives from Aristotle, he is always contemplating the human being in a Christian setting.

He did not distinguish the intellectual (*intellectus*) from the rational (*ratio*) as powers in the way he did for the cognitive and the appetitive; they are the same power distinguished by the way they function. The intellect immediately apprehends first principles as necessary truths; the reason is discursive in its operation, arguing from principles to conclusions.[20] Thus conscience as the interiorisation and personalisation of knowledge is identified with an aspect of practical reason. St Thomas asked, why is conscience not a faculty of the soul? The answer is that conscience can be set aside and disregarded but a faculty cannot! What conscience informs us should be done need not be done. It is possible to ignore conscience or in other ways to fail to act on what it prescribes. This would be impossible were it a power. He was aware that the term *contientia* was sometimes used to mean more than action as the application of knowledge. An act has a habit or *habitus* as its motivating principle. Sometimes the term nominates the first practical habit or *synderesis* which produces or causes acts of conscience. St Thomas therefore defined conscience in the narrow sense, but he also employed St Jerome's notion of *synderesis* to describe its ontological foundation. *Synderesis* warrants further attention. A habit is a fixed disposition or settled inclination of a faculty whereby it produces its acts spontaneously and readily. *Synderesis* is the very source of moral life and knowledge because it orients the intellect to good and away from evil. It contains the first principle of all practical moral living that inclines us to all the other human goods. *Synderesis*, then, is that practical intellectual habit which "contains the precepts of the natural law which are the first principles of human action". It therefore emerged in his thought as the habit used in making the act of judgement called *contientia*. It is a habit that is not acquired by the repeated performance of actions of a given kind. It is a habit that we could call innate, as given to humanity with the gift of reason at creation as a property of its nature. Not only does the human being have a natural inclination to the good and knowledge of first moral principles, but this habit cannot be lost or extinguished. The light of the agent intellect cannot be extinguished and so the habit of *synderesis* cannot be lost. There is another

characteristic most important for moral life. *Synderesis* is a
habit incapable of error or sin. Thus in explaining moral
failure or error the fault cannot be placed in the habitual
conscience. The first principles of practical reason by which
synderesis guides actual conscience can never fail or be false.

Synderesis is then a special inclination or disposition,
naturally possessed by all human beings, inextinguishable
and incapable of error; as a *habitus* it is the ontological base
and source of the actions of actual conscience. In this way
St Thomas grounded conscience in the fundamental and permanent features of human nature which make a moral being.

He viewed conscience as an activity of reason, but this in
a precise sense as can be seen from the following. Firstly,
St Thomas has been charged with making conscience something coldly, rationally divorced from emotional life. However, his description of conscience as having the power "to
accuse, to torment, to rebuke" shows he conceived it holistically
with the passions and emotions. Secondly, he restricted the
notion of conscience ontologically to that of *actus*. In contrast
with contemporary thought, that tends to treat conscience as
sentiment that reveals how a person reacts to a situation,
St Thomas thinks of it as deeper than its manifestations. We
speak of commands of conscience, of accusations of conscience, even metaphorically of the voice of conscience. For
him these all flow from *synderesis* which is something much
deeper, so that the relation of habitual and actual conscience is
that between a habit and its act.

After treating the ontological status of conscience, he passes
on to consider human actions as the object of its operation.
Here we are not concerned with conscience as "the application
of knowledge", but the application of knowledge "to that
which we do". We move now from the ontological to the
psychological realm and its dynamic, to how conscience functions and to what purpose.

No distinction is more basic for understanding conscience
as an act of reason than that between the speculative and the
practical intellect.[21] He thought of it as an act of reason func-
tioning practically rather than theoretically or speculatively.
He distinguishes the speculative intellect which has the

consideration of truth as such as its object from the practical intellect which has as object the truth precisely as action directed. Since this too is a function of reason, its object is also truth, but not truth as such but truth in so far as it appeals to the mind as good. The practical intellect, like the speculative, has first principles which it employs in reasoning to conclusions. But unlike the conclusions of the speculative intellect, the judgements of the practical intellect do not produce rigorously necessary conclusions, but result in contingent truths about what has to be done in order to attain given ends. They do not remain at the level of universal truths as in the speculative intellect, but are concerned with particular human actions. This distinction is important because conscience is practical. This has certain consequences that emerge from reflecting on the different types of act present in the phenomenon of conscience.

St Thomas set forth three categories for the act of conscience: (1) it witnesses that something has been done or has not been done; (2) it incites or binds: in its judgement it determines something should be done or should not be done; (3) its judgement excuses, accuses or torments: "We judge of something that has been done whether it has been done well or badly." These distinctions can be extended to the modern conceptions of antecedent and consequent conscience. Each of these three categories can produce what we would call a good or bad conscience. St Thomas, probably under the influence of Abelard and the questions he posed, centred his concern on the role of conscience in shaping the moral qualities of proposed actions.

Conscience was predominantly a part of the operation of the practical intellect as it reasoned to a decision about what was to be done in concrete situations confronting an individual. He did not pay great attention to its function as vindicator of past moral action, and paid even less to psychological guilt. The act of conscience itself is a particular act that judges the rightness or wrongness of a human act already in its own right. Many authors have sought to identify conscience as an isolatable phrase in the structure of the human act as a whole. It is better to see it as a reflexive assessment of the conformity of an act with moral principles, i.e., it is a judgement of how it is moral or fails to be so. The structure of the human act is not that of a temporal series but should be seen within an analytic framework that would seek to identify the causes of each partial act that goes to constitute the human act as a whole. St Thomas stressed the complex reciprocal interaction of intellect and will at every stage. They work together so that intention may achieve its *finis* through deliberation that specifies the means needed to that end. It is usually about these and how they correspond to moral principles that the act of actual conscience is concerned. An agent does not always require a reflexive act of conscience before proceeding to election. What prepares for election is the judgement that this act is to be done here and now.

This distinguished the judgement of conscience from that of free will that precedes election. "Therefore in both cases the matter of the judgement is a concrete act," says Philippe Delhaye, echoing St Thomas. "But the conscience makes its pronouncement in the name of reason *in pura cognitione*, whereas the judgement of free will puts truth into a personal context *in applicatione cognitionis ad affectionem*. It is no longer a question of knowing whether fornication is evil, but whether for the individual it represents a value even so."[22] The free act of choice or election is the immediate and effective determinant of the morality of the action, the "subject" of the moral act (*S.T.*, I-II, 19. 7-10). The judgement of conscience is much more an objective standing back from the situation the agent is involved in so as to measure it against moral principle than the judgement of free will or election that only happens in cooperation with the will. The external act is informed by the agent's intention which it puts into execution. The end of all action is thus the peace and joy that flow from achievement of one's purpose or end. The morality of the act is intrinsic to it in so far as it is rightly directed to realising this end. The supreme good which is sought, the beatitude which satisfies all human desires, is the God who has revealed himself in creation and redemption. But this is not the only end, for other human goods also function as genuine ends. Morality is intrinsic not only in the sense that all is directed to God, but in the sense that each act has its own proper goodness as measured by practical reason. What is objectively good for human beings is what benefits and befits their nature, perfecting them as rational beings. Of course, all of this falls within the intention of the final end. Conscience as seen in the perspective of faith is only complete when it is informed by charity and judges every act according to its intrinsic worth as enlivened by God's love. Conscience in its fullness goes beyond lawfulness such as we encounter it in systems of casuistry. It is a unique moment of encounter for the person in this, his or her *kairos* of decision before God. True conscience is thus guided by charity directing and drawing the agent to God, and is informed by prudence which integrates the person's unique situation and motivation into the supreme order of love. Conscience thus discerns what divine providence requires in every life-situation.

7. The authority of conscience

Providence is the task assigned to practical reason to guide one's life-plan to realisation in the totality of one's concrete life-situation. Within the practical intellect there is a knowledge of the natural law which St Thomas defined as "the sharing in the eternal law by creatures of reason". Thus human beings are fitted by reason to discover how God's own wisdom guides the world to himself and how their life is meant to share in his intimate happiness. Thus the rational creature participates in eternal reason through its natural inclination for the appropriate action and end. Reason shares in the divine light and truth. The proximate norm or rule of action is conscience and the remote or originative norm is the divine reason. The precepts of the natural law are for the practical reason what the axioms of science are for the speculative reason; they govern conduct in the same way that axioms govern conclusions. Moral principles are based upon and derived from the rationality present in reality; they are our human grasp or knowledge of the exemplary ideas present in the divine mind that imbue and permeate creation with a divine order. Natural law as a guide to conscience is an integral part of St Thomas' moderate realism.

Now the act of choice, which is the subject of voluntary action and hence the immediate determinant of its moral quality, is an act that either accepts or rejects the judgement of conscience. In the practical syllogism by which practical reason reaches a judgement about what is to be done we see the functional distinction of *synderesis* and conscience. The major is a universal proposition from natural law. Its first principle is that good is to be done and pursued, and evil avoided. The other specific principles are contained analogously in this first principle as its reflection in the human inclinations. The minor comes from factual knowledge about the situation and its circumstances. The conclusion is an action conforming to moral principles; the judgement of conscience is reached by reflection on the proposed act in the light of these principles. The precepts of the natural law in the major are universally certain *per se*. However, ignorance of some precepts of natural law may be possible *per accidens*, as in the case cited by St Thomas from an ancient Latin author of the German tribes who experienced no guilt of conscience over robbing others' property. Further, since actual conscience involves reasoning, it is obviously fallible. Prudence can be assisted by the other virtues, all of which derive their efficacy from *synderesis* enlightening and encouraging "the seeds of the natural virtues" to grow.

Conscience judgements which respect the integrity of human inclination toward goodness, truth and beatitude, i.e., those that genuinely personalise and internalise the natural law for the acting person in their real situation, are said to be of right conscience (*contientia recta*); those that do not are the product of a wrong or erroneous conscience (*contientia erronea*). It is in this context that St Thomas dealt with the problem of the authority of conscience. In his writings it seems he only considered the problem of the erroneous conscience at length. He did not have any major difficulties with the authority of the right conscience. In his treatment of the erroneous conscience he was responding to difficulties raised by Abelard, who said that unless one acts against one's conscience there is no sin, and to the early Franciscans who taught that ignorance excused only in morally indifferent actions. He treated erroneous conscience in the context of the goodness or malice of the interior act of the will (*S.T.*, I-II, 19. 5, 6). Is the will evil when it is at variance with right reason? Is the will good when it abides by an erring conscience?... "which is the same as to ask whether an erroneous conscience excuses".

To the first problem he answered that an erroneous conscience always obliges in a negative way. The object of the will is the good apprehended by the practical intellect. When the will refuses to accept what the intellect proposes as good, or when the will refuses to accept as evil what the intellect proposes as evil, the will is morally at fault, "absolutely speaking, every will at variance with reason, whether right or erring, is always evil". This is a very powerful statement of the absolute negative authority of conscience. To act against conscience is always wrong and objectively sinful.

To the second problem he replied that although an erroneous conscience may be binding on the will, nevertheless the will that follows it cannot always be excused from having committed evil. Now the conscience errs through ignorance either of the major or the minor premise in the practical syllogism. He was also aware that conscience could err through a mistake in reasoning to the conclusion. He concentrated his attention on the fact that ignorance of correct moral principles may be the source of error in the major term, or ignorance of factual circumstances of a particular case in the minor term. He maintained there is a distinction between ignorance which excuses the will from sinning and ignorance which does not. The ignorance which excuses is called invincible or incorrigible. It is of such a kind that the act committed in ignorance is involuntary. For example, ignorance of the factual nature of a particular case is such that the agent is unaware of the true nature of the act involved. He or she is unaware that this act is truly the type of act that it is. The example he gives, of a husband not being aware that the woman with whom he is having sexual intercourse is not his wife, seems quite fanciful to the modern imagination. When conscience is unaware of the nature of its action, the action becomes involuntary and falls outside the sphere of what we predicate as morally good or bad (*S.T.*, I-II, 6. 1).

But he did not think that all factual ignorance excused from sin. Ignorance that does not excuse was termed voluntary ignorance (*ignorantia voluntaria*). This ignorance is divided into two classes: directly voluntary, in which case the agent's ignorance itself becomes the object of the will and is consented to; and indirectly voluntary ignorance, in which case the agent is negligent in knowing what he or she ought to know. This point might be reduced to the following for St Thomas: ignorance does not excuse if it is ignorance of the moral principles all human beings are obliged to know, or if there is culpable neglect in perceiving the factual circumstances of the action in question. Right conscience binds *per se*, but erroneous conscience *per accidens* (*De Veritate*, 17. 4). "Actually, the binding force of conscience, even the erroneous conscience, is exactly the same thing as the binding force of the law of God" (*idem est ligamen conscientiae etiam erroneae et legis Dei*).[23]

This is the sense he gave to the authority of conscience, that is, it is always wrong to violate conscience, even if it is erroneous. It is sometimes said that he did not take this principle to its positive conclusion, the complete sovereignty of conscience. However, he did not believe that the state of a "perplexed conscience", which is so caught in a dilemma that it sins whatever it does, was a real dilemma. Such a perplexed person "has it in his power to get rid of his error; his ignorance is voluntary and not incorrigible". He cites the example of a priest who commits fornication and is obliged to say Mass. May he do so? Yes, by removing his error, by an act of conversion. St Thomas set out the moral principles underlying conscience without spelling out their pastoral implications fully. He did not want to excuse the corrupt conscience of those who act from deliberately chosen false principles or those who act carelessly. He qualified his statement on the liberty of conscience by principled reasoning, and not because he did not want to hand it over to ecclesiastical authority. However, he does hold that a person can be firmly convinced that his or her conscience binds even after being formally excommunicated by the Church. Such a person can have legitimate reason to fly from authority. St Thomas could not be expected to have entered into the modern discussion on freedom of conscience as a human right.

8. The redeemed conscience

The picture of conscience presented so far is fundamentally philosophical and rational. It has often been forgotten that St Thomas was also a great commentator on the Scriptures, as was required of all the medieval masters in theology. In his *Commentarium "ad Romanos"* he studied St Paul's ideas of conscience in depth. For him the heart is its biblical equivalent. He shows that conscience reproves us of nothing when we act for the glory of God. It is possible for a person to perform a good outward action that is not done for God's glory, and so it does not avail for the edification of others as St Paul requires (nn. 324-325). Through conscience Christ and the Holy Spirit witness personally in the heart of the believer (Rom 9:1; 2 Cor 1:12). The role of the Spirit is to redirect the erroneous conscience by arousing good desires. On Romans 2:15-16 he treats explicitly of the eschatological dimension of conscience. Its testimony yielded through its judgement on the morality of acts performed in this life shall be revealed as salvation or condemnation according as it approves or disapproves these acts. Conscience is thus the act of discernment of human acts in terms of salvation (nn. 220, 222-223).

There is a double theological norm of conscience, faith and charity as lived in the Church. Edification of our brothers and sisters in the faith is a Christian duty. St Thomas maintains that faith is the foundation on which each should construct their life as an architect would (Rom 14:19). "I know and am persuaded in the Lord" (Rom 14:14) implies that faith is the possession of such a knowledge as brings the Christian certainty and destroys the precept of the old law that prohibited, e.g., eating impure foods. Perfect faith is opposed to the law in the sense that "the word law here means the whole teaching of the law of Moses, that is, its legal and ceremonial precepts". Charity teaches conscience that a person is not to seek its own interests but those of its brothers and sisters. The

freedom of faith and the universality of charity are two
specifically Christian norms. As already stated, before God an
action is worth what a right conscience estimates it to be, so
that to act against conscience is always sinful (n. 1119). He
repeats his doctrine of the invincibly ignorant conscience. The
question of the person in good will who acts in invincible
ignorance becomes the test case down the centuries for the
understanding of conscience.

9. Conscience and casuistry

Scotus, following a voluntaristic notion of human action,
held that such an act done in good will was morally good and
meritorious. It was good because God had commanded it by
his will. This differs from St Thomas' notion that invincible
ignorance caused an involuntary act of which one could predicate neither moral good nor evil because ignorance as such
could cause neither of these. St Antoninus of Florence stands
between the traditional tutiorism of the Middle Ages and the
tendency toward casuistry. He followed a less stern line than
had been in vogue and said that when theologians differed
among themselves one did not always have to follow the most
sure or safe opinion, but could follow what seemed more
probable. On the one hand he subscribed to what St Paul said
about the qualities and defects of conscience. On the other
hand he saw that the certitude to act in the situation had to be
reached through human opinions and wise conjectures about
the best course of action, particularly in political matters.[24]
The voluntarist understanding of conscience was strengthened
by the whole nominalist movement with its emphasis away
from the universal to the individual. Nominalism understood
law as an imposition of a superior's will on the will of a
subject. Law called for obedience and submission and not for
intelligent cooperation in the plan and purpose that a superior
proposed for a community. Liberty was no longer essentially
linked to moral truth but was thought of as the will's absolute
freedom to determine itself by choosing as it would among the
alternatives available. Moral decision was degraded to a

conflict between being bound by God's command imposed as restrictive law on the will, or being free and untrammelled by external restraint so as to choose to do what one would. This conflict model projected by nominalism was a great stimulus to the growth of casuistry in moral theology.

The Council of Trent reformed pastoral practice and called for good confessors to be formed in the newly instituted seminaries it established for priestly education. The instrument for the renewal of confessional practice was the *Institutiones Morales,* which embodied casuistry as the way to resolve conflicts of conscience. Cultural historians point out that the golden era of casuistry, roughly 1570 to 1660, corresponds with the birth of the modern national State and its struggle to assume control in administering the welfare of its population. It is a period of acute conflict between the national State's new-won power and the awareness of individual rights awakened by the Renaissance. The same is also broadly true of the Church, which felt the need to regulate Christian life more thoroughly in the Counter-Reformation period. In fact the manuals began by being generally benign till they slipped into laxism. There was a massive reaction toward rigorism and this became decisive with Pascal's criticism of the Jesuits in the *Provincial Letters.* His victory in the battle of words assisted the spread of Jansenism in France, Belgium and then to most of the Church. Rigorism and even Jansenism were often enough favoured by the civil authorities and so penetrated deeply into the Church's life — particularly through morals' manuals and seminary education — in many countries. Jansenism fostered a return to what was considered the pure morality of the early Church and the Fathers, particularly St Augustine. For the Jansenist, ignorance cannot be invincible because it is the product of original sin. By original sin human nature is corrupted. In the present state of fallen nature, human beings have sufficient liberty to commit sin even though they are not placing a fully free or voluntary act. The free and voluntary character of their action is to be attributed *in causa* to the sinful will of Adam in original sin. Some of the more rigid probabiliorists espoused the Jansenist positions. There could be no invincible ignorance for a conscience in that state, since it had been corrupted sinfully and deliberately and so could only breed evil from whatever liberty remained to it. The Holy See intervened in the seventeenth century to condemn the excesses of laxism, rigorism and Jansenism in matters of conscience.

10. Solution to the crisis of conscience: St Alphonsus

St Alphonsus de' Liguori realised that the denial of invincible ignorance arose from Jansenist doctrine. He insisted on the necessity of freedom and making lack of knowledge sinful. In fact St Alphonsus does not begin his *Moral Theology* with the tract on law as authors usually did at that time, but with conscience, and this is the only tract in his *magnum opus* which is not a commentary on Busembaum. His ideas on conscience bear the mark of his genius more than any other tract. He says that the remote rule of action is God's eternal law. The proximate and formal rule of moral action is human reason or conscience. Conscience, enlightened by the gift of wisdom, assimilates the eternal law and makes the prudential act of conscience in the situation. Conscience, as can be seen from the hundreds of cases in his *Moral Theology*, is no mere mechanical syllogistic application of moral law to circumstances. It is an original stance taken by the person giving meaning to his or her life by this particular action in this situation. In the process of assimilation of the eternal law a person may fall into error because of psychological or sociological pressure, or because of a lack of education and instruction. St Alphonsus saw this type of person as fulfilling God's will because he or she followed conscience in good faith. The question then arises whether the action of such an invincibly ignorant person can be good. St Alphonsus' answer is brief and nuanced. He does not follow the rigorists who say that such a conscience is vitiated by its very disordered nature. Nor does he say that it is good because the person believes God has commanded it by his will as does Duns Scotus. St Alphonsus says:

The person who acts with an invincibly erroneous conscience, does not sin but more probably acquires even merits... The reason is that it is sufficient for an act to qualify as good, at least in an inadequate way, when it is directed with reason and prudence. When he who acts does so with prudence, without doubt he ought to merit, on account of the good end for which he acts, for example the glory of God or charity toward his neighbour [my translation].[25]

In other words, if such an act is really informed by charity it is hard to see how it cannot be meritorious before God. This is an assertion of God's recognition of the dignity of the poor for he is involved on their side in their struggle against ignorance and lack of power. Nowhere is St Alphonsus' compassion for the poor more evident than in the way he formulated his moral system as the middle ground between laxism which undermines moral teaching and rigorism that makes goodness unattainable for those struggling with doubts of conscience and moral weakness.

What is to be said of conscience in a state of doubt? The law must be followed where its truth and validity are obvious and it is clearly in possession. Where the law does not determine the case, then freedom obtains. But when law and liberty balance one another out evenly, then the mind wavers from side to side and neither part can claim to carry the conviction needed to act with moral certainty. This is the state of moral doubt strictly so called. When the mind is unsettled in this way, i.e., rationally and not just psychologically, law cannot bind the will. The result is that the law in question is uncertain and therefore doubtful and freedom is left in possession. St Alphonsus became the defender of liberty of conscience because of his moral teaching. This is most true in the confessional which is the forum of conscience.

Fr L. Vereecke[26] summarises the values in his equiprobabilism as: (1) the truth contained in the Gospel and the natural moral law is the rule for good living; (2) conscience discerns moral truth through its intrinsic evidence, thus transcending the disputes between moral authors and the weighing of authorities against each other; (3) freedom is given us in creation as the condition of our self-realisation as persons.

St Alphonsus' doctrine gradually spread and permeated the Church's thinking and pastoral practice, particularly after he was declared a Doctor of the Church by Pope Pius IX in 1871. Up till the Second Vatican Council most manuals of moral theology drew on St Alphonsus and St Thomas Aquinas. But a more rigid line sometimes appeared in some of the neo-scholastic manuals. The Church recognised in St Alphonsus' practical theology "solutions to problems of conscience worked out in the mind of a saint" as Father Laourdette said.[27] St Alphonsus had provided a model of sanctity that showed how the Gospel was to be lived by those in moral doubt, struggling with ignorance and bereft of so many advantages others enjoy.

11. Vatican Council II

The preparatory document on morality for the Second Vatican Council, *De Ordine Morali Christiano*, saw conscience as a practical judgement, the syllogistic application of the moral law to a contemplated action. Conscience mediated between the absolute demands of the objective moral order and the action of an individual agent. This rigid conception was turned on its head during the discussion on the Church in the Modern World and found its final formulation in *Gaudium et Spes*, n. 16. This paragraph is the very centre of the first chapter on "The dignity of the human person". This dignity is founded on the doctrine of man as the image of God (n. 12), in a history marked by the presence of sin (n. 13), composed of body and soul (n. 14). There are three characteristics of human dignity: intelligence which seeks the truth (n. 15), conscience that discerns the good (n. 16), and liberty as their undeniable presupposition (n. 17). The challenge of death (n. 18), and the queries raised by modern atheism (nn. 18-21), concludes the meditation on human dignity by leading all creation to Christ, the new man (n. 22).

Each sentence in the Council's statement on conscience must be interpreted against its background in the whole first chapter. Conscience is more than a practical judgement. It is "man's most secret core, and his sanctuary. There he is alone with God whose voice echoes in his depths" (n. 16). Because of this interiority, a person knows who he or she is, being "superior to bodily things" and "more than just a speck of nature or a nameless unit in the city of man". In Augustinian terms, "When he is drawn to think about his real self he turns to those deep recesses of his being where God who probes the heart awaits him and where he himself decides his own destiny in the sight of God" (n. 14).

This interiority is not closed in on itself, but as the image of God is open to be present with, to dialogue and commune not only with God but with all humanity. "God did not create man a solitary being... For by his innermost nature man is a social being, and if he does not enter into relations with others he can neither live nor develop his gifts" (n. 12). Here he experiences the moral "ought". "Deep within his conscience man discovers a law which he has not laid upon himself but which he must obey... For man has in his heart a law inscribed by God. His dignity lies in obeying this law, and by it he will be judged" (n. 16). This "ought" he "discovers" within his heart; it depends neither on his will nor is it the fruit of his creativity. It is the criterion against which he cannot appeal. But because it arises from his very depths it does not limit his freedom, but is its condition and foundation. This freedom is "an exceptional sign of the image of God in man" that enables human beings "to act out of conscious and free choice, as moved and drawn in a personal way from within" (n. 17).

The moral "ought" as a revelation of the truth cannot be reduced to experience, nor can science or technology on their own arrive at it. "The intellectual nature of man finds at last its perfection, as it should in wisdom." It attracts the human mind to what is true and good. "Filled with wisdom man is led through visible realities to those which cannot be seen." Conscience is the place of wisdom's dwelling. "It is by the gift of the Holy Spirit that man, through faith, comes to contemplate and savour the mystery of God's design" (n. 15). The ultimate meaning of this "ought" as man's inner law is love. "By conscience, in a wonderful way, that law is made known which is fulfilled in the love of God and one's neighbour" (n. 16). In the light of faith the believer discovers and interprets it as the presence and the voice of the Holy Spirit.

This imperative "ought" has two levels that are intimately connected, one general and foundational, the other particular and concrete. "Its voice, ever calling him to love and do what is good and avoid evil, tells him inwardly at the right moment: do this, shun that" (n. 16). These levels should not be divided, nor should they be confused and absorbed one into the other. The first is described by some authors as a fundamental option for the primary values most important in life; the second is the incarnation in the situation of this or that value through choice. Others speak of transcendental and categorical conscience in this context.

The doctrine of *Gaudium et Spes* is not what is called intuitionism in philosophy. It demands research, common effort, and dialogue. "Through loyalty to conscience Christians are joined to other men in the search for truth and the right solution of so many moral problems that arise both in the life of individuals and in social relationships" (n. 16). Conscience is based on truth and its effort is ever to bring humankind closer to the truth containing "objective standards of moral conduct". It is deeply social.

Paragraph 16 closes by drawing attention to erroneous conscience. "Yet it often happens that conscience goes astray through ignorance which it is unable to avoid, without thereby losing its dignity." A person does not lose his or her dignity, because such error does not involve just a concrete individual choice but a person's radical responsibility toward this value. It represents the moral "ought" or imperative to love the good and seek it. If a person acts against this basic commitment to goodness and so corrupts its truth for his or her mind he or she is diminished as a person. This happens through negligence to seek the good, or, "when conscience is by degrees almost blinded through the habit of committing sin".

In summary we may say that conscience is an essential element constitutive of human dignity because the human person is an image of God. Conscience is the core of the human person and the centre of encounter with God. It reveals the law of love to and in the human heart. It is the dynamic guide for everyone in the solution of the moral problems preoccupying humanity. Invincible error does not destroy the inclination to goodness and so the dignity of the person is preserved. The Council assimilated the thought of St Thomas, St Alphonsus and Cardinal Newman in order to show that the doctrine of conscience is a necessary constitutive of human dignity and is basic to all discussions on human rights.

In the Decree on Religious Liberty, *Dignitatis Humanae*, religious liberty is founded on two principles: firstly, every person is bound to search for truth, and in a particular way that of religion; and, secondly, conscience is to welcome and interiorise this truth when it discovers it. It is not to be frustrated in this function by civil authority. "It is through his conscience that man sees and recognises the demands of the divine law" (n. 3). This demand to seek the truth in conscience applies to social and professional life, to the apostolate of the laity, to the decisions that have to be taken in marriage etc. Conscience is a force that battles against all forms of exploitation, against every power that contradicts human dignity. The Council thus saw in conscience a new awareness of the worth of the person and his or her place in society.[28]

Pope John Paul II has commented at length on the teaching of the Council and applied it to many spheres of modern life. Conscience is where a human being finds a sanctuary to worship God and so constructs his or her life in adoration, or where if conscience nihilistically turns in on itself it begins to destroy all that is most deeply human. It is an inner eye that awakens the moral sense, the principal property of the person as a subject of rights. Conscience is the way along which to construct world peace. The Holy Spirit hovers over creation, moving in the human heart, convincing it of good and convicting it of evil. In the encyclical *Veritatis Splendor* the Pope repeats the Conciliar teaching but in the context of his criticism of an autonomous morality that would make conscience the creator of moral truth and of moral norms and thus its own moral law. Hence his critique of subjectivism and relativism when they penetrate thinking on conscience. True autonomy means not to deny, but to welcome the moral norm as truth to guide our steps through life. This teaching is to be held, but this does not detract even in the encyclical's own terms from other traditional explanations. In n. 61 of the encyclical he shows how moral truth and liberty meet to form the judgement of conscience.[29]

In the twentieth century the Catholic Church may be said to have discovered the value of conscience. This in many ways goes contrary to her reputation of defending her own rights, as when she tried to hold onto the Papal States or for the repression of thought, rightly or wrongly, in the Galileo case. By defending conscience she has become the advocate of the poor as they battle ignorance and exploitation.

NOTES

1. *Conscience in the New Testament*, SCM, London 1955, 54.
2. *The Journals of Søren Kierkegaard* (ed.), Alexander Dru, Oxford University Press, New York 1938, entry 560.
3. Ibid., entry 569.
4. See Calvin O. Schrag, *Existence and Freedom*, Northwest University Press, Purdue 1961, 158.
5. *Concluding Unscientific Postscript*, (tr.) David Swenson, Princeton University Press, Princeton, New Jersey 1941, 470.
6. J.H. Newman, *Certain Difficulties Felt by Anglicans in Catholic Teaching*, Longmans, Green and Co., New York 1891, 248.
7. Ibid., 248-249.
8. Ibid., 250.
9. Ibid., 252.
10. Ibid., 253.
11. Ibid., 254.
12. Ibid., 255.
13. Ibid., 256.
14. Ibid., 257.
15. Ibid., 257.
16. Ibid., 258.
17. *The Christian Conscience*, Desclée, New York 1968, 51-59.
18. Cited by Delhaye, 72-73.
19. *De Veritate*, 17. 2.
20. *S.T.*, I, 79. 8. As applied to practical reason, *S.T.*, I-II, 94. 2.
21. *S.T.*, I, 79. 11 and *De Veritate*, 16-17.

22. *The Christian Conscience*, 170, and 168 where he quotes *De Veritate*, 17. 1. ad 4 at length to explain this important distinction.
23. Quoted by Delhaye, *The Christian Conscience*, 159.
24. See Delhaye, *The Christian Conscience*, 119, 219-220.
25. *Theologia Moralis* (ed.) L. Gaude, Roma 1905, Lib. I, tr. 1, Cp 1, n. 6, p. 4.
26. "La coscienza nel pensiero di St Alfonso de' Liguori", in *Morale e redenzione*, (ed.) L. Alvarez and S. Majorano, EDACALF, Roma 1983, 176-183.
27. *Revue Thomiste*, 50 (1950), 230.
28. For a listing of the Council's concerns regarding conscience, see Thomas Srampickal, *The Concept of Conscience*, Resch Verlag, Innsbruck 1976, 344-355.
29. For a good treatment of Christian conscience see S. Majorano, *La coscienza: per una lettura cristiana*, Edizioni San Paolo, Milano 1994.

Character, culture and the Gospel

1. Life as pilgrimage

Every human life is a pilgrimage. This makes it out to be a search for religious meaning. As I have presented human destiny this means that it is a search for God. Others, such as St Bonaventure, calling on a long Christian tradition, have understood it as a journey into God. Well, how does this happen? The human person basically traces out the path already described of origin in God so that he or she is made to return to God. In this chapter I am going to describe the dynamics and the development of the person along this path.

The two points of reference, the extremes, beyond which one cannot go, are conception and death. Conception is when a person comes into being in this world as an act of love from his or her parents. It is only possible because God is at the origin of it all as Creator by bringing the soul into being *ex nihilo* and infusing it into the body prepared by the act of the parents. Death is the dissolution of the body and the return of the soul to the God who created it. There is then a tremendous interweaving of divine and human causing where God has the absolute initiative.

Our knowledge of the growth of the human person increases every day because of new discoveries. Life in the womb is not the mystery it once was. Doctors can even operate in the womb, diseases can be diagnosed and sometimes treated. There is a growing psychology of prenatal life. Medical ethics is much concerned with the moment of personalisation. This cannot mean the actual exercise of consciousness but the radical capacity, the power of consciousness that when properly developed will be able to choose its own destiny. Birth is the moment when the person enters the world as a separate entity and can be seen in his or her own right in society. Hence the importance of the feast of the Epiphany when Mary could present Christ to the world and the glory of the Lord began to shine before the nations. Here is the formal beginning of the life cycle as Erik H. Erikson calls it.[1] It is an outgrowth of ego psychology and seeks to trace the stages by which the self as the conscious centre of psychic life grows and develops. It is an essentially dynamic concept and hence serves as a basis for understanding moral maturation and as a framework for efforts in education throughout a person's total life span.

2. The life cycle

"Eight Ages of Man" is just such a phenomenological description:

1. *Basic trust versus basic distrust.* For a baby to be relaxed, to feed well and have easy bowel movements it needs to feel that the mother is "good" and that even when it cannot see her she is not far away so that it does not go into a rage. This internalisation of the mother as good and reliable establishes basic trust. People without this experience are forever looking for a mother who is ever present to nourish them. A feeling of distrust toward the outside world accompanies them through life.

2. *Autonomy versus shame and doubt.* Here the child has already acquired some ability to move about and so begins to explore the world. It learns to take hold of what it finds attractive and also to let things go or pass without being upset. This is the stage where it acquires control over bowel movements. It means it can acquire what it needs without shame so that a person who has not successfully achieved this ability looks on the world doubting its ability to achieve what it wants.

3. *Initiative versus guilt.* When children play games they are self-moving for themselves but within a set of rules.

By coming out in their own right they take initiative but when that attempt violates the rules of the game they can be penalised and so become guilty. Here we have the beginning of a sense of responsibility and failure before a group. If the tension between individual effort and group conformity is not resolved a person may live in fear of violating social conventions.

4. *Industry versus inferiority*. As the child continues to actualise its abilities it learns to apply its powers to ever new projects. It begins to be disciplined and methodic in its work especially at school. Without this achievement and its affirmation by others a person feels inferior or second rate and will hesitate to go out and meet the challenges of life.

5. *Identity and role confusion*. The adolescent starts to become its own person and to leave the family behind. Adolescents begin to realise they have a part, a role to play in the drama of life. People who have not made this transition are split between being what they are in the family and what they dream they might be in the wider world. They have not settled on being their own person with their unique role to perform.

6. *Intimacy versus isolation*. Friendship is the natural result of discovering other persons and other interests. Where there is a sharing of interests, activities and lifestyle then intimacy grows because two people are becoming part of each other's life. At this stage male-female attraction starts to blossom. If this stage is unsuccessful a person feels isolated and may be overcome by a sense of solitude. In fact intimacy and solitude need to be balanced so as to maintain individuality and sharing in friendship.

7. *Generativity versus stagnation*. Sexual union and marriage are natural outgrowths of intimacy and this becomes the foundation of a family with the birth of a child. Generativity is also expressed through artistic creativity, scientific discovery, the construction of buildings etc. For many people it means either coming to the top or being successful in their profes-

sion, or going perhaps neither forward nor backwards but being stuck in stagnation. Here they have a sense their career is not going anywhere. This stage lasts into the mid-years of life. When money or acclaim are not enough we are accustomed to speak of the mid-life crisis as a search for meaning.

8. *Integration versus despair*. When children have left home and one's working life comes to a close then one may assume a bird's-eye view of the whole of one's existence. This being able to bring it all together into unity so as to offer one's learning to others is wisdom. This is the stage at which the ego is truly integrated. But if there is no such inner meaning then life declines into despair and all seems to fall into fragments.

3. Patterns of education

This chart of eight stages emphasises infant and childhood development. It is an epigenetic chart and presumes there is a driving force at each stage to go ahead. This is the energy of life itself as it unfolds in a set of sociocultural circumstances which can in some ways vary the stages of development. Commentators point out that this chart should not be conceived mechanistically as a hurdle-race where a child has to leap each barrier dead on time and exactly at the right height. There are other psychological theories that have further developed Freud's thinking, for example the object-relations theory with its cycles of affirmation. It should be pointed out that all of these theories have a philosophy of the person and human behaviour behind them, and therefore can be and must be critically assessed from the point of view of a Christian philosophy.

The first extensive empirical study of moral development was Jean Piaget's *The Moral Development of the Child* in 1932. He examined children's stories and games and concluded that children go through two successive moral stages, a "morality of constraint" and a "morality of cooperation". At first, "right" is what conforms to the rules and "wrong" what does not. The intention of the agent does not feature in their awareness. From eight years old on cooperation develops as they learn respect for their peers and they begin to internalise rules as necessary for a common effort and enjoyment in games. Lawrence Kohlberg[2] has extended Piaget's theory into a six-stage schema with three levels:

The Preconventional Level:
Stage 1. *Heteronomous morality*: right is avoiding breaking rules so as not to do damage to persons or property.
Stage 2. *Individualism*: right is following rules when it is in one's interest and so being fair so that one gets one's go.

The Conventional Level:
Stage 3. *Conformity and interpersonal expectations*: right is living up to what people expect of someone who is "being good" by showing concern for others with loyalty and respect.
Stage 4. *Social system and conscience*: right is fulfilling one's actual duties as agreed upon with others.

The Postconventional Level:
Stage 5. *Social contact or utility and individual rights*: right means being aware that others may have other values and opinions so that right is relative to the group to which a person belongs. Some values such as life and liberty should be upheld in every society.
Stage 6. *Universal ethical principles*: right is following self-chosen ethical principles. Laws and social agreements are valid because they rest on such principles. When laws violate such principles one should act in accordance with the universal principles of justice, namely the equality of human rights and respect for the dignity of human beings as individual persons.

Kohlberg claims that this sequence of stages is invariant and universal and that each stage constitutes a "structured whole". There is no skipping stages or regression from one to the other. It applies to all individuals in all cultures, though individuals may go through them at their own speed. Each stage implies a distinct way of thinking, a "moral logic" of its own. This schema is obviously worked out in the framework of a Kantian philosophy and has been widely criticised as the moral picture of an upper-class, wealthy, white, Anglo-Saxon male in the United States. It is worth pointing out that there has never been empirical confirmation of the last stage which must remain as a true Kantian imperative not based in experience.

Carol Gilligan's *In Another Voice* from 1982 focuses on the difference in moral understanding between males and females. On the basis of a number of studies she argues that males and females usually interpret moral problems from two different orientations, involving distinct conceptions of the self and its relation to others. She says there is an ethic of care and responsibility found almost exclusively among females, and an ethic of right and justice that predominates among males. Gilligan describes development in three stages: (1) the self is the sole object of caring; the person is constrained by a lack of power, and survival is of prime importance; (2) as a sense of attachment and responsibility to others grows the self seeks social acceptance and moral judgement rests on shared norms and expectations and one is prepared for self-sacrifice; (3) when one can balance obligation to self and to others the tension between self and others is resolved in an ethic of non-violence which is expressed as universal responsibility to exercise care and avoid harm. While there is much truth in Gilligan's observations about care being overlooked her position is somewhat exaggerated since women can be well aware of justice and men can show care. She has sensitised scholars to women's point of view on education and moral development.

Martin Hoffman has shown how socialisation, especially that afforded by parents, has an important role in developing empathetic responses and overcoming egotistic needs and desires in the child. A child's sensitivity and motivation is increased by exposing it to a wide range of emotional experiences, by drawing its notice to the reaction of others. The aim of providing the child with much affection is to keep it open to the needs of others and not letting it become absorbed in its own needs. Hoffman emphasises disciplinary techniques by which parents intervene to change a child's behaviour by emphasising the adverse effects and the suffering it causes others. In this way an empathetic understanding of others and their needs should grow.

4. How education begins

All education is an attempt to draw out the hidden capacities of a child so that it can grow to the point of taking control of its own life by making free decisions for which it can be personally answerable. The psychological data and the patterns discernible in them all project an image of a child with tremendous energy and emotional capacity that awaits to be humanised by reason. At the beginning reason is not very evident but has to be awakened by the parent and other educators. The humanising of one's native capacities lasts a lifetime. This is a fact that philosophers and theologians have reflected upon quite deeply, and some of the theories from the past are quite helpful in drawing out the sense of what we have seen. In particular where do we begin, from what do we try to draw out the stuff that will form a mature, rounded personality? We need to return to the chapter on human action and the fact that it is voluntary. The influence that we have on a person, especially a child, is from outside but it impinges on its psyche and so we appeal to its inner powers and capacities. How do we awaken the power of voluntary action? Indeed, what is voluntary action? It is amazing how when we begin to speak of education we nearly automatically fall into metaphors of a sculptor releasing a figure just waiting to be discovered in the marble or of a gardener tending and directing a young plant's roots toward the water and its branches toward the life-giving sun. These metaphors do not happen just casually. We do start off with the most basic energies and we seek to give them a shape. We recognise that a child is not stone, nor a plant. Voluntary action is spontaneous action that arises from within: that is its classic definition from Aristotle and it can be applied to animals as sources of their own motion whether local or emotional; it applies more forcefully to children on whose behaviour we can impinge not only emotionally but rationally. However, the path to reason is through the emotions, as we have seen in Hoffman's evoking of empathetic responses from a child so that it recognises and respects another person through its actions. These voluntary acts of the child already display the glimmer of reason humanising emotion. Aristotle began his philosophy of education by considering how human action is caused, how it gets under way. Aristotle insists that we leave the human integrated into the animal kingdom and ask what is the common source of local motion, of going between here and there for animals. In spite of asking for a single common account he provides two quite different ones that are juxtaposed: one using the psychological language of perception, thought and desire, and another using the physiological account of tendons, bones and sinews. There is not anything obviously common between them nor is it apparent how they are related. Aristotle seems to be running together the purposive actions of human beings and the animal motions of swimming, running, flying. We do say that a person who is very hungry is ravenous "like a wolf", and there are a series of such terms that explain human acts in terms of animal motions without this degrading the human being. In fact there is a spectrum of actions from animal action, to animal-like human action, to rational virtuous human action, all with a common structure in them. In each case the animal moves because of a complex of desires and perceptions; because it sees that this movement will satisfy some need. The action is the way to the object desired. The two explanations therefore fall out as answers to different questions. "Why did he do it?" and "How did he do it?" The perception moves us to desire that object and desire in turn puts our physiology into motion. Perception, desire and action all form one logic being interlinked causally. The desires, beliefs or perceptions are all directed to a goal to which they are thereby logically connected. It is precisely the provoking of this *goal-directed action* that training and education is aimed at. We cannot give an explanation of our desires without mentioning the goal to which they are aimed. The physiological equipment is not introduced in answer to the question "why?" but "how was it able to move?" Aristotle therefore accepts neither Plato's explanation of a self-sufficient soul being totally in control of everything independent of the body, nor that the movement can be totally explained in a reductionist way by physiology.

There were two schools of thought in the ancient world that are still reflected in present-day opinions. Materialists such as Diogenes and Democritus believed that the soul was air composed of atoms and that all motion could be reduced to the movement of these atoms. Aristotle replied, "it seems that it is not in this way that the soul moves the body, but through some sort of choice and thinking".[3] What could he mean? Firstly, that the physiological explanation is not complete. It rightly identifies motion but only in physiological terms without attending to its intentionality and outward directedness to its goal that gives it purpose and meaning. They do not take into account how an animal, or a child, or an adult focuses on an external object. This has further results, namely that the distinction between different types of interior activities such as perceiving, imagining, thinking, and willing is lost. All of these intentional activities are given the same treatment as such non-intentional activities as automatic eye-movement or digestion. Without these "why" causes it is impossible to explain our moral and educational practices. In fact they then cannot amount to more than doctoring or conditioning. As Socrates taunted his naturalist enquirers: Why am I sitting here in prison? Because of my bones? Or because of delibera-tion and choice? Out of the voluntary at the source of move-ment it is possible to distinguish different types of cause: sensitive perception and desire, or rational insight and deliber-ate will or free choice as it is better called. There is, in fact, an affective and a cognitive element in every action that combine to form a unified cause. The key to the whole discussion is what Aristotle named *orexis*, that is, goal-directed behaviour which actively reaches out or stretches out to an end. It con-notes inclination to the fulfilment of needs and wants which is best expressed by the word desire. As Martha Nussbaum translates Aristotle's thought, "Intellect does not impart move-ment without *orexis* (desire), for *boulesis* (choice) is a type of *orexis* (desire), and when the creature moves according to reasoning, it also moves according to *boulesis* (choice)."[4] All such movement as a going out of the self betrays the non-autosufficiency of a self that has to be completed from the world about it and from others by friendship. In human action emotion and will carry us beyond ourselves toward goods also beyond ourselves. These are humanised by reason working through deliberation and decision moves toward the execution of an action. Now this spiritual process works itself out in the body so that there is a physiological expression of this desire; thus a scientist's description of an action is not so much false as very partial. Without intention mechanical motions of human organs and limbs lack scope and meaning. Alasdair MacIntyre has emphasised that the social sciences that research human behaviour are, at least, implicitly predicated on human intentionality. The agent is always the origin and explanation of an action. Thus when Oedipus in Euripides' drama strikes an old man so as to remove an obstacle in his way but in reality kills his father, there is no parricide because there was no informed desire of that crime. Intentionality, with its object, scope and direction, is what engages the person as such making him or her an agent. Desire, fantasy, intelligence, the drive for self-realisation are always realised in and constituted by some matter when they make up a completed human act. Such an act becomes connatural by its performance since the person easily and spontaneously realises his or her most basic values expressed by inclination in it. This process is called habituation since it forms a *habitus,* a way of being personally and socially in oneself in relation to others. *Habitus*[5] as a term has once again returned to vogue among psychologists and sociologists precisely because it focuses on human character with a depth denied by a positivist explanation. While it cannot be reduced merely to the mechanism of behaviour conditioning it, this reasoning does however appear to involve a vicious circle since we need to describe two distinct senses of *habitus* as of virtue: as origin it is the "seed" or inclination that is to be educated through habituation; as end it is the mature rounded virtue as character trait that indicates human fullness and self-dominion through reason and will. It is the point at

which a personality becomes full, balanced and solid in goodness. The process of going from one to the other by means of
habituation we call education. A child begins with a basic
inner desire and inclination which as an act can be described
as a *voluntarium* or voluntary act which gradually develops
into the autonomous stable choice of a virtuous adult. Education occurs through a child identifying with the practices
which its parents and teachers communicate to it.

5. The need for narrative

In all classic and heroic societies the chief means of moral
education was by telling stories. *The Odyssey* and *The Iliad*
were the real moral tutors of the Greeks, and Aeneas was the
model of heroic piety for the Romans. The legend of King
Arthur and his Knights of the Round Table has woken many
a youth to the values of courage and chivalry. Christian education is founded on the Bible as the history of salvation that
continues into the lives of the saints. Unfortunately, story-
telling does not seem to hold such prominence in contemporary moral education. The nearest we come would seem to
be the moral dilemma as a mind-teaser. These are usually
considered exercises in problem solving by trying to put a
person before a conflict of irreconcilable moral principles,
e.g., a person is left with a choice between murder or treason
against his country. Such problems are exercises in ethical
rationalism but not in character formation by habituation or
the exercise of virtue. Such teasers are often set down as
training in value clarification from a neutral point of view.
They usually presume a rather Kantian outlook on ethics as a
set of imperatives or rules to be worked out with a logic as
rigorous as that of science or mathematics. They are never
concerned with building up the moral resources that will see
one perform well and with dignity through the adventure of
one's whole life. Another difficulty is that the person in such a
dilemma is not tied to any social context such as traditions,
loyalties, localities or histories. In a Greek myth we know why
Ulysses is loyal to Penelope and how he belongs to his native

soil, homeland, tribe and hearth. It is strange that the loves and loyalties that make a good story should have become alien to moral dilemmas illustrating a clash of principles. The moral subject has not just disappeared from the scene, becoming invisible to the audience. His or her passing has meant the death of narrative because there is nothing left to link incidents in the intelligible teleology of a life-project as a person's own story. In contrast with classical and Christian stories, the current technique of education by moral conundrums is the work of psychologists who have concentrated on the stages of progress in rationality at the cost of emotional rootedness.

The telling of stories, as opposed to the presentation of open-ended dilemmas, implies in the first place that parents do have something to hand on to children, a valuable inheritance that children cannot come to themselves. An anthropologist who encountered a tribe where parents ceased to pass on to their offspring their customs and morality although they had a perfect right to do so would immediately conclude that they were ruined, pitiable, alienated from their own values and soon to self-destruct. That is true for other cultures, but there is tremendous resistance to recognising the failure of cultural transmission in many of the highly developed nations. Is it right to refer to the child as a mini-Socrates, a moral philosopher by spontaneous self-illumination? Kohlberg believed the child should be treated as a moral philosopher. Aristotle believed a person could not comprehend ethics before fifty for lack of the experience of life. To arrive at a realistic grasp of what morality means not in ideas but in substance is the fruit of a long education, much reflection and broad experience of people.

6. Practices basic to virtue

Aristotle also said that only those who have been well brought up can study ethics. Plato maintained that it is only the well-bred youth who will appreciate the Good and the Beautiful, "so that when reason at length comes to him, then bred as he has been, he will hold out his hands in welcome and recognise her because of the affinity he bears to her" (*Republic*, III).

A parent can get a child to brush his or her teeth and after a while he or she realises it is the best thing to do. Moral practices are not so easily learnt for they take much longer to take root and be nurtured. As Plato observed, one who does not learn just affections and sentiments as a child has little chance of ever fully comprehending them. Psychologists confirm the insight of virtue ethics that a subject perceives the world from the point of view of learnt habits. "The kind of knowledge available to a subject is directly related to the kind of attitudinal posture he is capable of assuming."[6] A person who is not well habituated in virtue cannot identify the fundamental principles of moral living easily, and so the goal of a happiness that will fulfil him or her through virtue becomes obscured. Moral education means being initiated into practices and customs, and not just analysing them objectively and scientifically at a distance as an anthropologist might study a tribe he has had to visit on the other side of the world. Habituation is important precisely because it generates the orientation of mind and affectivity from which one can judge moral reasons and stances. In this sense moral education cannot be neutral nor its categories empty, as so many would wish.

There is a Confucian saying: "With those who follow a different way, it is useless to take counsel." C.S. Lewis insisted on the initiation of "men transmitting manhood to men".[7] This might be effected by moral exhortation and preaching but the silent symbiosis of example and apprenticeship is much more effective. Gilbert Meilander has stated the truth of this tradition, "Lewis like Aristotle believes that moral principles are learnt indirectly from others, who serve as exemplars. And he, like Aristotle, suggests it will be extremely difficult to develop virtuous individuals apart from a virtuous society."[8] But even in the best societies people are aware of their personal shortcomings and so look to examples of moral wisdom and uprightness beyond themselves. Here we have heroic stories as the embodiment of a culture's ideals. *Everyman* and the morality plays of the Middle Ages certainly seem to embody Aristotle's dictum that the aim of education is to make the pupil like and dislike what he or she ought. Literature at present seems more interested in the inner workings of the psyche, often in dissociation from society, and concentrates on the stream of consciousness as the fleeting moments of a fragmented identity. It is out of this rupturing of tradition that the fragmented ego of postmodernism arises with a loss of moral sense usually typified by the loss of the sense of sin. In spite of all its contradictions as it seems to move "beyond good and evil", modern literature remains a moral teacher and former of culture. Written texts of plays and novels are most powerful masters when a person has already been introduced into a moral tradition.

7. The challenge of virtue ethics

Alasdair MacIntyre has written what has become the most challenging book in ethics in the last generation. *After Virtue* is precisely what its name implies, a description of the moral predicament of what happens to moral thinking after it has cut itself off from virtue. It either becomes all concentrated on our obligation to keep rules as in Kantianism, or a matter of satisfying our passional impulses as in the emotionalism that has dominated in Anglo-Saxon philosophy, where moral ideas do not allow of being scientifically verified by observation. We are in the end put before a choice between "Nietzsche or Aristotle?" There have been three main models of virtue in history: (1) for Homer a virtue is the quality that lets a person do what his or her social role in society requires particularly as a warrior; (2) for Aristotle it is the *telos* of the whole human species that tells us which qualities are virtues. The key is *phronesis* or prudence, which establishes the rational order of all one's powers to the *telos* or end of felicity as exemplified in the Athenian gentleman; (3) the New Testament sets before us faith, hope and love as the ideal and guiding principles in a life according to the Beatitudes. MacIntyre then suggests three stages or concentric circles that go to constitute a virtue. The first stage requires a background account of what I shall call a practice, the second an account of what I have already characterised as the narrative order of a single human life and the third an account a good deal fuller than I have given up to now of what constitutes a moral tradition.[9]

His definition of a practice is complicated and needs to be given in full so as to understand its intrinsic worth:

> By a "practice" I am going to mean any coherent and complex form of socially established cooperative human activity through which goods internal to that form of activity are realised in the course of trying to achieve those standards of excellence which are appropriate to, and partially definitive of, that form of activity, with the result that human powers to achieve excellence, and human conceptions of the ends and goods involved, are systematically extended.[10]

Examples of practices are playing football or chess, motherhood, and up till recent centuries the establishment of governments, counties and even institutions like banks. The aim is not the gaining of money, praise, fame or social esteem which are external and can be taken away from a person, but the conquest of an interior quality that makes one's life good. These are called "goods internal to the practice" which cannot be had in any other way than by participating in that exercise. A practice involves standards of excellence: this is the means between excess and defect and from a good practice is established the norm or measure according to which to act. To be initiated into a practice is to accept obedience to those standards and so to be judged by them. They can be adjusted, criticised and even changed through the development of a better practice. A virtue is an acquired human quality that empowers us to achieve these goods internal to our practices and makes such empowerment a permanent enrichment to life.

To grow in a virtue means submitting ourselves to the best standard so far achieved. This was the point made by Abraham Maslow when he said that psychology should not be about pathology of the human spirit but about what we can understand of the best standards made known to us by, as he called them, "peak-experiences", when top performers actualised their capacities to the maximum. This means taking risks and listening to what those more expert in the field say about our inadequacies. We are thereby connected to all those who share the same practice. It is in terms of the internal goods that constitute the practice that we define our relationship to others and so those standards are what is held in common in friendship in the community. We recognise merit and desert according to the goodness and the contribution of individuals to the community. It is impossible to think of an effective community where the members are not committed to justice, truthfulness and defence of their common life. We define our relationship to others in terms of these and other virtues, recognising at the same time that different societies will have and have had different codes for these virtues. For example, the standards of truth-telling of an Australian aborigine in the bush and a modern businessman striking a deal are considerably different. The virtues flourish in societies with different codes but not where they are not valued.

As Max Weber pointed out, the rationalisation of modern bureaucratic society has introduced more techniques of getting things done than ever before. It is more efficient in setting up technologies that produce a result or desired state of affairs. The intrinsic link whereby means exist in their goals and so constitute them through human purpose and intentionality has been lost, and so the notion of virtue has been replaced by that of technique. The expression of the goal of a virtue changes through time. Take for example the history of painting, or of courage in warfare, or of the vice of bribery as John Noonan Jr. has done. In fact every virtue has its own history defined by how its goal as a good is defined through time. A practice therefore means that we are in contact not only with its present practitioners but also with those who preceded us in the practice, that is, with its history and tradition. Practices are sustained by institutions that help ensure their continuance through time across the generations. Practices and institutions should not be confused. Institutions such as hospitals, clubs and universities have to think about monetary survival and the distribution of honours, tasks and burdens such as taxation. They are largely concerned with external goods that as an ideal they should put at the

service of the internal goods of practices. Without civic virtues
citizens would not resist the temptations of power and the
corrupting power of institution. "Institutions and practices
characteristically form a single causal order in which the ideals
and the creativity of the practice are always vulnerable to the
acquisitiveness of the institution, in which the cooperative care
for the common goods of the practice is always vulnerable to
the competitiveness of the institution."[11] It is therefore impossible to separate the practice of virtue from social and political
issues. The exercise of good government and sound leadership
of the community has been acclaimed as the highest form of
prudence. There has been a deep change in the conception of
virtue here too. For the ancients and medievals there was a
common search for the good life as a shared project in virtue. In
liberal society each person is not only encouraged but required
to choose his or her own conception of the good life and this
liberal ideal has been incorporated in Western law and philosophy over the last few centuries till it has become the predominant tradition today. It claims to be neutral as regards moral
ideals and the conception of the good. MacIntyre concludes
"that we shall be unable to write a true history of practices and
institutions unless that history is also one of the virtues and
vices".[12] He therefore believes it should be possible to restore
Aristotle's teleology to society without necessarily subscribing
to his biological imaging of nature and society. He notes that
virtue ethics proposes a model of practical reasoning that
involves desire and emotion in its progress, that is non-utilitar-
ian because it distinguishes goods internal and external to an
action, and that links moral evaluation with the type of explanation we have become familiar with in the social sciences.

8. Character and the sentiments

He asserts that training in virtue is an "education
sentimentale" where virtues are "dispositions not only to act in
particular ways but to feel in particular ways". A good man or
woman instinctively loves good and hates evil. This is the
connaturality of virtue. A result of dispassionate discussions of

virtue such as advocated by Kohlberg would then serve to undercut moral sentiments. They condition students to think that moral questions are merely intellectual problems rather than human problems that evoke strong emotional reactions. The idea that everything is open to discussion and all values should receive equal respect subtly weakens the virtuous instinct that some things are repugnant and contemptible to the well-brought-up person. Character can easily be undermined by the non-judgemental approach, especially in its natural anger at what one sees as immoral. This abhorrence and burning indignation at a felt threatening evil is too often dismissed as an idiosyncratic quirk or personal preference that is merely subjective. Vice is also a matter of habituation just as much as virtue, and neutral value discussions can and do easily become forms of desensitising to virtue or vice talk and practice. One becomes habituated instead to rights, needs and wants talk without engagement in the actions needed to realise them. This has happened in a massive way in television and radio chat shows that invade areas of privacy and personal living previously thought too important to be publicly aired for entertainment. The depiction of sex and violence on the screen at children's viewing time are also cases at point. The psychological and sociological explanation of crime without reference to moral standards is also seriously offensive. The loss of a sense of shame is a phenomenon of this value-free culture often enough commented upon. When C.S. Lewis contemplated "the abolition of man" he foresaw that the first step would be "the stifling of all deep-set repugnancies".[13] The greatest danger of this desensitising to evil is that the more we become habituated to it the less aware we are of its destructiveness.

Stories appeal to our need for identification, they habituate our minds to the good and defend against evil. They present children with the ideal of what they can become if they fulfil their potential for goodness. It is interesting that the stories that influence children most deeply set goals for them that are repeated till they are in fact known by heart. Are these goals arbitrarily instilled by conditioning? Not really, although they cannot be argued about. Like axioms in mathematics, they are statements that cannot be demonstrated but without which all the rest is rendered senseless. Virtues are starting-points, definitions of what it means to be human. They are not arbitrary inventions of our fantasy but state the fundamental truths about our moral nature. Now a virtue is only understood by engaging in it. One may preach the goodness of virtue but a child does not see it until he or she lives it, that is, until he or she participates fully in a human life. The virtues of friendship, loyalty, courage and justice are simply what constitutes a good person in a good society. To say "good" or "bad", "right" or "wrong", implies that we know the way people ought to behave and that they are or are not fulfilling their function or purpose.

9. Character and life's purpose

This notion was embedded in the classic and Christian notion of virtue. Aristotle described life's trajectory as a movement from "man-as-he-is" to "man-as-he-could-be-if-heful-filled-his-purpose". Humanity's purpose was to journey from the one to the other, from its natural gifts and capacities to the gaining of happiness through the practice of the virtues. The Christian scheme added the three theological virtues of faith, hope and charity because humanity's *telos* was to live with God. When the idea of purpose was expelled from moral theory with the Enlightenment, says MacIntyre, there was no longer a unified point of reference for human nature, and thriving and ethics descended into an endless debate between irreconcilably contradictory parties. The idea of *telos* helps us understand why the telling of stories is necessary to the transmission of tradition. When we ask "what is the point of a story?", we are in fact asking, "what is a person living for?" or, "what is the point of this life?" G.K. Chesterton recognised this truth. "You cannot tell a story without the idea of pursuing a purpose and sticking to a point."[14] It is impossible to live life as it ought to be lived without sticking to the point, without staying to the narrative. Contemporary psychology confirms this conception as should be obvious from Erik Erikson's description of the life cycle as I rendered it. The life cycle is nothing else than the life story of "the eight ages of man", each with its more appropriate virtues. Story-telling always occurs in a social context. Stories are learnt in the family or local community and are handed down from generation to generation. A baby's life story begins in the hands of others, in the middle of others' life stories, and unfolds within and takes on the character of those other narratives. Although we are players in the drama we find ourselves playing "roles into which we have been drafted", such as family work or religious affiliation or nationality. A sense of identity and vocation grows out of this rootedness in history, nation, religion. As MacIntyre says, "I can only answer the question 'What am I to do?' if I can answer the prior question 'Of what story or stories do I find myself a part?'"[15]

It follows that we are both determined and free, or better that our freedom is historically situated and thereby limited. We are determined by the time and place of birth, by those with whom we live and on whom we depend. The self while free is always inextricably bound up with other selves and their stories without which it would have no identity. There is no Archimedean point outside history from which one can watch its progress without being involved. To stand back in pure objectivity without being involved in social particularity is to cease to play a role and to have no character.

Erikson escaped the notion of a self-centred autonomous self that is now so prevalent by invoking the Greek idea of virtue as a strength or quality that is both inherited and developed. We do not invent virtues but learn them from a tradition of living the virtues. In fact for Erikson it is the continuity of a life story that establishes identity through the stages of growth. Identity gives "a sense of sameness, a unity of personality now felt by the individual and recognised by others as having consistency in time – of being, as it were, an irreversible historical fact".[16] "Unity of personality" means not only inner harmony but coherence over time, and so consistency in our relationship with others. One should be able to look back to one's youth and look forward to the future and see them joined by the one thread. The virtue that ensures continuity in identity is fidelity, which means one may be relied upon to be true to oneself and so true to others. Shared fidelity is what makes friendship, so that just as life is a story, so love and friendship are best treated as a shared story. Without fidelity as constancy all the other virtues seem to lose their point. Erikson teaches us that one of the virtues one must develop early in life is that of "purpose", for when that is missing we lose the thread and life itself become unintelligible. There is no longer a sense that life has a point. It is an unfortunate and sad fact that what was once thought impossibility has now become a fashionable cultural experiment – the vision of an individual so absolutely free as to be bound by no story. But it is an unworkable idea, as MacIntyre notes, "All attempts to elucidate the notion of personal identity independently of, and in isolation from, the notions of narrative, intelligibility, and accountability are bound to fail."[17] The unity of a life is built up from what the unity of the narrative requires to make it intelligible. In the end a virtue ethic is a choice between rival stories we could choose to guide us in living out our life.

10. Christian character

Identification with the Christian story produces Christian virtue as the life pattern and life cycle of the Christian in the Pasch of Christ. "If we have died with him we have also risen with him", says St Paul. Stanley Hauerwas has made a strong case for a specifically Christian ethics that is not mere human ethics but ethics purified, criticised and corrected by the Gospel till it is transcended in grace. The Bible as the story of salvation calls together in assembly the Church as the community of faith in which is found salvation. In his conception the Church is a community of virtue that is counterpoised to the world, it proposes a programme of life and virtuous living that separates it from the world through the forgiveness of sin in Christ. Hauerwas has empirically observed the community of faith and interpreted its faith commitment to be a community of virtue as that of a denomination, others would say a sect, destined to stand out and be different from all others. She is in service of the world by being different from the world. While he has brilliantly applied MacIntyre's idea of narrative to the life of the Church as living the virtues of Christ, he does not share MacIntyre's idea of nature with its teleology and a species-based natural law. In other words he does not hold with the idea that the universal human community could value the same virtues in however different codes they might be expressed. Christian virtues set Christians off from the rest of the race, he says. It is here that he has failed to discern the genius of MacIntyre's insight that recognises common virtues and human values without detracting from, but in fact reinforcing the specificity of how these virtues are lived and defined. The idea of natural law is always "in Christ" for the believer and in no way diminishes the specificity of the powers of the agent and his virtues as being fashioned to the purposes learnt from salvation history. The Christian story is the vision of the world we accept. It is then the way we have learnt to see the world as saved in the passion, death and resurrection of Christ.

> We can only act in the world we can envision, and we can envision the world rightly only as we are trained to see. We do not come to see merely by looking, but must develop disciplines and skills through initiation into that community that attempts to live faithful to the story of God. Furthermore we cannot see the world rightly unless we are changed, for as sinners we do not desire to see truthfully. Therefore Christian ethics must assert that by learning to be faithful disciples, we are more able to see the world as it is, namely God's creation.[18]

Hauerwas put great emphasis on the reality of sin as radically spoiling humanity so that redemption separates the community of the believers as those inserted into God's story for the world from the great mass of humanity that is still in rebellion against God. The Church is a critical community with "the virtues necessary for remembering and telling the story of a crucified saviour".[19] Because of the nature of the Christian story the nature of the virtues is essentially changed for Christians. He settles on non-violence as what distinguishes Christian ethics from general human ethics, particularly that in a Kantian mould. He realises that the Church as much as any institution is supported by these virtues, "But that does not mean that what is meant by faith, hope, and love is the same for the Christian as for other people." His objection to natural law as the starting-point for Christian ethics is that it observes the agent from outside and does not consider virtue as an ethic in the first person, and so does not take Christian convictions as being truly moral in content and motive force.[20] This is a valid criticism of a Catholic morality that reduced all to natural law without integrating it as but one element in God's providence and his redemption in Christ. But to see natural law only as the result of sinful reason in rebellion against God does not do it justice.

Bernard Häring has developed a position based on an innovative interpretation of the "eschatological virtues" that distinguish Christian moral life. These virtues correlate features of the story of God in Christ with the moral character of believing existence. That existence consists in humility in gratitude which includes a grateful memory of God's saving work and an accompanying readiness always to witness in thanks to both giver and gift. Faith is the acceptance in gratitude of the *mirabilia Dei*, of God's marvellous deeds in our regard, of his love toward us. But such a memory is also future-orientated, because it includes attention to God's promise and the mission it implies. In hope the believer is enabled to respond in trust to the truth of that promise, and with the "courage to be, to grow, to take risks in the midst of uncertainty and suffering".[21] Vigilance empowers the agent, considered in his or her present involvement in the history of salvation and redemption, "to appraise correctly the objective realities, and to discern and command the actions which are appropriate as a response to God's gift and human needs".[22] The harvest of gratitude and hope, vigilance is "the ability to see the present moment in the light of the great moments of salvation history", which "enables one to enter in that history as a co-creator".[23] The wholeness and integrity of the agent is more certainly secured across his or her past, present and future, and thus in serenity and joy one may accept the gifts and burdens of each moment without anguish or worry. The eschatological virtues thus signify the range of social skills operative in the members of a community that lives in its time in response to the divine gift and promise. In Häring's vision the virtues are the realisation of God's love for us concretised in our loving response to him.

The eschatological virtues may be said to make the four cardinal virtues blossom into their complete or perfect form. Häring explicitly links hope with courage, and vigilance with prudence. St Thomas Aquinas treats virtue as an analogous term in the *Summa Theologiae*, I-II, 61. 1, ad 1. It therefore has to apply to different categories and cases, there being different authorities giving different definitions. Aristotle has already been cited. St Augustine defined virtue as that which God does in us without us and so made the theological virtues the primary reference, then the infused moral virtues and lastly the cardinal virtues of prudence, justice, courage and moderation. "Virtue is a good quality of mind, by which one lives rightly and which no one uses badly, that God alone works in man", is a definition heavily under Augustinian auspices through the influence of Peter Lombard. There is unity in difference and difference in unity, so that humanly acquired abilities and infused capacities can all come within the range of the one conception of virtue. It has often been forgotten that the term virtue has been predicated in radically different ways of the civic virtues of the pagans, of the qualities of the disciple of Christ and of the autonomous character of a secular humanist. In fact, all the virtues and thus the moral and intellectual culture of the well-educated person should lead to God and terminate in contemplation of him. This is the fullness of charity as in the unifying vision of wisdom, to see all in God and then to see the world in his light.

There is a difficulty here in so far as the infused moral virtues differ in kind from the acquired moral virtues precisely because they prepare human beings to be citizens of the heavenly city and not of the earthly one (*S.T.*, I-II, 63. 4). The three theological virtues are also ordered to an end, a *telos* different from the acquired virtues. They have God as their object, they are infused only by God, and are taught only by divine revelation (62. 1). The difference is not only formal for it also has consequences for action. The theological virtues do not have a standard measured by the mean but find their standard is God himself (64. 4). This has an influence on the infused moral virtues which, for example, require a degree of asceticism not called for by the moral virtues (63. 4). By examining the intellectual tradition of the virtues from Aristotle, through the Stoics and Augustine, St Thomas posits a distinction between complete and incomplete virtue. The acquired virtues remain inadequately defined as virtue if they are not motivated and informed by charity as love of God and neighbour (65. 2). With charity they do indeed make for a balanced and well-rounded life and so are authentic virtues only when embraced by grace and properly directed to happiness in God. In this way human effort is taken up into the working out of God's providence in Christ. For St Thomas no single inclination toward the good taken by itself can be called a virtue without qualification. It is only an incomplete or anticipated virtue that needs to be taken up into the unity of the virtues centred on charity. Aristotle's virtues were ordered to goods that were not the complete and final good of human life. This leads to the substitution of a theological for a philosophical definition, or, as the medievals were wont to say, to change the water of philosophy into the wine of theology.

Recent research has demonstrated that the analogical notion of virtue is very important for studies in comparative ethics and religion. Lee Yearley's *Mencius and Aquinas* illustrated the fruitfulness of dialogue between different philosophical and cultural traditions. By comparing St Thomas' tract on fortitude with the Confucian treatment of courage in Mencius he has been able to get a fuller view of both traditions and bring out features of agency, self and purpose in life not readily discerned except when put in contrast with another presentation of the same virtue. Yearley stated his aim as "to chart similarities within differences and differences within similarities", and this illustrates that two traditions separated by time, geography and culture can indeed talk to each other and this not only in terms of wide world-views but about precise ethical themes.

11. Culture and the Gospel

The social, political and educational investigation into virtue can be extended to the study of culture. Culture used to be identified with the Greek *Paideia* or Cicero's *Cultura animi* as the cultivation of the mind or, as we would say, higher education or even civilisation. This definition held good till just over a century ago, when it was discovered that all peoples and groups had their own distinctive culture that could be researched by the new science of anthropology. The beginnings of this science as with so many of the modern empirical sciences was agnostic, if not atheistic. Its founders, E.B. Tylor and James Frazer, were firm believers in social evolution. Tylor saw in the word "anthropology" a convenient term for the non-biological transmitted heritage of a people, covering material artifacts, customs, skills, beliefs, morality, art, religion etc. "Culture or civilisation is that *complex whole* which includes knowledge, belief, art, morals, law, custom and any other capabilities and habits acquired by man as a member of society."[24] Catholic philosophers and theologians had great difficulty with what E. Evans-Pritchard called the "absolute relativism" of many in the functionalist school, a relativism that "makes nonsense not only of the history itself but of all thought".[25] The polarising differences in definition that used to exist have tended to fade because of the studies of Claude Levi-Strauss, Victor Turner and Mary Douglas. A broadly acceptable definition would be Clifford Geertz's:

> An historically transmitted pattern of meanings embodied in symbols, a system of inherited conceptions expressed in symbolic forms by means of which men communicate, perpetuate and develop their knowledge about and attitudes toward life.[26]

The new awareness of culture is behind many of the liberation movements for national freedom as the expression of a nation's identity. Julius Nyerere put this very strongly and directly:

Of all the crimes of colonialism there is none worse than the attempt to make us believe we have no indigenous culture of our own, or that what we have is worthless – something of which we should be ashamed instead of a source of pride.[27]

The theme of cultural anthropology was the force behind what Roberto Tucci called "the anthropological turn" of the Second Vatican Council. The Pastoral Constitution *Gaudium et Spes* had a chapter added on this theme. With time it is being recognised that culture is the focus and context for the Church's liturgy, proclamation and work in social justice.

The Council treated "The Promotion of Culture" under three headings. Firstly, the cultural situation today discerned through "the signs of the times". There was a very keen awareness of change, of the fact that humanity is the creator of its own culture and that there is a grave danger of rapid technological advances destroying wisdom. Secondly, the fundamental principles for the proper promotion of culture, i.e., culture seen in the light of faith. There is a manifold relationship between the Gospel and culture so that they should be mutually helpful to each other. Only in faith can culture become integral and fully human. And, thirdly, the urgent duties of Christians in regard to culture, i.e., the right to equal participation in culture and the actualisation of this right; education to human dignity through an integral culture; the harmonising of human culture with Christian education, particularly of secular with ecclesiastical disciplines. The Council highlights ministry to the poor and victims of injustice.

In 1983 Pope Paul II established a Pontifical Council for Culture, which some ten years later was fused with another Pontifical Council, that for Dialogue with Non-Believers. The description of culture accepts the best of the current sociological and anthropological definitions, thus bringing those disciplines into the circle of the Church's concern. They are seen against the background of a theology of man as the image of God and the cosmology of Genesis, of St Irenaeus' theory of "seeds of the Word" spread in every culture before the coming of Christ, and especially of the eschatological perspective when all will be brought under the Lordship of Christ. The Council's main aim was to show that faith was a positive force and not a hindrance to the promotion of culture. In short the Council recognised that there was work to be done in a new age so that the Gospel could be heard in contemporary culture. The ambiguity and the autonomy of culture were both affirmed, so that there was need of an ongoing critical assessment of culture. This was done in the documents *Justice in the World* in 1971 and *Octagesima Adveniens* which was a call to action for Christian communities, "to analyse with objectivity the situation which is proper to their own country, to shed on it the light of the Gospel's unalterable words and to draw principles of reflection, norms of judgement and directives for action from the social teaching of the Church". Paul VI intervened strongly with the Apostolic Exhortation *Evangelii Nuntiandi* in 1975. "The split between the Gospel and culture is without a doubt the drama of our time, just as it was of other times."

NOTES

1. For the following see *Childhood and Society*, Norton, New York and London 1963, especially 187-284.
2. *Essays in Moral Development*, Vols. 1-2, Harper and Row, San Francisco 1981-1983.
3. *De Anima*, 406b 24-5.
4. *The Fragility of Goodness*, Cambridge University Press, Cambridge 1986, 275.
5. See Charles Tayor, "To Follow a Rule...", *Cahiers d'épistemologie*, n. 9019, Université du Québec à Montréal 1990, 6.
6. F.E. Ellrod, G.F. McLean, D. Schindler, J. Mann, *Act and Agent: Philosophical Foundations for Moral education and Character Development*, University Press of America, Washington 1986, 79.
7. *The Abolition of Man*, Macmillan, New York 1947, 43.
8. *The Taste for the Other: The Social and Ethical Thought of C.S. Lewis*, Eerdmans, Grand Rapids 1978, 212.
9. *After Virtue*, University of Notre Dame Press, Notre Dame, Indiana 1981, 174.
10. Ibid., 175.
11. Ibid., 181.
12. Ibid., 182.
13. *That Hideous Strength*, Macmillan, New York 1946, 203.
14. *Francis Versus Fads*, Dodd, Mead and Company, New York 1923, 121.

15. *After Virtue*, 201.
16. Erikson, 11.
17. *After Virtue*, 203.
18. S. Hauerwas, *The Peaceable Kingdom*, SCM, London 1983, 29-30.
19. Ibid., 103.
20. See ibid., 63 for a fuller argument.
21. *Free and Faithful in Christ*, Vol. 2, St Paul Publications, Slough/Crossroad, New York 1979, 398.
22. Ibid., 254.
23. *Free and Faithful in Christ*, Vol. 1, St Paul Publications, Slough/Crossroad, New York 1978, 207.
24. *Primitive Culture*, John Murray, London 1971, 1.
25. "Social Anthropology: Past and Present", in *Essays*, Faber and Faber, London 1962, 20.
26. *The Interpretation of Cultures*, Basic Books, New York 1983, 89.
27. *Ujamana*, Oxford University Press, Oxford, 1974, 66.

9

Guilt and "the mystery of evil"

The deepest, darkest enigma that humanity has ever faced is evil. Not only where does it come from, but why is it at all? The type of evil that we focus on here is called sin. It is something that we just cannot talk about neutrally and with indifference: somehow we are always involved even when we deny it outright. For Nietschze the concept of sin passed away as well when God died. It has disappeared from everyday speech except in the throw-away expression "a night of sin" or worse the down-putting "a sinful woman" because men have not got to sin yet. Even among philosophers and intellectuals the word "sin" has become a stumbling-block. It has had to be rationalised in psychology and materialised and statisticised in sociology and economics. Only in the catechism and in a religious setting can we expect to use the word with ease because it is a religious term about our relationship with God.

1. Can we speak of sin?

The dynamics of our use of the word "sin" is well brought out by TS Eliot in his drama *The Cocktail Party*, which reveals how he sees through life's superficiality. Everyone wants to talk to the unidentified guest, especially the anxious party-giver, EDWARD:

I only wanted to relieve my mind
By telling someone what I'd been concealing.

The UNIDENTIFED GUEST turns this self-manifestation back on Edward:

And I knew that all you wanted was the luxury
Of an intimate disclosure to a stranger.

Let me, therefore, remain the stranger.
But let me tell you, that to approach the stranger
Is to invite the unexpected, release a new force,
Or let the genie out of the bottle.
It is to start a train of events
Beyond your control. So let me continue.
I will say then, you experience some relief
Of which you're not aware. It will come to you slowly:

Here we have an excellent example of how psychotherapy and spirituality overlap. To name sin is to release a horrendous hidden force. It is also its undoing, disillusionment and unbinding. Seen from the point of view of psychology, we can say, "the subject, the centre of reality". But when we name sin, God is the one and only centre. This was the problem which Miss Celia Copelstone could not articulate in her loneliness, her world of illusion with another woman's husband. She came to the unidentified guest not just as to a doctor but as to a guide of souls. After floundering about she breaks through to what her education had denied her, a confession of her real condition,

It sounds ridiculous – but the only word for it
That I can find, is a sense of sin.

She then goes on to explain how this just does not fit with what she has taken as the typical human condition:

Well, my bringing up was pretty conventional –
I had always been taught to disbelieve in sin.
Oh, I don't mean that it was ever mentioned!
But anything wrong, from our point of view,
Was either bad form, or was psychological.
And bad form always led to disaster
Because the people one knew disapproved of it.
I don't worry much about form, myself –
But when everything's bad form, or mental kinks,
You either become bad form, and cease to care,
Or else, if you care, you must be kinky.

CELIA's reflection on her condition is both terrifying and truthful:

But I don't see why mistakes should make one feel sinful!
And yet I can't find any other word for it.

It must be some kind of hallucination;
Yet, at the same time, I'm frightened by the fear
That it is more real than anything I believed in.

REILLY, the unidentified guest, the medic of the soul, can only note how very few have this unique and extraordinary insight, "a sense of sin". He puts his question in such a way as to bring Celia back to herself:

What is more real than anything you believed in?

The end of the conversation transcends the power of words:

Go in peace, my daughter.
Work out your salvation with diligence.[1]

How often is it the case that those who use the word "sin" so easily have never experienced a true sense of sin? How often have the Church's catechesis and preaching on sin not brought people to their genuine selves but plastered another layer of alienation over their already false selves?

2. Symbols of sin

What are the symbols, the words and the ways of conceptualising sin that people today may find convincing? Where sin, particularly of the sexual sort, used to be so clear, confusion and ambiguity seem to reign now. This silence about sin is not deafening in the confessional box. As the psychiatrist Karl Menninger asks, "Whatever became of sin?" Clearly the idea of sin has not evaporated, yet the symbols and models of our thinking have changed profoundly. Sin is fundamentally a mystery not only because it is finally contrary to reason and places a great puzzle at the heart of our existence, but simply because it is a datum of experience on which we can only throw light from God's revelation. Only his brightness can penetrate the murky depths where I do the evil that I do not want to do. That we should turn in freedom to the doing of evil is a part of ourselves that we call sin as the use and abuse of freedom all at the one time. It takes freedom to turn away from God and rupture our relationship with him so that we lose the freedom of relating to him. Freedom becomes slavery when it turns to sin. And there is no way out except a new, recreating intervention by the all-powerful and all-loving God that we call grace. It too is a mystery, for "where sin abounds grace abounds all the more". We must never think that the tragedy of sin is greater than the mercy of God. As the psalmist knew, God's mercy is greater than his justice. Sin has traditionally been symbolised as stain, as crime, as a personal affront. In experiential terms it seems to be a downward spiral in our lives, a disease that saps our life energy and resources, an addiction from which we cannot release ourselves.

3. Scriptural terms

In the Old Testament there is no single word in English that can stand behind all the Hebrew words representing sin. *Hattah* in a secular context meant "to miss" or "to miss the mark". In a religious setting it came to mean failure to fulfil one's duty in a relationship. It thus came to mean being unfaithful to one's duty to the covenant, and thus to sin *against* in the sense of going against the God who established and offered us the covenant. *Awon* refers to being crooked, twisted or bent. It is a defect of character, a disorder that weighs and bends us down. In religion it came to refer to sin as a burden that could be handed over or put onto a scapegoat and so removed by expiation. Guilt thus became a paradigm for sin. *Pesha* means rebellion, like Satan, setting oneself up against God by coming into conflict with his given order. In religion it points out disloyalty and becoming hard-hearted toward God.

4. Stain and dread

The earliest level of awareness of sin is that of dread, a sense of being unclean before the Holy. This is a spontaneous sentiment that should be reckoned pre-ethical. It is violations of religious cult that provoke the wrath of the Holy. In this way sins tend to be external acts breaking cultic taboos, regardless of the intent of the violator. Such breaches of holiness usually refer to cultic purity, sexual conduct and laws of worship. This type of thinking is typical of the Book of Leviticus. It shows up a profound sense of being unworthy and unholy before the face of God. This type of sense of sin needs to be radically purified and rethought as happened through the ministry of the prophets to Israel. Sin is then no longer identified with failure to attend to the external details of cult but with the internal stance of being unfaithful, hard and rebellious toward Jahweh, their covenanted God. The concept also comes to include ordinary, non-sacred behaviour that runs contrary to Jahweh's will, e.g., the mistreatment of the widow, the orphan and the foreigner. There was a growth of legalism in post-exilic Israel because of fear of the Holy; it put a barrier of laws around itself and ceased to experience sin as alienation, rupture and loss of covenant relationship. The Old Testament understanding of sin moves from the corporate to the personal. Since Israel was covenanted to God as a nation and not as individual persons, sin was what threatened its good relations with God. The one who sins is Israel by infidelity. At the same time there is a growing awareness that this occurs through the transgressions or acts of individuals. Jeremiah and Ezekiel were the first to suggest that God will not punish children for the sins of their parents. The discovery of personal responsibility does not mean a downplaying of the social aspect but a developing grammar of sin which is seen ever more clearly to reside in the rebellious will of the person who breaks Israel's alliance with Jahweh.

5. New Testament description

The New Testament presents the life and ministry of Jesus as a confrontation with and conquest of the power of evil expressed in human sinfulness. He comes to "save Israel from its sins", and this is evident in the temptation in the desert, through the proclamation of the Kingdom and his message of repentance, healing, liberation and forgiveness, all of which become effective in the paschal mystery. Christ demonstrates a profound awareness of the power, malice and tyranny of sin; he calls for a radical break with sin and adhesion to the Kingdom with the offer of forgiveness to those who repent turning in faith and trust to God. The challenge to "sin no more" and "come follow me" is issued to individuals and to the whole community of Israel. It means to die to self, to be reborn to God. This call to conversion reveals the incredible compassion of Christ for those imprisoned by their own sinfulness. See his gentleness to the woman at the well and the woman taken in adultery. He could also confront the hardheartedness and blindness of the leaders in order to lead them into insight into their condition.

John's Gospel is famous for its transpersonal awareness of sin. Christ has come not only to expiate the sin of individuals, but he is "the lamb of God who takes away the sin of the world" (Jn 1:29). This idea moves beyond the individual experience of sin to the total state of hostility, rejection and outright denial of Jesus and his message. Here is a state of things that precedes individual wrongdoing, that tempts one to join Satan and the power of darkness, that leads to eternal death. Paul too dramatises this power as personified evil that takes possession of a person, making him or her a slave to sin. The human heart is divided between what I want to do but do not because I disobey my conscience when "sin lives in me".

6. Pastoral of curing sin

The Church reacted to the "mystery of iniquity" by baptising infants who could not possibly have committed serious personal sin. Baptism as "the plank of salvation" meant the remission of original sin through which one is identified with the alienated state of humanity before God. The sacrament of penance was the remedy, "the second plank of salvation" for those who sinned after baptism. The power of Christ over evil in all its aspects, physical, social and moral, was expressed in the anointing of the sick and especially the Eucharist where

Christ the healer, reconciler and sustenance in face of evil, suffering and death was active. The Church's consciousness of sin and its identification developed around the sacrament of penance first as public penance in the early Church, then in the penitentials spread across Europe by the Anglo-Irish monks. From these the distinction of mortal and venial sin came into vogue and was incorporated in the manuals for confessors particularly after the Fourth Lateran Council's reform of the pastoral life of the Church in 1215. After Trent the distinction was strengthened even further in the manuals of moral theology that sought more than ever to calculate the guilty malice of sins, their type, number and circumstances. Casuistry tended to become legalism because it reduced moral theology just exactly to this calculation of sins as measured by law in all its kinds. Awareness of sin focused on the individual's choice of an isolated bad action without paying attention to the person as agent nor to the social context of action. The cure for this exaggeration requires a return to a notion of sin as a social and symbolic reality.

7. Stain

In his great tragedy *Macbeth*, Shakespeare touched depths of the human psyche unreachable by conscious moral awareness, especially in Lady Macbeth's dreamwalking scene. "Yet who would have thought the old man had so much blood in him? ... What, will these hands ne'er be clean? Here's the smell of blood still: all the perfumes of Arabia will not sweeten this little hand" (Act V, Scene 1). It is the murkiness of hell's punishment that renders her act so evil. One is sorry simply because one is going to be punished in such an awful way. Literature is rich with scenes treating guilty humanity as tainted, stained, marked, and contaminated by the unclean and impure that somehow violates the taboos of the Holy. Leviticus 11-16 gives a detailed description of sin as stain and the sinner as tainted and unfit for contact with the community of salvation. The corrosive power of the unclean is imaged for us in the figure of *Dracula*. Some characteristics of this model of sin are: the language that measures the separation of good from evil is that of pure/impure or clean/unclean; defilement is conceived of as our shame and dread before the face of God as in Isaiah's recognising himself unworthy as a "man of unclean lips" to approach the divine presence; contamination comes by physical even casual contact with a corpse or a woman giving birth so that guilt is felt as a material presence; sickness such as leprosy becomes a metaphor for sin as contaminating the community.

This model is pre-ethical in three ways: it does not distinguish voluntary from involuntary action, because it does not focus on intention but on taboo; it has no sense of moral wrongness, so that many sexual and ritual prohibitions from the past cannot honestly be retained in contemporary ethical codes; at the level of motivation sin as stain speaks to the experience of fear, dread and guilt, of blood as a life-force but not of the dignity or sanctity of the person. This conception of sin is thoroughly religious, for it treats the Holy as dreadful, as what is separate and should never be touched. The Holy is what is beyond human control and authority. One should not wander into the mysterious forbidding world of the Holy. Human sexuality expresses the vitality of human life, especially in association with the body fluids of blood and semen.

Stain can be removed by washing through the rites of purification. Thus persons, altars etc. were sprinkled with water or blood in preparation for sacred actions. The experience of being stained by sin cried out for atonement as in Psalm 51:7:

Purge me with hyssop, and I shall be clean.
Wash me, and I shall be whiter than snow.

The ritual bath of baptism not only removes sin but guards against its contamination. When Isaiah speaks of himself as a man of unclean lips, an angel of the Lord is sent to purify those lips with a living coal. Fire can cleanse the blemish of sin through burning. The idea of purgatory is based on the idea of non-mortal sins being purged and burnt away by fire.

Finally, sin may be undone by some sacrifice of expiation. The sin-driven are forever trying to satisfy the divine justice, to pay back in kind what was wrongly done, to offer goods in order to win God's good will toward themselves. The exile from the community is finished only when the divine wrath has been pacified. The greatest problem with the idea of sin as blemish is that it is exterior and therefore does not invite conversion from the depth of one's heart. The prophets replace the demand for ritual cleanliness with the promise of a new heart, a recreation of the human spirit by means of the Holy Spirit poured into our hearts. It is precisely this new heart that brings about a genuine, interior awareness of sin. Dread of contact with blood is now transformed into moral rage against the shedding of innocent blood. The image of an awful God even needing to be placated by sacrificing needs to be rethought through our drawing near to the throne of grace in Jesus. Love and contact need to replace fear and distance which have been so harmful in pastoral practice.

8. Crime

The catechism definition of sin was as a breach of the law. If this was serious then sin meant crime. This idea was based on Augustine's definition repeated by Aquinas as "fittingly defined as a word, deed, or desire which is against eternal law" (*S.T.*, I-II, 71. 6). This has been a constant theme and has been badly understood by identifying law with the civil penal code or with any of law's positive aims or features. In the Our Father we asked God to forgive us "our trespasses" as we forgave others. Sin was then a freely chosen rebellion against the God-given order of reality. While stain is the most primitive insight, criminality is the most common image for sin. Until recently the sinner was thought of as a criminal, and it was against this legalism that the Second Vatican Council asked for a reform in moral theology and its application to people's lives. In particular God was seen as a lawgiver imposing his will on our rebellious tendencies by curbing our will by his law. In the legal model sin was seen primarily as a

free, conscious and competent decision to break the law of
God by being disobedient to one of his commandments. Sin as
crime involves: (1) that it be understood in juridical terms and
in a penal context; (2) that the one who sins is the individual;
(3) he or she becomes lawless by rebelling against the divinely
sanctioned order. As a breaking of law it invites some sort of
just punishment as its desert. Both Menninger the psychiatrist
and Dostoevsky the novelist have noted separately how crime
and punishment are paired terms, the first crying out for the
latter. Cain's blood crying out for vengeance describes this
relation very well. Patrick McCormick has pointed out a number
of cultural factors that have made this conception predominate
in the Western world and particularly in Catholic theology and
practice.

The first has been the extreme individualism of thought
and the analytic ability to isolate an essence apart from its
ambience, circumstances or context. In this way of thinking
the importance of community and context were lost from the
cosmic wholeness of experience. Politics and life in the
Church too are organised around the individual and the inviolability of his or her rights. As a consequence the concept
of sin was individualised and privatised so that it was easily
treated in a legal framework. Confessional practice reflected
the trial of a criminal rather too exactly by: (1) determining
that a crime had been committed; (2) ascertaining the culpability of the defendant; and (3) assigning an appropriate
penalty or punishment.

The second factor was the intermeshing of Church and
State as institutions. This had a particular effect on the concepts of crime and sin, which tended to become identified.
From the time of Constantine up to the French Revolution
crimes against the State were often seen as immoral and
irreligious acts. At the same time the Church employed sanctions against sins that rendered the sinner an "out-law" in civil
society, so that such a person did not enjoy the protection of
law and the privileges of citizenship. Theocracy was in vigour
in Israel before David, and Jewish law still tends to identify an
offence against God with a civil crime, as does Islam where its
law is still applied as originally conceived. If this line of

thinking is followed to the bitter end the moral law is enforced with all the might of the State and no room is left to individual conscience in social matters. In Catholic cultures canon law tended to favour casuistry and thereby the growth of legalism. As already said, this mentality took deep root in the penitentials and then in the manuals from which priests learnt their moral theology. "In fact, the whole of moral theology, confined to an act-analysis of the sins of individuals, was conceived by many to be the partner or stepchild of canon law."[2] There are many objections to this way of conceptualising sin. It lacks a theology of grace and the mercy of God as revealed in his saving and liberating interventions in Scripture. It renders moral theology dangerously insensitive to issues of justice and un-critical of law-making institutions. Its philosophy of law is voluntaristic to the point where might is right. It seems to make divine justice arbitrary and unforgiving as well. Perhaps one of its worst effects is the way it precipitates a division between the innocent and the guilty. The violence of the innocent is too easily turned against those who have commit-ted a criminal act, so that they become scapegoats for the moral evil of the community. By applying the letter of the law people could with great facility be condemned to hell-fire for what would seem minor offences. Patrick McCormick puts it bluntly: "That Catholics believed a youth would, in the normal course of events, merit eternal damnation for intentionally missing mass on *one* Sunday or for a single act of mastur-bation is but a symptom of a deeper and more pervasive disorder – the drive to be innocent, achieved through the condemnation of the guilty."[3] Ironically, this sort of sense of sin released large parts of the community from any responsi-bility for the evil that they did. It was all too easy to remain in a comfortable state of infantilism. As the Gospel says, a person can see the speck in another's eye without perceiving the plank in his own. In pastoral practice not enough attention was given to biological, psychological and social factors that either removed or diminished guilt. What was lacking, of course, was the awareness of what St Paul says. We have all sinned and fallen short of the glory of God. We all stand in need of his gracious mercy.

9. Personal sin

Crime means an actual choice against the law. As well as being an act it also engages or involves the person. It is impossible to understand sin without a personal reference-point because it is impossible to sin without human agency. Sin is no laboratory experiment or abstract case discussion but the repudiation of God's will by a human person. If sin alienates us from God and our neighbour then the experience of being a person is radically affected by sin. The personal dimension of sin is deeply written into Christian tradition because sin as a free act is a personal commitment with alienating effects on one's relations with God and neighbour. Not only is an evil deed done, but it must be a genuine expression of the person who finds himself or herself in an interpersonal context. Without this interpersonal context one cannot claim responsibility for the act as working out one's life plan and destiny. The Council proposed that moral theology dissociate itself from the extrinsicist and legalist ethic to one nourished by Scripture and dogmatic theology. Morality is not external conformity to law but a personal relationship between God and humanity. As a consequence theologians assumed the language of personalist and existentialist philosophy which put morality into the context of covenant and of personal vocation to follow the call to imitate Jesus in his lifestyle. The harsh courtroom language of punishment seemed altogether out of place with a loving, compassionate God and Father. "Hell and brimstone" as motives for right action simply disappeared and the quality of relationship replaced the detailed analysis of individual acts. In a personalist morality the sinful act was perceived as an expression of a deeper decision to repudiate one's own vocation at the core or heart of the human person. It was a change in or a new fundamental option in one's life. It was not only personal malice but offence against the God of covenant and those one was bound to love in the covenant relationship. Responsibility meant being answerable for the harm done to others in relationship with them. This was in part a recovery of the biblical idea of sin as alienation and could theoretically be extended to societal, communal, ecological and cosmic dimensions so often forgotten by focusing on the person. In fact the full force of the idea of sin as alienation was not realised by this type of personalism which concentrated too narrowly on the rights of the individual, thereby privatising morality. The Council was not the only inspiration for personalist thinking. The liberal movement in the Western world was reflected in the call for the liberation of the individual from all legal restraints, putting his or her claims above those of the organised political community. Personalism is often a defence against mass or even totalitarian society in ever increasingly technological and specialised global conglomerates. This tendency to defend the dignity of the person has become a struggle for individual rights in the political realm. In the *Roe vs. Wade* decision in the U.S. the Supreme Court discovered a rather absolute boundary between so called public realm law and the private sphere of morality. The cry is "You cannot legislate morality", and this is true if what is legislated is unacceptable to the community and so utterly inefficacious, but that should not mean that law may cut all links with what is morally right. A radical separation of the two realms means that sin becomes a purely private matter, addressing only issues of personal concern over which civil authority has no jurisdiction. Sexual ethics and religious belief then belong to the private realm so that the religious community has no right to cry out against social ills or injustice. This is often the response of congregations unhappy with a priest or minister's excursion into the social realm. An unhappy side-effect of the shift from legalism to personalism has been the growth of individualistic morality in the Western world. Personal sin became private sin. What is true is that sin always involves a personal subject as agent who expresses and experiences responsibility through his or her action. Sin underscores the malice and harm done in interpersonal relations as an expression of disordered freedom. The excessively privatistic practice of the sacramental confession has put the focus on sin as private to the exclusion of social sin.

10. Private and/or social

We are all well aware that the alienated, destructive state of human sinfulness is not explainable within the parameters of a narrow individualism. The Bible presents a growing awareness of the social sense of sin not as a taboo or ritual breaking of the covenant, but as a personal intentionality and responsibility in bringing about alienation, hurt relationships and destruction of the covenant even through an individual act. While there is a growth in awareness of conscience and culpability in the Old Testament, this never diminishes the social reality of sin. This social sense of sin is necessary to grasp the New Testament concept of sin not just as an act, but as a state and condition of alienation from God and others. In dogmatic theology a move away from a quantified to a relational idea of grace leads us to think of sin in the social categories of oppression, hostility and injustice. Sin, as Schoonenberg recognised, is more than the accumulation of individual acts of sinfulness. This concept of sin embraces sin writ large and encoded into institutional and societal structures. Political theology has criticised the privatisation of the Gospel and this has been a major force in the growth of individualism in the West. The corporate "blindness" that Jesus criticised in the Pharisees is also to be found in the lack of a social sense of sin because of the lack of an adequately social sense of the person. The awareness of doing evil by cooperating with government programmes that disadvantage, or worse oppress, the poor is often wanted by those who benefit unfairly. In other words the continued reliance on a privatised idea of sinful action may itself be group cooperation in social sin and evil. Of course, such groups are usually quite unconscious of the evil they are projecting onto others they see as "lazy" or inadequate.

Psychologists have had to move beyond looking at the individual patient and his or her problem to the social system in which he or she is inserted and how that is dysfunctional. It often happens that a child with a problem is "acting out" the group's problem and turns out to be the healthiest member of the whole when a thorough analysis is done. In morality as in therapy, an awareness of "contextualised responsibility" is a help to see the issue in its wider and more real dimensions. Persons are often only able to change and therefore come to conversion when they are prepared to put all their social relationships into question because they believe in Christ as the purpose of their life. It has been recognised for a long time that an alcoholic is both the cause and the result of an "alcoholic family". Sinful action both causes and is caused by the situation of social sin and the alienated state of humanity.

There is a lack of realism in treating sin merely as an act for that goes against human experience. Sin as a specimen that can be photographed all in one moment in one act does not correspond to the history, the psychology and the social dynamics of sin which persist like a virus in the bloodstream of an individual and of society for years and for generations. Sin takes on a habitual character that repeats itself over and over again. In St Paul's terms sin is a power fighting for dominion over our lives. Sin in this sense becomes malignity, the mystery of evil that expands itself and unfolds in a Pandora's box of sins. It is more than a single deed, an isolated act, however freely chosen. It is experienced as a habit, a deep-rooted way of things that takes control and disorders the will, as a power or a demon with a will of its own. In Saints Paul and John it is a tenacious power fighting for dominion of our lives. We do not have to fall into anthropomorphism to appreciate that this inner battle for the soul and destiny of the person is quite real. There is another aspect, in so far as this habitual conditioning to evil becomes contagious for others. In human relations it becomes noxious and infectious. The attitude of being inclined to evil, of being comprehensive of the evil done, easily passes from one generation to another. The mystique of sin is, as it were, whispered from parent to child and down through history. Then by cooperating in sin the whole social atmosphere of combined and common human effort becomes poisoned. The net result of all these factors for the person is that he or she feels unfree, paralysed within, as it were, and unable to move against the forces from without. This is what St Paul so rightly named "the slavery of sin".

I can will what is right but I cannot do it. For I do not do the good I want, but the evil I do not want is what I do. Now if I do what I do not want, it is no longer I that do it, but sin that dwells within me. So I find it to be a law that when I want to do what is good, evil lies close at hand. For I delight in the law of God in my inmost self, but I see in my members another law at war with the law of my mind, making me captive to the law of sin that dwells in my members (Rom 7:18-23).

Sin must be seen as vice that precipitates solidarity in sin for the whole human race. This is a pessimistic picture of humanity that St Augustine projected as a "massa damnata". The concentric waves of sin spreading from the origin of the race to the whole of history is pictured like a virus contaminating the whole population in Genesis 3-11 and Romans 1-2 and 5. We have become particularly aware of "group evil", or "groupthink", as M. Scott Peck calls it.[4] There is a penetration of evil into organisations, families, groups etc. that would never be tolerated in the behaviour of an individual. It is repetitive and so ingrained that most individuals being so overwhelmed by the flood of malice become unaware of their unfreedom.

11. Sickness

Another symbol of sin that comes readily to mind is that of sickness and disease. One who violates a taboo is smitten down, is punished by becoming ill. This is a very primitive sense of having done wrong, of having defiled the sacred, the reaction to which is a loss of health and vitality. By sinning one experiences the wrath of God. This may be experienced in earthquakes and natural disasters or in handicaps handed on from parent to child. Health and wealth were taken as signs of God's benevolence, and evil as a proof of being afflicted and punished by God. The disciples ask Christ whether the man born blind or his parents had sinned. Christ answers, "neither"! Sickness was seen as the consequence of sin and miracles of healing as turning back the tide of evil by making liberation present to the most oppressed. Christ therefore radically modified the Jewish over-materialist concept of sin while drawing close to the poor in their misery. A similar problem occurs today in the psychological field, where emotional un-freedom becomes confused with moral responsibility for one's psychic state. Thus it is sometimes said that had some person expressed their emotions freely they would not be sick. A net result of this approach can be to psychologise the morality of liberty and responsibility. We need to recognise that there are mechanisms beyond liberty and free choice from which we may also require release. Salvation therefore means liberation from all the forces that enchain humanity in all the dimensions of personality. The mystery of sin as spiritual slavery goes beyond the range of psychological therapy. The most important aspect is making the will free to achieve the good it desires, and this only comes by grace. Advances in medicine and in the understanding of psychological disorders have redimensioned our idea of sin as sickness in the direction of viewing Christ as the healer of evil in all its dimensions and meanings. We realise that certain psychological and social forces impinge on the psyche without the person being morally responsible for such. In this way the medical or disease model is more convincing than the criminal model of human behaviour. However, the disease model has been largely demythologised by medical advances so that although it is still very powerful, because it plugs into human well-being, it should be invoked with critical discrimination.

We fight cancer and other diseases. We have campaigns of vaccination against diphtheria and other contagious diseases which we want "to wipe out in this generation". No one has ever seriously thought of wiping out sin in their lifetime. Kevin O'Shea has described its power and violence.

Biblical thought about sin is dominated by the theme of Sin of the World. We should write it with a capital: the Sin, the Sinfulness of the world. Modern thought about sin is dominated by the idea of the "human act" in which "sin" happens. St Paul would have called that a "transgression", he would not have called it "Sin". Sin is a deeper thing, a powerful virus of evil which has a history of its own on the cosmic plane. The Sin of the world is a virus of evil which entered the world as a personal force through original sin and dynamically unfolds itself and tightens its grip on humanity and on the world in an escalating fashion down the ages of history. It is the hidden power which multiplies transgressions in the history of mankind. They are merely its symptoms; it is deeper and greater than all of them. It forms human history into what we call "perdition history" (to coin the opposite of "salvation history").[5]

Experience teaches us, if we have faith, that none of us was the first sinner, but that we were conceived in sin, born into sin as the Scripture puts it, and raised in an environment made noxious and life-threatening because of the contagion of sin. Many people have instead thought of denying that this whole conception is true at all. This is the challenge of modernity. Is the Christian account of sin true? We might even go as far as to ask, given the tidal wave of evil in the world, can we say that God has been responsible by not exercising his omnipotence to our advantage? Is the Christian idea of sin not just another myth that means that ultimately we humans must take complete responsibility for the progress of the world? Is not this the postmodern, postchristian stance?

12. The sense of sin

The underlying force in contemporary culture which has led to the loss of "the sense of sin" is without doubt the loss of "the sense of God". Since nihilism and value-free thinking have become predominant it is so difficult for people to think of themselves in relation to God. Their ingrained scepticism tells them such a relationship is unreal in spite of their acute sense of evil ruining the world and spoiling their personal existence. The loss of the sense of God must be understood against the background of the nihilism as it were cleaning all religious presuppositions and world-views from the human mind. This does not always happen by a formal commitment to atheism, or even by assuming an agnostic stance. The culture is so changed in its literary, artistic, scientific and technological expressions that traditional God-talk no longer seems to make sense. The most devastating effect of nihilism is that the desire for God as purpose and meaning in life becomes corrupted. "If there is no God, everything becomes possible", hardly needs repeating. This is what Pius XII was aware of when he said that people in this century had lost the sense of sin,[6] and Paul VI that this happened because they had lost the sense of God. This new state of things has thrown the traditional theology of sin into confusion so that people are emotionally overwhelmed by the brooding sense of evil and wrongness in the world, while not being able to name it as sin because the culture has closed the ways to God and called off the search for transcendence.

It needs to be noted that the expression "sense of sin" is new in theology and arose precisely as a reaction to this situation. By examining the experience of evil and conflict phenomenologically in modern culture we see that they are absurd and cry out for sense and explanation beyond themselves. Our sense of justice and human solidarity says that the war in Bosnia, inter-tribal conflict in Africa and endless civil wars and international conflicts "just cannot go on!" There must be a better justice, a higher love and commitment to make sense of things, and this is true also for the secular humanist. Sin is, to use a mathematical image, a surd, something we can put in numbers or words that do not add up and introduce a contradiction into the core of human action. The mistake is only resolved from outside by getting our thinking and acting right so that the mistake is exposed and expelled. Theologians give various reasons for the loss of the sense of sin. M. Vidal concentrates his discussion on ambiguity, others such as J.M. Pohier, L. Monden, R.A. McCormick, C. Curran[7] focus on the negatives in the culture without wanting to fall into a black-white distinction between pessimism and optimism in modern culture. B. Häring emphasises how the legalism that has penetrated Church teaching in its catechesis and preaching on sin was a contradiction of the Gospel that tried to impose outdated rules on social realities that have radically

changed. Somewhat in the same way as capital punishment
has disappeared from the penal code in many countries, sin in
its old forms and definitions has vanished from the mentality
of many moderns.[8] These experiences all lead back to guilt as
loss of meaning, as the unavoidable question that is somehow
always part of the human condition. D. Tettamanzi speaks of a
certain "constellation of the sense of sin"[9] which leads to a
diffused sense of fault and failure. In psychological terms the
Freudian sense of guilt as a psychic sickness to be cured by the
therapist is only possible once God has been expelled from
our cultural horizon. Such a notion of sin is reductionist, as
nearly all the commentators on Freud would acknowledge
without devaluing his discoveries of how psychological guilt
can falsify a person's living and view of the world. The idea of
autonomous liberty that contains everything within the closed
circle of human effort has effectively diminished if not done
away with the notion of sin. This problem has been well
analysed in *Reconciliatio et Paenitentia*, n. 18. One of the
causes identified by this document for the loss of the sense of
sin is an exaggerated idea of conscience as unrestricted freedom that does not need to refer to God's revealed law to find
the path of right living. However, the argument for such
freedom is self-defeating since it ultimately turns on itself, and
because, being nihilistic, it becomes self-destructive. Here we
see how an investment in freedom as absolute, indeed as the
one absolute on which to construct human progress, inevitably
ends in emptiness and a void at the centre of personal existence. In this way it should be recognised as a denial of the
dignity of the person in his or her individual and personal
existence. Described in phenomenological terms E. Chiavacci
finds that sin is experienced as a closing of the self against the
call of the Other and finally against the call of God as absolute
Other.[10] The philosophies of the Other inspired by the experience of Auschwitz and the mass horror of the twentieth
century have broken out of the subjectivist boundaries of the
Cartesian ego to awaken in us a reverence of the face of
the stranger. On this basis sin as a contemporary experience
can be reassessed because it demands a rebellion against
every form of dominion of any person over an-other. Sin is a

necessary theme in a personalistic ethic properly conceived, since by taking guilt seriously one reaches the limits of the ego and finds that release and salvation must be gifted and given from outside, not impersonally through scientific, psychological or social techniques but by An-other whom we allow to enter and save us from our misery.

13. Christ and the true face of sin

It is necessary to recall how well this fits with the traditional dogmas in Christian faith. The true face of sin is only revealed when we are released from it by Christ the Redeemer. The Church has always given a personal, existential answer to the personal problem of sin. Beneath the Cross of Christ the human race has been able to view what sin has done to the body of Christ. It is here that "the constellation of the sense of sin", as Tettamanzi calls it, is unmasked to the view of humanity. It reveals a double loss, that of the reality of the God of salvation history and that of human liberty to relate freely to him.

Sin formally defined separates us from God by rupturing our relationship with him. It is saying "No!" to his creative and redemptive love. Sin is manifested materially by all the ways that love is lacking and wanting in the universe. It is thereby experienced in two forms: as moral guilt which is the absence and nothingness of "turning away from God", *aversio a Deo*; and as the harm, the pain and the damage consequent on this loss by "turning to a creature" in preference to the Creator, *conversio ad creaturam*. "The constellation of sin" is a deep shadow thrown over the radiant revelation of God's goodness. It contradicts his covenant with the universe, with the world he wanted and the people he chose as his very own. Goodness is an analogous notion that draws together into unity all the levels of the covenant in our unique destiny in God. Sin is the evil that shatters that analogy and destroys that unity by dispersing humanity, leading it away from its destiny and thereby ruining the many beautiful faces of goodness in the universe. "The constellation of sin" includes the concepts of the cosmic dimensions of sin, of ecological sin, of sin against humanity, of "the sin of the world" (Jn 1:29), of social

sin and the structures of sin in society, of personal and community sin, and worst of all "sin unto death" (1 Jn 5:16) that
brings about the eternal loss of God and separation from Christ.

In this constellation we can discover what has traditionally
been called original sin as the alienated state of humanity in its
existential condition. We may speak of the sin of Adam as the
original guilty act from which the history of sin derived. This
should be done with discretion since we cannot imagine what
the "state of original justice" was like, nor do we need to
become lost in fantasising about what the Garden of Eden
looked like or how our first parents lived. Here there are
countless historical and scientific problems which need not
detract from the awareness of the human condition being that of
existential alienation as a historical reality that touches the
whole race as we know it. Original sin is real to us as the basic
existential not being right with others as a sign of not being
right with the Other. And this is something we experience as
conditioning our whole existence without our ever having
caused it or being guilty for it. It is, however, the basic weakness
within us that leads us to personally affirm and carry that state into
act as our very own. It is the contradiction we encounter at the
deepest point of our identity. As St Paul identifies it in Romans 7,
"what I want to do I do not do" because sin dwells in me.

14. The distinction of sins

The personal involvement and affirmation of the power of
sin that dominates and lives in me occurs in two modes according to traditional Catholic theology. These are called mortal and venial sin. They are two quite distinct categories and
realities, and not just a way of quantifying the seriousness of
sin according to more or less. Mortal sin is the death of charity
as the love of God and neighbour within us. In venial sin we
remain alive to God but our relationship with him is not as
healthy as it should be, although our existence is still directed
to him as our destiny. Casuistry was accustomed to identify
mortal sin with a breach of God's law. This can too easily be
conceived legalistically as any material crime that contra-

venes any written law, civil or ecclesiastical. The person is either not involved or is stigmatised as a criminal. St Augustine, however, who formulated the original definition, said that it was any thought, word, deed or omission against the divine law. It is therefore against God. But in what sense? In its negating, neutralising or in any way harming the deepest desire of the human heart for meaning and so for God. It is therefore in contradiction with our own existence as openness, desire and attraction toward the Other. We rarely find ourselves directly rising up against or even being conscious of touching on such a relationship. Blasphemy, sacrilege, perjury are among the few occasions when a human directly directs his or her act against the divinity. Mostly the relation is broken by cutting our good relationships with others and so with the Other. The transcendent relationship to God as Other is implicit and tacit in all human relationships as loving or hating, as positive or negative, as good or evil. As the name suggests, mortal sin is an act through which the doer dies within. Usually it is more like a series of acts all of the same kind multiplying the same type of malice that as a cancer eats away our spiritual life till all affection, relationship and link to the living God expires. Like cancer, the reality of sin as a negation of the transcendent source of life is often not seen, recognised or perceived. Indeed, when we speak of sin we are using God-language negatively, that is, as a contradiction of the inexpressible mystery of God as Love. For this reason St Paul was right to speak of "the mystery of iniquity". Sin in its proper sense is a contradiction of the transcendental relationship to God as the source of life, love and justice, but in a way deeper than words or laws. Even if we take the symbols of sin as stain, sickness, crime, addiction, or as a spiral that draws the whole world into its vortex, and do not advert to the contradiction of eternal love that opens onto mystery, we remain lost in empty signs and stuck in a mere word-game. But how do we become aware of this mystery in the concrete? Perhaps the last judgement scene in Matthew 25 will help, since it gives a divine criterion in human realities: "Whatever you do to these, the least of my brethren, you do to me." The human way of knowing how we treat God is how we behave toward Christ,

and we treat Christ well or badly in every person we encounter. The awareness of sin flows through the unconditional
respect we render to the dignity of every human person without exception, the unrestricted condemnation of the evils that
bedevil our planet, any lack of the love that should enliven
human relationships. You will notice that this awareness is
unconditional, unrestricted and can never be denied. This is a
reflection of how it opens onto and points into the infinite
mysterious life of divine Love. When these wounds to human
dignity and well-being are perceived as wounds done to the
body of Christ, when they are seen as the burden and suffering
he willingly bore by assuming upon himself this contradiction
of love, then the notion of sin is personalised and becomes a
felt, existential reality. Sin is what makes our openness to
infinite love fail by turning back on itself. In this sense mortal
sin is the loss of charity, the misdirecting of the deepest urge
of our total being. Of course, this reality is so deep that it is
hidden to every human eye, nor does the human intellect ever
penetrate the murky darkness and bottomless depth of a heart
fallen into such evil, so as to be able to say with finality the
definitive word that such a soul is in mortal sin and is separated from its Lord even while it lives on physically. We can
judge mortal sin in an objective manner with the realistic
criteria that must be applied to every human act as human. A
sin is considered to be mortal when it: (1) concerns grave
matter; (2) is done with full knowledge; and (3) is done with
full consent. Grave matter means that the intention of the act is
aimed at something that in itself is serious, that is, the object
of the act; its matter is such that it could not be an expression
of love and esteem for God. As measured by moral law it is
against the genuinely human good as willed by God. In this
way acts classed as intrinsically evil, e.g., the killing of the
innocent, torture of children etc., are always seriously wrong
and thus objectively mortal sins. In contradistinction to grave
matter we have the category of light matter, i.e., the object
may be wrong but only in a slight or small way or is such that
it only lessens the fervour of our rapport with God but would
not break it, e.g., a white lie, or stealing a small sum of money.
Grave matter is such that it is against charity, e.g., a lie that

does irreparable damage to reputation, a large robbery. The point of grave matter is that as the object of the act it cannot be a proportionate means to loving God and therefore when freely, deliberately chosen ruins our relationship with him. It must be said that the determination of grave matter is not always easy and may require great discrimination on the part of the agent, as in cases of justice requiring retribution or the righting of wrongs etc. There is a tradition that has considered sexual matter as always grave matter for sin. This tradition needs to be taken seriously without becoming too rigid, since in practice when too strictly applied it can easily become the cause of scrupulosity. It should be understood in a formal sense, i.e., it only applies to the sexual act when it is a sexual act as such whether in fantasy, thought or performance. A sexual fantasy may arrive without invitation and should be considered temptation till such time as it is deliberately consented to. Day-dreaming and the normal psychological attraction to the other sex are not in question here. It is only when these become the object and cause of sexual sin formally considered that they can be defined as grave matter of sin. If a person sways in doubt as to whether it was grave matter or not then the act is not mortally sinful. While the principle of sexual matter being grave matter properly defined is correct, great care should be taken in sexual education and upbringing of children and adolescents to ensure that they do not become anxious about normal sexual reactions and fantasies so as always or even quite often to associate them with sin but without sound moral reasons. Where a sane, mature attitude to sexuality is not maintained, various obsessions easily result because the idea of grave matter has been misapplied.

The other two conditions for mortal sin are no less important. Full knowledge means that a person recognises and personally owns the evil of the act he or she performs. Unawareness, being half asleep or day-dreaming all undermine this requirement. Of course one should not be negligent in having knowledge one should have, e.g., a married person is presumed to understand what marriage essentially involves; a business person should not be unaware of the basic requirements of justice in commerce. A person should have the basic information and knowledge needed in their state or condition or vocation. In spite of these requirements people do often have moral blind spots even about the most fundamental moral principles and values. St Thomas Aquinas cited Cicero's example of the German tribes who could not see that stealing was really wrong. The same is still true today for some groups and in some parts of the world. Public polls on sexual and bioethics issues show that a high percentage of the public just do not seem to understand what is morally involved in IVF or contraception and no amount of arguing will make them change their point of view. They are in no way motivated by disregard or disrespect for the moral law and have nothing but good will toward the Church and her moral teaching. This is what is called invincible ignorance. Certainly it is not a condition to be praised, but it does excuse such persons from moral guilt. The reason for them being in that condition is usually either their familial upbringing or the values of the predominant culture which they have assimilated uncritically by symbiosis. These values can be changed over the long term by wise education and by critical reflection on the culture. Where these false values penetrate institutions, governments, schools, industry, the economy and the universities their social force for evil has been described as "social sin" or "structures of sin". Since such evil corrupts and corrodes the common good it cannot be excused and tolerated in the same way as in the case of the individual. It is necessary to take a harder stance against entrenched bad will, where people begin to want not to know or consider the evil they are doing. Such public ignorance when it is deliberate avoidance of moral obligation in the wider community is not to be tolerated. One still needs to respect the conscience of public officials where in good faith they cannot see they are doing wrong. This respect for another's conscience does not absolve other officials or citizens from making their moral opinion publicly known. Feigned or hypocritical ignorance is obviously to be condemned.

Full consent depends on proper knowledge and means that a person can put their will into choosing the good and avoiding the evil. There are factors which can diminish the will's commitment to the good, e.g., being swayed by passion, being

subject to mental illness or terrorised by fear. It is obvious that
there are psychotic states where a person may intellectually
know what should be done but still cannot be held responsible
for their actions. In general, since emotion should be subject
to and should be humanised by reason a person has a moral
obligation to express their emotions responsibly. Nevertheless, a person may be overcome by an avalanche of vindictive
anger and commit a crime of passion, a murder, for example.
In such a case, the person is still held responsible for their
action but the passion becomes a mitigating circumstance. If
reason was completely obliterated, however, this may excuse
from moral guilt though the damage done is horrendous. Where
a person over time lets their emotions take unreasonable control of their life, so that weakness of character and various
forms of viciousness grow out of that weakness, such an
attitude must be considered a vice and indeed gravely sinful.

The action of the will as the engagement of freedom remains something of an enigma to us. A choice that changes
the direction of a person's life away from God by the loss of
charity is clearly a mortal sin. For most people the problem is
to know when this happens. It presumes that persons commit
themselves from the depth of their heart with and by their
freedom. Where persons do not commit themselves in this
way there cannot be mortal sin, and the evil act that results is
called venial sin. Mortal sin in an objective sense means that
the three above conditions must all be fulfilled. Failure to
fulfil any one of them means that the sin becomes venial.
Venial sin is when one remains God-directed in love but acts
in a way somehow inconsistent with that love without losing
it. It weakens but does not destroy love for God and others. Of
course, the basic relationship may almost unconsciously be
undermined by persistent inattention to the love relationship.
Such disengagement when it has done its work is mortal sin,
for the relationship is dead. For that reason we should be quite
attentive to the growth of small sins in our lives. For this
reason some theologians have made a threefold distinction
that is more psychological than philosophical in its intent.
They describe everyday sin which almost passes unnoticed;
venial sin that has some important impact on our lives without

changing its direction; and mortal sin as a commitment of freedom against God. One of the deepest mysteries of sin is knowing whether our will is really directed to God or not. St Augustine expressed the undeniable truth of a fundamental option when one is fully and truly committed to sin. His famous and much quoted passage from the *City of God* shows that how and what we love determines our life's value. "Two loves make two cities. Self-love to the despite of God made the earthly city, love of God to the despite of self the heavenly."[11] We are rarely so clear about where we stand with God, and yet we know from the depths of ourselves that the choice can only be one way or the other. Where we stand in regard to the constellation of sin as a condition of alienation, as a going the wrong way in life so as to lose God and reinforce the evil in the world, and as a silent lessening of our intent toward God are all summed up in the scriptural challenge: "I have set before you today life and prosperity, death and adversity... I call heaven and earth to witness against you today that I have set before you life and death, blessings and a curse. Choose life so that you and your descendants may live" (cf. Deut 30:15-19). Salvation from sin is a free gift of God that we can only have by freely choosing to embrace i God's last word on sin is the Cross, where he revealed himself as superabundant love.

NOTES

1. TS Eliot, *The Cocktail Party. A Comedy.* Faber and Faber, London 1950.
2. Patrick McCormick, CM., *Sin as Addiction,* Paulist, New York 1989, 61.
3. Ibid., 65.
4. *The People of the Lie,* Simon and Schuster, New York, 183, 223-226.
5. "The Reality of Sin: A Theological and Pastoral Critique", in *The Mystery of Sin and Forgiveness,* Alba House, New York 1971, 9495.
6. *Discorsi e radiomessaggi,* VIII (1946) 584.
7. See Ivan Fucek S.J., *Il peccato oggi,* P.U.G., Rome 1991, 54.
8. See *Sin in a Secular Age,* St Paul Publications, Slough, 1974.
9. "Teologia morale e peecato: alcuni discussioni attuali", in *La Scuola Cattolica* 115 (1987), 601.
10. "Il peccato", in *Teologia Morale,* Cittadella, Assisi 1977, I, 232-265.
11. Oliver O'Donovan's rendition of *De Civitate Dei,* lib. XIV, cap. 28 in *The Problem of Self-Love in St Augustine,* Yale University Press, New Haven and London 1980, 93.

Moral dimensions of the Gospel vision

10

The law according to the Gospel

1. A moral order

When things go wrong, we immediately think that some-one did not follow the right rules for their performance. It is a universal instinct and conviction that there is a rationality in life that makes the universe go right with what John Dryden in another age called "the harmony of the spheres". To be right with ourselves or with others or with God is a matter of following the right order. When this belief is exaggerated it becomes an obsession with "law and order". But at its best it shows how deep the search for the moral truth is within us. It is witnessed to by the way we respect the truth of things and of ourselves as persons. When we speak of human action we are the agents responsible for putting the right order into our acts by our decisions. It is by right action that we construct the moral order of our lives.

2. God's Word creates rational order

The Christian idea of law is that of following the right order God has infused in our hearts. It means responding positively, saying "Yes" to his Word of creation and re-demption. We have often heard law defined as *logos* or the rationality inherent in humanity and the world; it is some-thing that demands our respect. This word "law" for a Jew and a Christian is God's creative Word, his *dabah* that he spoke at creation, and because of it we have an intelligence like God's which can recognise the intelligibility of things. It should be noted that *torah* and *nomos* are subsequent to or follow on the notion of God's Word that causes the creation to be intelligible. They are practical ways of measuring that intelligibility in view of action. In the Old Testament the faithfulness of the God of revelation is guaranteed by the regular working and permanence of a nature created by God. The stars, the sun, the moon and all the animals are consigned to Adam as the steward of creation. On the seventh day God saw that his work was pleasing, it was "good". God tells his people he will be as constant with them as he has made creation firm and secure. It is absurd to think that the order of the world would break up under their feet, and so it is inconceivable that God would abandon his people. This most basic idea of God's creative Word being his law permeating material and spiritual creation is a constant theme in the psalms.

Your word is firmly fixed in heaven.
Your faithfulness endures to all generations;
you have established the earth,
and it stands fast (Ps 119:89-90).

3. Law is based on wisdom

This meditation on the rightness we feel is inherent to creation leads to a celebration of the divine wisdom. This wisdom is personified as working through providence and in the New Testament it is identified with the person and mission of the Holy Spirit.

The LORD created me at the beginning of his work,
the first of his acts of long ago...
when he marked out the foundations of the earth,
then I was beside him, like a master worker;
and I was daily his delight,
rejoicing before him always,
rejoicing in his inhabited world
and delighting in the human race (Prov 8:22, 29-31).

God loves all he has made and rules his creation with concern and affection. Here is a positive image of God who creates through love. His providence is simply the extension, the continuation of this creative love through time so as to permeate and structure history with his personal planning and concern for the whole creation. The Jewish and Christian tradition has always been able to visualise God as the creative artist who conceived in his mind the conception of his master work. If he is the Creator who alone could bring forth from nothing his master work, then that master work can have no other name than THE creation. And the sum total of all that is created is called the universe. To be a created universe means to be totally dependent on God for existence and so to be limited by one's dependence on the infinite God. To lose contact with God implies the loss of existence, to fall back into nothingness, to be annihilated. Hence "the mystery of sin". The very fact of existence is the proof of God's goodness that is confirmed by his rational plan for our fulfilment.

4. Leadership in the community

"As an exemplar of the things he makes by his art pre-exists in an artist's mind, so an exemplar of the ordered actions to be done by those subject to his sway pre-exists in a governor's mind... Through his wisdom God is the founder of the universe of things, and in relation to them he is like an artist in relation to the things he makes... he is the governor of all acts and motions to be found in each and every creature. And so as being the principle through which the universe is created, divine wisdom means art, or exemplar or idea, and likewise it also means law, as moving all things to their due end. Accordingly the Eternal Law is nothing other than the exemplar of divine wisdom as directing the motions and acts of everything... Law is nothing but a dictate of practical reason issued by a sovereign who governs a complete community... It is evident that the whole community of the universe is governed by God's mind. Therefore the ruling idea of things which exist in God as the effective sovereign of them all has the nature of law. Then since God's mind does not conceive in time, but has an eternal concept... it follows that this law should be called eternal... A human authority imparts a kind of inward principle of activity to its subjects; so also God impresses on the whole of nature the principles of the proper activity of things. Accordingly God is said to command the whole of nature... That is why every motion and every act in the whole universe is subject to the eternal law" (*S.T.*, I-II, 93. 1,3,5). Creation, redemption and *parousia* are all part of his eternal law.

5. Eternal law

What does the eternal law tell us of our relationship with God? Firstly, that in creating God acts in a way that conforms to the eternal law which is himself. In scriptural terms he is faithful to himself and therefore just. But he is also merciful, for his loving concern for his creatures is also identified with himself and so is compatible with his justice. God therefore respects creatures, giving them all that is their due, and more, for from his superabundant goodness he gifts them his mercy which they could never merit. The whole of creation is subject to God's just and merciful governing. His love is demonstrated in an extraordinary way because human beings are not just subject to this providence but are themselves consciously and freely the realisers of this providence. They are a providence for themselves through their dominion over their lives and actions. All of this is contained in his eternal law. Their participation in God's providence is through reason, "et ipsa fit providentiae particeps, sibi ipsi et aliis providens" (*S.T.*, I-II, 90. 2). The human being is an image of God by sharing in the exemplarity of divine wisdom. In moral action the divine wisdom is reflected through synderesis and the virtue of prudence. A person with practical wisdom exercises a personal providence through foresight and planning over the achievement of one's destiny to happiness. Prudence is the elaboration of practical reason that realises the eternal law in one's personal existence.

Eternal law is the perfect model or primary analogue of Aquinas' four-point definition of law as: (1) a precept of practical reason, i.e., a rational plan formulated by reason; (2) for the achievement of the common good of the community; this is its purpose or teleological principle toward the realisation of which it strives dynamically; (3) made by the proper authority which is responsible for looking after the good of the whole community; and (4) promulgated, i.e., communicated as binding to those whom it concerns.

6. Law as analogous

This definition of law is then realised, in different and various ways, in all the strata of creation. It is a concept capable of use at various levels, in different perspectives and against a variety of horizons. It is necessary not to think of law too univocally, as we do when we refer to it simply as positive civil law which furnishes our first experience of explicitly formulated law. Eternal law exists and is actual to us before we advert to any of its explicit formulations. It is first of all providence encountered through the good and benign order of the world which supports our existence and self-realisation as persons. Law grows out of our sense of a rightness in the world and in ourselves. The tendency to goodness and the dynamic toward fulfilment are "measured" according to this rightness that we recognise radiating from God's providential wisdom. Law is thereby "regula et mensura" that reveals to us how the world is dynamically unfolding and how the human person should integrate and situate him or herself within this cosmic harmony of goodness. Law, as we are only too well aware, comes from outside ourselves and is a revealing light that shows us ourselves as we truly are, sin included, and how we should become what we ought to be in God.

Law therefore has an important role to play in Christian life as an instrument of God's self-communication. It guides graced natures to a share in divine life through love. This notion is reflected in the definitions of law given by St Thomas. From the point of view of the lawmaker, "Law is an ordinance of reason for the common good made by the one who has care of the community and promulgated" (*S.T.*, I-II, 90. 1). From the point of view of the one subject to it, "law is a rule and measure of acts". The notions of regulator and regulated complement each other in seeking a common goal so that law should be seen as the sharing in a common effort for a common benefit. In the simplest terms law is an action of a superior that sets down a measure or rule to be followed by all in view of the common good. A lawmaker acts through legislation to determine how the community should act to attain its goal. It means commanding, forbidding or permitting conduct by community members.

God's providence is realised in humanity's unfolding and developing its capacities and dynamisms according to the measure in which it has been loved by God. The measure of human destiny is God's law expressed as providence. By recognising this plan the human person discovers the right manner and measure of being human. But this measure is not different from God himself; it is not something that God has left to anyone else to think out and measure. It is a plan that has been promulgated and made manifest in the Word of the Father, in whom and according to whom all things are "constituted" as what they are, and are called to be what they are meant to become. In the Father's love for the Son we find the secret of creation as his plan of love for us as "sons in the Son". Eternal law rests on the fact that God knows all the things he has created individually and so how they must act to fulfil their destiny. His willing of that order of beings and its operation is eternal, the dictate of practical reason by which God rules the community of "the universe". God alone knows his law directly and immediately, yet by reason and revelation humans are able to participate in his eternal law and thus fulfil their destiny. There is but one eternal law and in it humans have but one destiny. God's plan is that law in all its forms should work together so that their actualisation in history will bring us to God himself in his eternal Kingdom. God wants to lead creation to its goal. To do this in the fullness of time he sent his Son, who by his resurrection gifted us the Holy Spirit to recreate his work when it had been deformed by sin.

The different participations of the eternal law in humanity, that is, natural law, human law, the divine law of the Old and

New Testaments and the law of sin or concupiscence, all sketch out basic structures constituting the human person in salvation history. To fragment this complex reality of law is to falsify human nature as a unified whole and its constitutive elements as well. The autonomy of reason has its proper place, but this does not mean it can be separated from the law of grace or that civil law exists independently of our relationship with God. To take any element separately from every other one is to impoverish its true significance which can only be perceived against the background of God's overall intention. In this unitary perspective of St Thomas' theology of law there is a remarkable parallel with chapter 1 of *Dei Verbum*, which concerns the synthetic sense and meaning of the history of salvation. As Father Mongillo points out, this progress toward the absolute good is precisely what the history of salvation aims at and so it is well described as the "revelatio morum".[1] Each type of law must be considered not only in itself but in its relationship to the whole complex of law.

7. The natural law

God has given us reason to guide us to our destiny. In its light we make the fundamental option of the way of life we are going to follow. By following the insights into what is truly good for us we discern what we think are basic human values and the primary principles in whose terms we judge human affairs. We run our lives on these principles of moral realism and rationality.

The natural law is human participation in the eternal law through the light of reason. It is our ability to ask and answer questions, seeking the laws or rules of human conduct. Here we come up against all the problems of interpreting norms and of understanding natural law. It is possible to consider these topics from a biological, psychological, cultural, historical or philosophical perspective. All of those are valid and should be taken into account. Here we are looking for an anthropological vision of the good of the human person, a global and existential conception of human destiny where all of these by implication should find their place. Natural law is essentially linked to the vision of the human person as created by God, inserted into a world also created by him and meant to achieve its purpose in harmony with the whole universe. St Thomas conceived of God as an external cause instructing or educating us in goodness through his law and enabling us to perform all it required through grace. Natural law, however, goes deeper than any form of education we can conceive of, since it involves the transcendent God operating in the intimacy of the human heart to draw it by attraction to himself as its complete realisation.

Reflection on natural law is not an abstract ideal, but seeing what the concrete realisation of men and women inserted in the universe as it really is requires. What is God's real plan for our fulfilment? To understand human nature properly it cannot be separated from its setting, its home and indwelling in the universe. Human nature participates in the universe in all its aspects. Men and women are part of the universe in the strictest sense; they share its destiny; and also its powers and forces pass through them forming part of their nature and make-up. In this sense natural law oscillates between what is proper and distinctively human, namely reason; what the human person has in common with all living things, that is, vital animal forces, and what it shares with all physical existence, the fact of existing in its own right. Now natural law is specifically the law of human reason, since it is reason that makes our nature human. So our animal forces and our hold on existence itself are a rational animality and a rational permanence and preservation of existence. For instance, our sexuality has a community with all species that propagate by reproduction but it is human because it is permeated and animated by reason. It looks not just to the material and vital preservation of the species but to satisfying the deepest human desire to express and receive love physically. These inclinations or instincts that drive us toward self-preservation and the fulfilment of our vital powers, as well as to opening us to the whole horizon of meaning with God and others, instruct us about what is genuinely human when we reflect long and hard on them.

Natural law is not monolithic but is made up of several diverse elements, all distinct but occurring in a hierarchical order recognised by reason's insights into the structure existing in our basic inclinations. These insights may be seen as evident *per se* to those who have made their conquest in this reflex form. Philosophers can show that these insights are always active in any moral reasoning and cannot in fact be denied without falling into contradiction. They are indemonstrable and are in fact axiomatic assertions. The natural law has one root, one common source for all its principles: do good and pursue it, and avoid evil. All the other principles outlined above are based on this orientation to the good. The primary principles are universal, absolute and immutable. They cannot be obliterated from the human mind, since the drive toward sociality, marriage and self-preservation are necessary to human nature itself. The principles very close to them that reason deduces from them are valid for the most part or *ut in pluribus* since our basic drives do not always realise their object in a contingent, changeable world. The common principles which are obvious to everyone are to be distinguished from more particular conclusions which are not only more difficult to work out but must involve a large measure of flexibility in practice. These inclinations, although essential to human nature, are sometimes frustrated. This type of exception does not disprove their universality as constitutive of our humanity but is the necessary consequence of living in a mutable environment where we as rational beings can intervene freely. Moral theology, like ethics, is not an exact science. It is possible to have invincible ignorance even of natural law, not in its common most general principles but in the conclusions that flow very closely from them. As mentioned previously, St Thomas gives the example of some of the German tribes who were incorrigibly mistaken in the matter of stealing. Many cases of people not being able to see the point in the Church's moral teaching, e.g., on contraception, while retaining respect and good will toward her, come under the heading of invincible ignorance. Education, public values that become corrupted, emotional blocks and false reasoning may contribute to such ignorance. Another insight that follows from reflecting on humanity in a changing world is the realisation that human nature not only undergoes evolution as every animal species does, but that reason can err and that its reflection on human affairs has a power of self-correction and growth in insight over time. We call this the historicity of human nature. The history of such institutions as slavery and usury shows how we can grow in insight into human dignity and worth through becoming aware of our deeper humanity. Natural inclinations become, through reason's interpreting activity, sources of human growth both individually and socially, as well as provoking institutional reform and personal conversion when enlivened by grace.

The principles of natural law all represent forms of revelation, because God has manifested our deepest moral nature to us by infusing the light of reason into our minds at creation. God has enlightened our reason with his own light. This illumination means that our reason participates in God's reason which is his eternal law. We do not see God face to face, but in his light our minds become sources of light by which we see. We cannot look directly at the sun but we see the sun's light illumining the objects of our vision. Just so the light of our minds makes what we see intelligible because God who is light has enlightened our minds. This does not imply Augustinian illuminism such that I glance up to catch a glimpse of God's light. God has put his light in my mind as my proper possession, as my agent intellect by which I can choose to illumine my path through the world toward him. The encyclical *Veritatis Splendor* (n. 42) repeats one of St Thomas' favourite verses from the psalms,

> There are many who say,
> "O that we might see some good!
> Let the light of your face shine on us, O LORD!" (Ps 4:6).

Natural law refers to humanity in its concrete historical reality in God's plan of salvation. It is a participation in the eternal law which is reflected into immutably human and universal structures of our action. It occurs formally through the light of reason, and materially through the inclinations to conviviality, to marriage and the family, and to self-preservation in existence. Natural law is not univocal, then, but operates at as many levels as go to make human nature good and that good intelligible. It is a true case of analogy of "unum ex pluribus". The inclinations become law through reason which discerns in them the demands of human nature open to its ultimate purpose and fulfilment. They reveal the universal goods that are to be sought as purposes worthy of the dignity of the human person. It is only in view of beatitude that they make final sense as participating in the fullness of humanity. So God governs humanity with a universal providence and this he does through reason. Each human person is capable of knowing God's will precisely by the fact of being blessed with reason. God has a plan, a vocation and a destiny for me that I can discern and faithfully carry out by following the inclinations indicated by reason. The natural law is for humanity the law constitutive of the good of the person individually and socially; because of it the human person has a connatural orientation to develop him or herself precisely as a person and so to become a doer of good, helping others develop their personhood also. Everything in human life that can be regulated by reason is a matter for natural law. But natural law is not a written law which can be identified with the collection of principles and formulations to which the textbook morality of the last few centuries reduced it. It is identified with the very rationality of our nature, what guides us from the depth of our being.

> Historically the appeal to natural law has arisen precisely from the resistance of personal conscience to the arbitrariness of written laws; it appealed to an *unwritten law*, an inward knowledge of what man ought to do and ought not to do in order to be and to become authentically himself.[2]

8. Human-made law

Moral laws are moral precisely in as far as they are reasonable. Such laws arise through insight into inclination or by further precisioning such insight or insights. The empirical conception of law only as the fruit of experience established by induction which discovers the same pattern constantly repeated in the data of experience has to be severely questioned. The basic idea here is that laws can be established by experiment through the scientific interpretation of data. A more sophisticated variant of the same positivist philosophy is found in considering a statistical mean in human behaviour as a law. Besides there being a gross confusion between physical laws of nature and natural law, a collection of data never of itself yields an insight into the intelligibility of human conduct. Human ingenuity has to devise ways in which the universal demands of natural law will be lived out concretely in these circumstances. These do not belong to the first promptings of human reason but are based on them. The making of these particular arrangements is the function of human law. St Thomas sees in this sort of law a going beyond basic natural law principles to a schooling in virtue. Human law aims not only at producing outer order in society, but at encouraging inner goodness. For him the aspect of interiority is primary, so much so that if a human law stands in contradiction with natural law it lacks all validity as law, being but the corruption of genuine law (*S.T.*, I-II, 95. 2). Most philosophers of law follow a more positivist interpretation today, saying that an unjust law if properly legislated and in the proper legal form is genuinely law, but that it should be brought into line with what is moral. They work from a strong distinction between the moral and the legal orders, seeing law as autonomous and therefore neither based on nor derived from moral principles. The possibility for conflict between legislation and morality in a liberal democratic society, and between Church and civil authority becomes very obvious.

Human law can depend on natural law in either of two ways: (1) it can be directly based on it like laws forbidding murder or theft; these are contrary to right reason in themselves; (2) it can determine an issue in a way that is required by natural law. This is akin to an artistic invention of how to bring a work of imagination into existence. For instance, reason demands that traffic be regulated so as to protect human life, but it is the competent human authority which determines how this is to be done in a particular time and place. The particularities as such do not have the force of natural law. It was pointed out above that St Thomas did not apply the word "law" to an ordinance that was against natural law. For him the word has such a connotation of goodness and rationality that he would not apply it to something bad. Human law is the mediation of something greater, something to be found in God himself. He was, nevertheless, aware of the limitations of human law. Its role is educational and disciplinary, and it is to be employed only to the extent it is useful to this purpose. It does not have to forbid all evildoing but only the greater vices, and in particular those that need to be restrained to protect society. As regards virtue, human law enjoins only those acts that are necessary to achieve and preserve the common good.

The letter of the law is not sacrosanct, but we should take the legislator's intention into account and not just his or her words, presuming that his or her intention is to promote the common good. Legislation can usually only take the majority of cases into account, so that it is reasonable to foresee that there will be exceptions to be covered by the higher justice of *epicheia*. Material norms never succeed in covering every conceivable case.

We can see then how God, as it were, had good reason not to make the law of the Holy Spirit a written law. Even human law, although it is written, is not such without qualification. There will be cases where the law can only be kept by breaking the letter of the law, because natural law, right reason and the legislator's intention to serve the common good take priority over written legislation.

9. Civil law

Human or man-made law is for the most part made by legislators. Judges can, however, sometimes make law. This is done when, in applying statutes, they have to fill gaps left by the statute, or when they decide cases of "first impression", or when as members of a higher court they render decision by way of judicial review. The executive branch of government may also in certain circumstances make law by proclamation. Finally the people themselves, the source of all political law-making authority, make laws by means of the customs they have established. Customs are ways of acting that are necessary for the common good, have been accepted and used by the people over a long time, and are recognised as binding by legislators and judges. The landmark judgements of law-makers past or long dead continue as law in as much as it is a matter of recorded fact they did so directively judge, and succeeding legislators are assumed to have made the judgement of their predecessors their own unless they show their disagreement by attempted amendment or appeal. Legal tradition as a consistently reasoned and stable argument over time is very important for society. Most of the great institutions of a free society are tradition-dependent in this sense, e.g., the law itself, the medical profession, universities and commerce. There are reasons and arguments that support and in fact justify these institutions and without which they would not continue to exist. Legislation has the power of committing a society to maintaining those institutions that are needed for its common welfare. The premises that support society's institutions reveal the basic values to which the society subscribes. Legislation can also reform social institutions according to moral criteria, e.g., the abolition of slavery, the non-proliferation of atomic weapons etc.

The promulgation of human-made law to the people is a condition of its effectiveness in directing the people to their common welfare. Custom has its own particular form of promulgation. It is made known by the publicly repeated acts of people which manifest their estimation or judgement that some practice is necessary to the common welfare. The end of human law, the common welfare, is a unique kind of good. It is not the sum of all goods proper to all individuals such as the total of all producer and consumer goods. Nor is it a collective good such as the family fortune which diminishes as it is communicated to each member. The common good is the type of good that is communicated to all and is not lessened by being so communicated. The peace, protection and security of the law are good examples. They are not lessened by the number of participants, nor does this number cause each to have less. The common good is effective according to the amount of cooperation put forward by the members of the society. The content of civil law includes whatever is necessary for the common welfare, either absolutely, such as police protection, or relatively, such as having direction indicators on motor vehicles. Statutes that would purport to dictate what people should believe or how they should worship would invade the private life and private welfare of people and do not pertain to the common welfare. Such an invasion is the embodiment of tyranny and thought control. On the basis of content, laws are either substantive or procedural, depending on whether they are concerned with claims themselves or with methods of enforcing these claims. Laws are also either private or public. Private laws concern the private claims of one citizen against another and other laws are concerned with the public claims of all the citizens against one or many. The field of private law covers torts, property, contracts, domestic relations etc. Public law deals with the constitution, administration, crimes and legal procedure.

10. The obligation of law

The obligation of law derives from the necessity of the content of the law for the common good. This means that law is binding in conscience. For obligation arises from the moral necessity of choosing a means that is necessary for a desired end. It should be noted that this necessity is intrinsic, i.e., the means contributes to the end constituted and without it the end would lack an essential constitutive. If I desire the safety of myself and others then I must drive within the speed limit. If I exceed the limit then my and others' safety is at stake.

In the long history of jurisprudence, this end-means foundation of obligation has often been lost sight of. Some said that obligation had a subjective foundation in the will of the lawgiver. A statute obliged only if the lawmaker so desired. Otherwise, the law was merely indicative of what the lawmakers wanted done but it was not obligatory. This type of thinking gave rise to the "purely penal theory of law". This was a type of law that did not oblige me to do what was commanded but merely to the payment of a penalty or fine if I were discovered violating the law. This type of reasoning was sometimes used in the heyday of casuistry. Others, in a more Kantian line, considering human will or practical reason to be autonomous and incapable of being put under any determination by an objective end-means relationship, said that obligation derived from the interior reverence and respect I should have for the law itself. In this theory obligation is for obligation's sake.

Still others rejected all philosophical explanations and said that obligation was the same as sanction, that the obligation of the law was the same as its enforcement by power. Some who took this line did not deny the need for morality but wanted to keep moral and legal obligations separate in the debate over the enforcement of morals. Others took this position because they believed morals rested on an emotional basis and were consequently non-cognitivist and non-scientific. Morals had no place in scientific thinking.

The movement to moral realism has shown that once obligation is cut adrift from its end-means anchor, it becomes meaningless. Time as the great tester of ethical and legal theories shows that obligation then becomes either the lawmaker's will or my own, or it becomes the same as force or power which means that might is right. Obligation is determined by my desire for an end. There is one end for which I have a natural desire and which I cannot help desiring, my happiness as my self-realisation and fulfilment. Obligation is the objective relation between this particular situation of fact and my happiness as my end. The sanction of law is a different matter from obligation. Sanctions are either rewards for keeping the law or punishments for breaking it. They may be extrinsic, i.e., they are affixed or added to the law, or they may be intrinsic, i.e., they flow from the very content of the law itself. In Church law, the penalty of mortal sin for missing Sunday's Mass is a good example of an extrinsic sanction in the sphere of religious practice. Other examples of extrinsic sanctions would be rewards for the apprehension of criminals, and the deprivation of property by fine, or of freedom by imprisonment. Capital punishment is also an extrinsic sanction attached to the law. Examples of intrinsic sanctions would be the safety that results from observing the speed limit, or the harm done by dangerous driving that violates the law. In so far as intrinsic sanctions are connected to the end of the law, obligation and sanction logically have to do with one another. Extrinsic sanctions such as force and imprisonment are undoubtedly needed to ensure the enforcement of law, human perversity being what it is. But these sanctions are not the essence of the law, for there are many good laws without a punishment being stipulated for their violation. Every effort should be made to abolish capital punishment as well as every barbaric form of corporal punishment. For the Church's part she can give a very false impression of what motivates her in her mission when sanctions become the primary moving force for religious practice. Such sanctions may reinforce a cultural Christianity but hardly a mature decision in faith.

Law then is a directive for humans regarding those things necessary for the common good, and obligation to observe the law is based on this end-means relationship. This conception of law is verified not only in the written codes of literate people but also in the unwritten customs of preliterate peoples. Anthropologists have shown that these peoples often observe regulations without the threatened sanction of physical force such as imprisonment. Many times the threat of public ridicule is more than sufficient. This is a mechanism that has been largely lost in a society without shame, which then has to have recourse to brutal means to protect itself. It is much better where implicit recognition is given to the necessity of regulations for the common good of society and this is upheld by a common public spirit.

11. Revealed law

In its primary sense law is a guide or directive of human action. Specifically defined, it is a directive judgement of a lawmaker regarding means necessary for the common welfare. This conception is found at least implicitly in all cultures and is part of the great tradition of human wisdom handed down from generation to generation. The Bible also knew of law as necessary to our relationship with God.

> Teach me, O LORD, the way of your statutes,
> and I will observe it to the end.
> Give me understanding, that I may keep your law
> and observe it with my whole heart.
> Lead me in the path of your commandments,
> for I delight in it...
> Your word is a lamp to my feet
> and a light to my path...
> Truly I direct my steps by all your precepts;
> I hate every false way (Ps 119:33-35, 105, 128).

In discussing the varieties of law St Thomas gives four reasons for the necessity of divine law: (1) human judgement is uncertain, especially in regard to more detailed matters. Divine law carries the assurance of being certain and without error and so provides a sure guide for conduct; (2) human law, particularly in its civil form in a pluralistic society, can only deal with externals, but true virtue and character require inner goodness as well, and this is guided by divine law; (3) it is impossible for human-made law to forbid all wrongdoing. Divine law, however, misses nothing and covers all sins and causes all virtues to grow; (4) the fundamental reason for God's giving his own divine law is that it is necessary to direct us in those acts proper to our ultimate end, that is, happiness with God. Only God can reveal everything that is necessary to fulfil the deepest desires of the human heart, and he has done this by educating us in his law. In this sense divine law is an outside intervention, a revelation of God's loving plan in our regard. It is God as it were evoking, even provoking, and calling forth our deepest human desires to respond to him. His law, although external as given by him, corresponds to what is deepest in us for in a mysterious way, as St Augustine says, he is closer to us than we are to ourselves. This law is, to use

St Thomas' word, impressed on or into us by God's creation and by his action in grace. In both ways the face of God is revealed for our salvation. He explains that while natural law is a universal sharing in the eternal law proportionate to the capacity of human nature, the divine law is a higher sharing that is proportioned to our supernatural happiness with God. The divine law is twofold, what we call the old and the new covenant. What is involved here is a theology of the Old Testament and then of the New. They are both concerned with our relationship with God as we see it in the light of his self-manifestation. There is not a difference in kind between the Testaments, because they both involve our revealed relationship with God. They involve our interiorising, as a personal inner reality in faith and love, God's intervention, what he has "impressed" onto us through his action in salvation history. They are like the shadow and then the full presence of the one foreshadowed. They are related as imperfect to the perfect, as the incomplete to its completion. They are related as child to adult. The child is under a tutor, the law of Moses; the adult must answer for him or herself, having grown in the power of the Spirit. The progress from the old to the new law may be seen particularly in three areas: (1) Both are concerned with the common good. The Old Testament was directed to the common welfare of the Jewish people and the State of Israel as the land God had given to his chosen people. They were aware of a universal mission to the nations through their national identity as being chosen as a "pars pro toto". The new law concerns the heavenly and the spiritual. It is aimed at bringing all humanity into the Kingdom of God. The new law is that of grace, the Magna Carta of the Kingdom set out in the Sermon on the Mount by St Matthew. (2) Both laws set out to establish justice among the members of society as is the purpose of law, peace in the common good. The justice of the old law is an external justice, that of the society of Israel. That of the new law is internal, "the greater justice" Christ proclaimed in the Sermon on the Mount. (3) In both laws men and women are induced to keep the commandments. In the old law the strongest motive is fear, e.g., the sanctions against a criminal such as exclusion from the Jewish people or execution; in the new law it is love because the Spirit poured into our hearts through faith in Christ moves us to fulfil the law spontaneously and joyfully and therefore without force or constraining us against our will.

12. The old law

St Thomas gave a remarkable answer to the question as to whether the old law was good. Yes! he says. But not because it is God's law or expresses his will, but because it accords with right reason. This conception runs through all of the types and conceptions of law. The new law does go beyond reason, transcending reason, integrating it into a larger plan and horizon without denying its integrity or autonomy. The old law was given to the people of Israel to prepare them for the coming of the Messiah. The revelation of the covenant on Sinai clearly manifests the ten commandments as the requirements of the covenant relationship with God for his elect people. The precepts of this revealed law contain the demands of the natural law which in fact bind the whole of humanity. It also contained precepts that are culturally specific to the Jewish people and their political state at that time. The old law contained many precepts but it was unified by the fact that they all were focused on charity as love of the God who had chosen them as his own and love of one another as belonging to his people. There are moral, ceremonial and juridic precepts. The ceremonial precepts concern worship of God which prefigure the person and redemption of Christ in the New Testament. This liturgy is a figure, a shadow of a person whose outline appears on the horizon, a sign pointing to what is yet to come. The juridic precepts concerned the social relationships between the Jews and formed the mechanisms for their casuistry. They are to be distinguished from the natural law as its determination and specification to their conditions of life. Now all the precepts of the old law pertain to the natural law, but this in three ways that specify three ways of progressively achieving more efficacious access to the natural law: (1) There are some precepts that every person should spontaneously and without difficulty recognise by reason as to be done or not to be done. Examples are the prohibition of killing and stealing which we say belong to the natural law absolutely. (2) There are other precepts that belong to natural law but can only be worked out by the wise and well educated after long consideration and reflection. An example would be that one should honour the aged, or the duty to care for the handicapped. (3) There are actions that belong to natural law which we only succeed in rightly assessing with the help of divine instruction. Examples are the prohibition of making images of the divinity and on taking God's name in vain. These are moral precepts because they belong to the virtue of religion which is a moral virtue for the performance and organising of worship as part of the normal life of society. This theory does not follow the hard distinction between religion and morality so as to privatise religion effectively by excluding it from all public political discussion. According to St Thomas the moral precepts of the old law are all reducible to the Decalogue. He says that the Decalogue was given directly by God to the people, whereas the other precepts were given through Moses as intermediary. This is something that is not always adverted to as it should be, namely, that the revelation of the Decalogue is given directly to each person by the very fact of his or her being created. Each person endowed with reason images his or her creator precisely through the light he has infused into their mind. It is in this light that we recognise the Decalogue as God's will for moral living. The Decalogue concerns those things about which we have knowledge in ourselves from God (*S.T.*, I-II, 100. 3). Some can be known straight away with little reflection and there are others which are known by divinely infused faith. He further says there are two kinds of precepts not contained in the Decalogue: those that concern first principles of natural law that are the basis from which the Decalogue is derived and so do not require human promulgation, and those that are in turn derived from the Decalogue and are so detailed as to be available only to the well educated and wise who should instruct the community in them.

There is a certain ambiguity and unclarity about the theology of the Old Testament because it remains unfinished, a venture awaiting its Saviour. On the one hand it enjoins and commands charity as the fullness of moral life. "You shall love the LORD your God with all your heart, and with all your soul, and with all your might" (Deut 6:5), and "you shall love your neighbour as yourself" (Lev 19:18). To fulfil this command would mean to be justified before God. To the question as to whether the oral and written precepts of the old law were efficacious in making the Jews right with God, St Thomas answers that they dispose to but cannot cause such justification which comes with grace. The law that communicates justification is the new law of grace in the Holy Spirit. The old law which came before Christ had the limited goal of preparing a people from which he could be born. "The end of the divine law is to bring people to that end which is everlasting happiness", and this, he adds, "cannot be done without the Holy Spirit" (*S.T.*, I-II, 98. 1).

13. "Lex Evangelii", the Gospel law

Perhaps the greatest breakthrough in moral theology this century was Bernard Häring's realisation that Christ himself is the one, the only one in whom Christian morality is set forth the way God wants it for all of humanity. Not only is he the model and thereby the norm and standard by which we should measure ourselves, he is also "life", for he alone fills us with divine life and gives us the strength and power to live unto God as we should. The Gospel calls us to live and be energised, divinised and live with and in Christ. The new law is precisely this *law of Christ* which became the formula for the reform of moral theology leading up to the Second Vatican Council. How did this law which is the Gospel enter the world and penetrate our hearts?

The Father has sent the Son and the Holy Spirit into the world so that they may be present in a way that goes beyond their presence here simply as divine. We can understand the Son and Spirit because the Father has sent them to be present to us as persons. The divine missions into the world are therefore necessary for us to grasp God as a Trinity of persons.

The Son came to us in the incarnation whereby Christ, the second person of the Trinity, was conceived in time. From the death of Christ on the Cross by which he redeemed the world the Spirit flowed from his pierced side out over the whole of humanity to cause the new creation. After the death of Christ the Spirit was sent as a power causing grace in those who believed in him. It is precisely this sending of the Spirit of the Father through Christ that brings about the transition from the old to the new law. "The New Law consists chiefly in the grace of the Holy Spirit, which is shown forth by faith working through love... People become recipients of this grace through God's Son become man, whose humanity was first filled with grace, and his grace then flowed forth to us" (*S.T.*, I-II, 108. 1).

Belonging to the new covenant is not just a matter of having lived after the coming of Christ but of giving a welcome to God's presence as grace in our hearts. There were saints among the pagans and in the Old Testament who because of their faith showed hospitality to Christ before they knew his name. They were "justified by faith in the Passion of Christ as we ourselves are" (*S.T.*, III, 62. 6). St Augustine and St Thomas both came to understand the Church's tradition through the prophet Jeremiah,

> The days are surely coming, says the LORD, when I will make a new covenant with the house of Israel and the house of Judah. It will not be like the covenant I made with their ancestors when I took them by the hand to bring them out of the land of Egypt – a covenant they broke, though I was their husband, says the LORD. But this is the covenant that I will make with the house of Israel after those days, says the LORD: I will put my law within them, and I will write it on their hearts; and I will be their God and they shall be my people. No longer shall they teach one another, or say to each other, "Know the LORD," for they shall all know me, from the least of them to the greatest, says the LORD; for I will forgive their iniquity, and remember their sin no more (Jer 31:31-34).

In the New Testament this passage is cited in the epistle to the Hebrews in the sense that since the coming of the Son and the Spirit people are able to love with God's own love and are not limited just to obeying him. St Augustine discovered in the same passage an answer to the self-sufficient morality of the Pelagians. In his master work *On the Spirit and the Letter* he shows how human and even Old Testament law remains at the level of exterior imposition. It can show up how we fail but it never gives us the strength to succeed in pleasing God. The New Testament law, by contrast, is that of the Spirit who has "instilled it in our hearts" so that it has its effect "not only by indicating to us what we should do, but also by helping us to accomplish it" (*S.T.*, I-II, 106. 1). For the Fathers of the Church and for its continuing tradition the new law represented the making of the perfect response to God our Father in the Son through the outpouring of their Spirit in our hearts. In this sense Christians are said to have virtue as strength given by God.

> Those who are possessed of virtue are inclined to do virtuous deeds through love of virtue, not on account of some extrinsic punishment or reward. Hence the New Law which derives its pre-eminence from the spiritual grace instilled into our hearts, is called *the Law of Love*.[3]

The perfect response to all God has done for us in creation and redemption is nothing other than to love him with our whole being. This has been made possible not only by what Jesus taught but also by what he did. What then is the content of this new law that enables our full and perfect response of love to God? The tradition of treating the new law as the basis of following Christ points out that the Christian religion is not a purely spiritual one. The new law is the law of faith, but faith works through charity and faith without works is dead, as St James has so clearly asserted. The contents of this law are not just external actions, but include the instructions given by Christ about our internal acts, attitudes and dispositions. The Kingdom of God with its basic law of freedom must find its appropriate external human expression.

Now the new law primarily consists in the grace of the Holy Spirit. But this grace comes through Christ, the incarnate Son of God. So it is not only appropriate but in a certain way a human necessity that the incarnational principle continue to act in our lives, the invisible being expressed in the visible. The new law concerns external actions in two ways. Firstly, with the sacraments through which we receive grace, and, secondly, with the good actions we do as a result of the grace we have received. So the content of the new law consists in the sacraments and in Christ's moral teaching. In both cases St Thomas refers to the practical requirements of the new law as "fides per dilectionem operans" (*S.T.*, I-II, 108.1). It is the inner life of faith, working through love, which, being the primary aspect of the new law, determines the secondary external aspect. This means that the whole external life of the Church in the world should be nothing else than her witnessing to charity as her very soul and animating principle. The new law is also called the *Lex libertatis*, the law of freedom, because it gives its possessor the power to decide for him or herself what to do about acts neither necessarily required nor prohibited by faith acting through love. There is another, more fundamental, reason for calling it the law of liberty. It is the Holy Spirit who activates our freedom by making us truly free to act from within ourselves. This is because the grace of the Holy Spirit so wonderfully harmonised our nature to his own action that the consequent act is our act through his energising, inspiring, drawing us to cry from our inner self, "Abba, Father, your will be done" (cf. Mk 14:36).

We receive grace through the sacraments and we make use of it in works of charity. The Church has enumerated baptism, confirmation, eucharist, penance, anointing of the sick, order, and marriage as the sacraments of the new law. Now these sacraments all go back to the mystery of Christ's pasch as their foundation. Now while they have to follow the express will of Christ where this is clearly Christ's intention, for example, regarding eucharist and baptism, there are many decisions about details, for example, the consecration of altars, the age of admission to the sacraments of initiation, which Christ left his disciples free to arrange for themselves.

We see here the necessity of canon law for the good order of ecclesial life.

St Thomas taught that the entire substance of the precepts of the new law is contained in the old law and that the moral teaching of the old law is still valid for Christians. This seems remarkable from two points of view. It allows little ground for a specifically Christian morality in terms of specifically Christian behavioural norms. And these same norms are not essentially different from those of Jewish morality. The new law gave more explicit teaching in matters of faith because they are beyond human understanding. But this is not so in matters of morality. All the moral precepts of the new law come under natural law and so are contained in the Decalogue.

Just as the Decalogue summed up the old law, so the Sermon on the Mount occupies a similar position in New Testament teaching as the core of Jesus' moral teaching. John P. Meier, commenting on Matthew's Gospel, calls the Sermon on the Mount the "charter of the Kingdom" and "the law of discipleship".[4] He points out that the saying of Jesus, "Everyone then who hears these words of mine and acts on them will be like a wise man who built his house on rock" (Mt 7:24), means that the disciple is to base his or her whole life on this discourse in particular. Father Bernard Häring identified in St Matthew's Beatitudes what he called the goal commandments of the Christian. These are not commandments as restrictions on freedom but openings to transcendence that show us how to share in divine life and so point us toward such goodness as will only be complete in God's final Kingdom. "Poor in spirit" means complete dependence and confidence in God to fill the existential emptiness of our lives with his gifts of goodness. "Those who mourn" experience repentance for their faults, turning to God for healing and not to self in self-pity. "Blessed the meek" is the capacity to grow gentle at God's approach and not resist his coming. "Those who hunger and thirst for righteousness" are those who know their desire for a new world order where every person will receive full human dignity can only be satisfied in God. "The merciful" are those whose forgiveness of enemies and help of the downtrodden are reflections of God's unlimited love. "The pure of heart" means a simplicity of vision that penetrates to the core of things to see them as God does. "The peacemakers" alone are called "the children of God" because they share God's *shalom* by harmonising the forces of creation into his plan and purpose. As it were they bring creation back to the family home in the Father's dwelling-place. Lastly, "those who are persecuted for righteousness' sake" are those who, having persevered through all sorts of tribulations for their faith in God, are assured that they belong to "the Kingdom of heaven". The Beatitudes are a full picture of Christian life in all its stages. They are blessings poured out by God that transform hearts of stone into hearts of flesh, that liberate us from our hard unfreedom for the liberty of the children of the Kingdom. The encyclical *Veritatis Splendor* used St Augustine's vision of the Beatitudes as the law of freedom to show that, when properly developed, morality is a spirituality since the movement of the Spirit harmonises everything genuinely human in our going to the eternal Father. Ultimately morality should become the work of grace leading to self-fulfilment in God.

NOTES

1. "L'elemento primario della legge naturale in S. Tommaso", in *La legge naturale*, (ed.) L. Lorenzetti, EDB, Bologna 1970, 109.
2. Louis Monden, *Sin, Liberty and Law*, Geoffrey Chapman, London 1966, 89.
3. Quoted in this way by Brian Davies, *The Thought of Thomas Aquinas*, Clarendon Press, Oxford 1992, 261.
4. *Matthew*, Veritas Publications, Dublin 1980, 38.

11

Christ the "pleroma" of the Kingdom

Once a person accepts the grace of the Holy Spirit he or she lives from charity according to the new law. The centre of the new law is the acceptance of Christ in faith which releases the Holy Spirit into every aspect of the life of the believer. In this chapter we shall consider the transformation operated by God through grace and how this is communicated through the Lordship of Christ over Church and world. Moral theology is a service to the truth that will only be fully revealed in the Kingdom. Key concepts in its elaboration are conversion to Christ and following after him in discipleship. All theology is therefore essentially christocentric. In our world the mission of the Church is to follow Christ in his *kenosis*, his emptying himself for the world's salvation.

1. The transformation operated by grace

A theme that has been missing from moral theology since the disintegration of St Thomas' synthesis and the more empiric concerns of the moral manuals has been that of grace. It was handed over to dogmatic theology as a matter of belief. It does come through faith, but what was tragic was that grace was lost to view as the principle of moral life, for without grace we cannot do good and please God. The word *charis* in Greek means favour, graciousness toward, to show goodness to. It means sharing what is most loved and precious in oneself with someone who does not have it. In the New Testament it means God's free giving, especially in the work of Christ and of the Gospel. It means God's action in us, leading us to union with himself. Now grace and the new law go together because the new law involves nothing less than God sharing himself, that is, what he has as God or his divine nature, with us the people he has chosen by predilection. Now this sharing is something that cannot be brought about by human capacities. It is not something open to human abilities. It can only be achieved with God's assistance and at his free initiative when he chooses to set our hearts aflame with the fire of his own passionate love for us. Christian theologians have always argued that the capacities we develop that make existence in this world full as far as it goes, the moral virtues as they are called, do not satisfy the desire for final meaning. We feel the need of something necessary but impossible to us through these capacities. In short, our happiness lies in God and not in any nor all the goods we can possess here and now. We need another kind of strength, the virtue it takes to possess God as a gift infused by God into our deepest being. "Our reason and our will by nature go out to God in that he is the cause and the end of nature... Yet this is not enough for them to reach out to him as the object of supernatural happiness."[1] By the theological virtues of faith, hope and charity we receive divine energy and the capacity to share in God's knowledge, his hope and confidence for us and all creation, and most of all in his own love for himself and so for us. Grace therefore is sharing and cooperating with God so that we transcend our capacities not by leaving them behind but by his raising them above themselves so that they become wonderfully capable of him. God has not only created us to be open to himself; he has also in his mercy filled the void that openness caused with the mystery of his own presence, his indwelling in the human person as in a sanctuary. Hence the respect we show to conscience as our place of encounter with the living God. Grace is also necessary because of sin. The existential condition of humanity gone off course and institutions forced to restrain human perversity are evidence of what the Church's tradition calls original sin. It is, as it were, handed down to the present generation which is born into it without being its originating cause though it communicates and furthers it through every actual sin. It is necessary for God then to intervene by his goodness to lift the shadow of "the mystery of iniquity" from the human race. "In the state of corrupt nature people fall short of what they could do by their nature so that they are unable to fulfil it by their own natural powers" (*S.T.*, I-II, 109. 2). If this seems a negative picture of humanity that cannot even get its natural powers to achieve their natural potential as they should, it is a partial impression, for grace has been given fully. Christ is God's final and absolute Word of love on the world. In Christ human nature has been remade. Grace is not just a help for us to do what we finally do on our own. Grace is totally a work of God, and human freedom is not something tolerated by God but is caused and brought to life in us by God. Grace does not just make things easier for us and soften the circumstances in which we battle to do good; it actually transforms us to be "new creatures" capable of true goodness.

2. The Lordship of Christ

The new creature is part of the new creation brought into being by Christ as Lord. The gift of grace of which I have spoken flows from Christ as head and leader of the new creation. No event in the life of Christ or of the Church has more significance than his resurrection. After the tragic death on the Cross to which his ministry led, God's raising of Jesus from the dead vindicated him as Lord, vindicated his life and ministry, and revealed that Jesus had in fact been sent by God, that he was "of God", that he was God's Servant. The resurrection of Christ was a revelation event that made Christ known to his disciples as the Messiah, "the anointed one", the awaited Saviour. St Paul centred the history of the world in the paschal mystery, in the passion, death and resurrection of Christ. The risen Lord was the new Adam, the source of the new humanity that was to be his body in the world with him being the principle of the Christian life. By his resurrection Christ assumed authority as head and leader not only of the Church but of the world as its principle of life unto God. Yves Congar produced two studies relevant to this very notion. They are "Christ, Invisible Leader of the Visible Church", and "The Lordship of Christ over the Church and the World".[2] The first thing to note is that by grace we enter the invisible sphere of

God, we are united to him. In the Church this mystery of grace is made incarnate and historically visible through the bodily union of Christians in the paschal body of Christ. Christians preserve union among themselves by being one with the sacrificed and risen Christ. This idea of body has taken on two senses even in Scripture. It can be used to apply the image of the body as an organism with the one life ensouled in head and members. "I am the vine, you are the branches" (Jn 15:5) is an assertion of mystical identity. In this sense the head is the highest, the most noble, the thinking and commanding part of the body. This image was often used to illustrate the social unity of all the citizens in a city state. But from the time of the captivity epistles St Paul had another insight into the significance of the body, based on the marriage image where there is unity of husband and wife without the two ceasing to be two separate persons. Here the husband is head because in the anthropology of the ancient world he had authority over his wife. This image and way of thinking is no longer acceptable. Nevertheless, St Paul extended it, maintaining that Christ is above the powers (Col 1:16) as their vanquisher (Col 2:15; Phil 2:9f.). "And he [the Father] has put all things under his feet and has made him the head over all things for the church, which is his body, the fullness of him who fills all in all" (Eph 1:22-23). Being above all, he is the summit of creation. As being the leader above he has all the evil powers under his feet. Congar points out that the Church is the reflection, image, representative and glory of her Lord. This being the head means he is first not just chronologically but ontologically as well. He is the first as the principle of creation, first-born from the dead by resurrection and cause of our resurrection. He is first in the order of creation, of redemption and of eschatology if we understand all the implications of what St Paul proclaims about Christ in Colossians 1:15-20. But he is also the End because in view of him creation was brought into being, the world was redeemed and the *eschata* will effect union with him when God is "all in all". Christ "thus constitutes something like a space within being, a reference both of origin and of finality, in relation to which it is possible to receive a new existence (*in Christo*...)."[3]

Recapitulation of all in Christ means that all is summed up in him, all is reduced to its essential elements and converges so as to be concentrated completely in him. In this sense everything that is good converges into him as its final realisation. This occurs in two modalities, as the furthest limit of all the capacities of the totality of creation, and as the positive element of salvation. The idea of *pleroma* or fullness involves the totality, a restoration to creation of its being according to God. This is the object of the divine plan, "the mystery of his will, according to his good pleasure that he set forth in Christ" (Eph 1:9), "the mystery" (Eph 3:3, 9), "the wisdom of God in its rich variety", "the eternal purpose that he has carried out in Christ Jesus" (Eph 3:10-11). Congar gives the following wonderful analysis: "The plan of divine wisdom is to restore to the world a being-according-to-God, through Christ, by making the whole dwell in Christ as in its summit, principle, and summing-up, as its summit-summary. The position of Christ, thus become filled by the whole, Paul calls *pleroma*."[4] From his fullness as principle he communicates his fullness to us and to the whole world. In this sense we can speak of a new ontology, a filial being by existing to God our Father. The person who is filled from Christ's fullness begins to participate in a redeemed world where all has been embraced by grace "so that you may be filled with all the fullness of God" (Eph 3:19). Christ is thus for Christians and for the world the principle of participation in the whole. Because of Christ the Church becomes his *pleroma*, his body of the whole, that is, of the new existence according to God that is possible for all things since Christ's resurrection. The Church therefore exists for the whole, *ta panta,* which by God's action in Christ through the Church can become the whole in which God dwells. In this process of being filled by God communicating his life and strength, persons become sons and daughters of God and creation his home with us. For the human person this identification is effected on the foundation of baptism, by the faith and love that constitute the Church. Christ is the One sent into the world by which God exercises his sovereignty of grace. He truly acts as God in regard to his creatures to bring everything to its final conclusion, in spite of sin, and so achieve the plan designed from eternity by his Father. "For us there is one God, the Father, from whom are all things, and for whom we exist, and one Lord, Jesus Christ, through whom are all things and through whom we exist" (1 Cor 8:6). Christ is in himself the coming of the *eschata*, the last times of fulfilment. He is the Lord of time who fashions history to the Father's design by closing the distance between the now of the present perishable world and the *parousia*, between the "already" and the "not yet", that is too great for us to imagine. He is the means whose service fills creation with the creative and saving presence of God "so that God may be all in all" (1 Cor 15: 28).

3. Christocentrism

Theology has traditionally understood the coming of God's final Kingdom as the completion and fulfilment of God's purpose in the incarnation. It is an event totally of God's making and initiative that closes the circle begun at creation. This, of course, corresponds to and confirms by fulfilment the philosophical notion of the mind returning to itself by reflection, *reditio completa*, of knowing itself in knowing reality, and even more in St Paul's terms for "then we will see face to face. Now I know only in part; then I will know fully, even as I have been fully known" (1 Cor 13:12). St Thomas, commenting on the famous passage of Ecclesiastes 1:7 which was thought to refer to the rivers of creation that returned to their source, said,

> It is the mystery of the Incarnation that is meant by this return of these rivers to their source... These rivers are in effect the natural goods with which God has filled his creatures, being, life, intelligence... and the source from which they flow is God... Now while they may be found spread throughout the whole of creation, these goods all meet together in the human person who is as it were the horizon within whose limits both corporeal and spiritual nature converge: being as it were at the interface of the spiritual and temporal the human being shares in both

spheres... It is for this reason that when human nature has once again been united to God through the mystery of the Incarnation, all the rivers of natural goodness returned to their origin (*Sent. III Prol.*, my translation).

This is the traditional explanation of the Christocentrism that should inform moral theology as a properly theological discipline. It should be pointed out that it in no way compromises the rightful autonomy of ethics nor the place of the basic natural goods in a theocentric vision of reality. It avoids the dangers of absorbing the natural order without trace into the supernatural order of redemption. The distinction of orders, of natural and supernatural, and of creation and redemption, are preserved without being at all confused. They are reconciled and brought into unity in a higher vision, the eschatological reality of God's *parousia*. We already share this reality through grace that makes us "new creatures" awaiting the time when we will live with God under a "new heaven" on a "new earth". We have become capable of acting according to our divine filiation through the infused divine gifts of faith, hope and charity. It should be pointed out that the proper character of Christian morality cannot be established merely by philosophical reflection or comparison of the concepts of Christian morality with those of secular ethics. This is a vain enterprise since Christian ethics is founded in a history of God's presence and intervention in the world. The content and power of the history of God's relation with the whole creation can only be understood in faith and interpreted by the same faith collaborating with reason to reflect on itself and return to the wonderful reality of whom we are as God's children in God's universe. Christian ethics and moral theology are impossible for any philosophy that looks to interpret them as an ideal schema outside history to be applied to pure nature as such. Moral theology is not an exercise of pure reason, but of reason immersed in history that on the basis of faith can discover the universal intent of God both in natural creation and in personal salvation worked by Christ in the Holy Spirit. In this process the human person has a unique role to play, a role which it is the mission of moral theology to reflect upon and in so far as possible explain. This role of the human person within the total unfolding of the universe till it all converges in God is well expressed by St Thomas. "The totality of the divine work comes to completion in a certain way, since the human person who was the last being to be created returns to its source in a circular movement because the Incarnation has rejoined it back to the very source from which everything flows" (*Compendium theol.* 201, my translation).

4. The domains of Christ's headship

In the epistles to the Colossians and the Ephesians St Paul delineates two domains over which Christ exercises Lordship as leader: firstly, everything, *ta panta* (Col 1:15-18; 2:10; Eph 3:3; 4:9); and, secondly, the Church (Col 1:18; Eph 1:22). Christ is the first-born of all creation (Col 1:15) but also the first-born from the dead (Col 1:18; 1 Cor 15:20). There are, as it were, two concentric circles or zones over which Christ is Lord and leader. One is absolutely universal in view of his creative power as God. It embraces everything created, even the angelic and cosmic powers which struggle against his reign even when they know their power is utterly broken but not yet finished. The other more restricted sphere is made up of those persons who accept the Gospel and is properly referred to as the Church as the body of Christ. The cosmos, the "everything", is not called the body of Christ but it comes under Christ as head in as much as he contains everything. He communicates meaning to it and subjects it to himself even when it resists him. The power of evil as sin and death has been defeated but the "mopping up" after the great cosmic battle at the Cross is still going on in the in-between time till the *parousia*. Those who accept Christ by faith submit to his Lordship in baptism and are joined to his paschal body in the Eucharist. The relationship between Christ and the Church is unique, going well beyond the idea of head over creation to show there is a personal relationship between Christ and his body.

This relationship for St Paul in the captivity epistles is not that between head and trunk that form the complete body. This was stressed by St Augustine in his conception of the *Christus totus, unus homo,* as the cause not so much of grace which belonged to God alone, but of his humanity through which Christ had authority over the Church and through which he communicated grace. St Paul's idea of the body was much more Semitic. It included the place or sphere of one's vital activity as well as the means of making manifest the action of a person. The body of Christ is that gathering of men and women in whom by the actions of faith, baptism and the Eucharist Christ effects what he had experienced once for all in the Cross and resurrection. He underwent the Passover experience of death and rising in his body on behalf of all. The Church then is the zone where Christ communicates to his disciples in the faith his own destiny of death and resurrection as the paschal mystery. The principle of the Church's life is Christ himself, dead and risen, but now hidden in God and available only to the eyes of faith. The Church is meant to be the image, reflection and glory manifesting her living Lord to a world that does not believe. It is precisely the communication of the paschal mystery to the faithful that makes the Church into the body of Christ.

The first result of this is that Christ possesses and exercises and is known by his followers to exercise complete authority over the Church. Not only does he communicate his life as interiority, but the external structure of the Church is also contained in the will of Christ and determined by his authority. In this sense what has been developed down the centuries by way of Church structure is the unfolding with the help of rational reflection and ingenuity of what was contained in the events of the paschal mystery. As the peak or summit of a cone contains all the lines that can extend out from it and be projected into space always in the same fundamental pattern, so Christ contains the future development in time of the Church. We should remember that we have constantly to strive for identity with Christ. The history of the Church has ample evidence of those who failed to live according to the holiness embodied in the Church. While the

Church is the sinless spouse of Christ, his members often fall short of their vocation as is so obvious in the violence, dishonesty and lust for power that have typified much of Christian history.

5. The ministry of moral theology in the Church

The paschal mystery is the source of the triple ministry of Christ as priest, king and prophet which is communicated to the Church as the ministries of sanctifying, governing and announcing the coming of the Kingdom at the end of time. Moral theology is the Church's service of Christ by proclaiming his evangelical morality of complete human fulfilment in the *parousia*. The Pope and bishops are formally charged with preserving and proclaiming the message of salvation in history. The Pope in particular enjoys the charism of infallibility when he formally defines truths of faith and morals under the conditions laid down by the First Vatican Council. The bishops in union with the Pope can also teach the faith in an infallible manner when they are united in repeating the same truth of faith consistently in history. These truths of faith may be defined as dogma. Similarly the faithful can also proclaim the faith infallibly through the *sensus fidelium* which could be confirmed in a formal definition by the magisterium. The moral teaching of the magisterium is of several types. A moral truth could be defined as being contained in Scripture, e.g., Pope John Paul II's declaration in *Evangelium Vitae* on the directly intentional killing of an innocent person. Other truths can be declared as true and unchangeably or irreformably so because they are drawn on the basis or foundation of Scripture, e.g., *Evangelium Vitae*'s teaching on abortion relies on Scripture. There are other truths, that are more remotely deduced from revealed truth, e.g., on euthanasia. These require a religious consent of mind and heart as the Conciliar Constitution on the Church *Lumen Gentium*, n. 25, provides. Scholars, when convinced that a position may be mistaken, are asked not to dissent from the Church's teaching authority so as not to disturb the life of the Church, but to continue their research so as to throw more light on the difficulty and when appropriate to bring the issue to the notice of the teaching authority itself. Moral theology is a ministry that shares in the teaching mission of Christ and the Church. As a kingly ministry it also provides a service to the world since it aims at implanting the criterion of Gospel love in the lives not only of individuals but of the whole community. The ideal of being *doers of the Word* applies not only to the life of the Church but to all the affairs of society. This service to the whole of humanity is emphasised in social ethics, which has become more pressing than ever before. The greatest achievement of moral theology is to bring forth sanctity and present an image of how the world we know can be united with God. It is for this reason that the Church honours as saints and Doctors the outstanding moral teachers who have illumined the pilgrim path of the faithful through history, especially St Augustine, St Thomas Aquinas and St Alphonsus de' Liguori. These have shown how Christ is the source of moral good and holiness for everyone, priest, laity and religious.

6. The Church is where Christ is acknowledged as Lord

Christ's authority over the Church is completely different from his power over the cosmos. He will constrain the powers of evil to submit to his Lordship. He also works through grace in an unseen and unacknowledged fashion in the world. But his relationship to the Church is personal; in her he is received with loving obedience. Christ cares for his Church with tenderness and generosity, even to sacrificing himself for her (Eph 5:21-33).

The Church on her part is assimilated and conformed to him so that she reflects the light on the face of Christ into the world. The world where rebellious forces still reign remains in darkness till illumined by the light of Christ. Christ as head is the principle of life and growth for the Church. "We must grow up in every way into him who is the head, into Christ, from whom the whole body, joined and knit together by every ligament with which it is equipped, as each part is working properly, promotes the body's growth in building itself up in love" (Eph 4:15-16). The heavenly glorified Christ is present in his Church to produce the holiness he hopes to find on his return. In this way the body receives an influx of divine life that leads it back to conform itself to Christ till it be completely united to him; it grows toward him, into his fullness.

Now if Christ is its standard of existence and norm of life, it follows that growth takes place according to the structures which he has set in place. Christ's action in the Church occurs in two manners that could be described in Max Scheler's terms as him being leader and pattern of existence. He acts in the whole body of humanity indeed by teaching or example, but also by vital influx and movement. This movement begins as a type of begetting, for baptism has been compared to a second birth in John 3:3 and Titus 3:5. The treasures of the covenant are communicated to us through our faith in Christ. This is the meaning of *ex opere operato*, namely, that God has guaranteed the structures of the covenant of grace for those who enter it freely with faith.

The Fathers of the Church and the best of subsequent theology have always insisted that every gift of grace made to humanity passes through the understanding and love of the God-man, that it is perfectly conformed and in agreement with the divine will, for, as St John repeats, the Son knows the Father and always does his will. This benevolence of God toward us is the basis for devotion to the humanity of Christ symbolised in the Sacred Heart. Biblically speaking, then, Christ is the absolute "Yes" to all God's promises (2 Cor 1:20). In him is concentrated the whole plan of God's salvation for the whole world. Yves Congar articulated this truth quite forcefully.

In a humanity which is like to ours in all respects, save sin, He is constituted leader not only over the Church of the redeemed, but over the world as well. He is filled, from God, with all the energy and perfection corresponding to this mission. Jesus himself has fully opened and offered his consciousness, His soul, His understanding, His will,

His heart, and finally His body, so as to be perfectly what God wanted Him to be, namely the minister and the leader of the world's salvation.[5]

The humanity of Christ with the grace of the hypostatic union and the limitations of human nature was always bent on "bringing many children to glory" (Heb 2:10).

As the God-man, Christ could introduce sinful humanity into the covenant of grace and cause it to grow into the Kingdom of God. God has filled us with every heavenly blessing "in Christ" (Eph 1:3). "In Christ" means Christ's causality in realising the design of grace. The "new creation" starts from Christ and it depends on him as its cause and principle. He is also in his humanness the means and instrument by which it happens. He is said to be seated in heaven at the right hand of his Father and from there he builds up his body. Baptism unites us to his sacrificed and risen body in heaven (Rom 6:3-11; Col 1:12; Eph 5:26-27). The ecclesial body of Christ is established on earth by means of physical bodily mediations that put our bodies, that is, our whole persons, into contact with the paschal body of Christ which thereby grows and increases in heaven for, "your life is hidden with Christ in God" (Col 3:3). The ecclesial body on earth grows toward the fullness of Christ in his paschal body in heaven. The Church functions on earth through sensible, visible signs, particularly the sacraments. Within the world's cosmic time the Church lives her own history of grace. She participates in her head's fullness which he gives her and communicates from heaven. This is truly the mission of the divine persons, of the Son and the Spirit into the world to confer holiness. The whole of salvation history is, in the words of the Creed, "for us and for our salvation". God gives his gifts in response to the needs of the world, especially new developments and advances in human history. It is precisely from these divine initiatives that we perceive through faith the "signs of the times" as manifestations of God's presence and concern for our welfare in the world.

Christ is the invisible head of the visible Church. We speak of him being invisible in biblical terms, that is, in reference to the New Testament God who is the Father as the source of the communication of the divinity. Christ is his image (Col 1:15), the one in whom and by whom he is manifested (Jn 1:18), so as to bring about a creation different from the present one marked by sin by introducing us into the final "eon", the time of salvation. We already have the Spirit as the pledge of God's final victory when our entire being will be transformed. Christ by his resurrection has become "life-giving-Spirit" whose action still has to be received by carnal humans, that is, persons who still belong to this creation prone to ignorance, weakness and error. The Church, then, in her members is not immune to temptation, to the seduction of power and self-seeking. The Spirit does assure the Church as the spouse of Christ that she will be indefectible in holiness. Nevertheless, she has to exist in a darkened world where her individual members are not unaffected by evil and must therefore ever open themselves to conversion. Hence St Paul's warnings to the community in Corinth. When we think of the Church as a moral person it is true that she enjoys mystical union with Christ and we may think of them as one body. But it is also true that the faithful who make up the Church are individual persons who must respond freely to grace and that therefore they do not always by any means live up to their ideal type. What is done by the Church is not always adequate or up to the measure of what is done by Christ. In this way wickedness may be found in the Church through the sins of her members. Up till the *parousia* a tension, even a duality, will always exist between the present state of the Church in a sinful world and the spotless spouse in her heavenly existence. There is an ongoing struggle to preserve the spirit of Christ down the centuries, a struggle witnessed to in the reform movements that strive to bring the all too human side of the Church back to her ideal image, to Christ and his Gospel as her norm of life. We can say then that while Christ is a transcendent principle, the Church is a defined and socially organised organism here on earth. The field of Christ's influence and of the Church's activity will converge eschatologically when the visible and the invisible coalesce. The ultimate point of reference for the relations of

Christ and the Church is therefore eschatological, God's final Kingdom.

7. The Kingdom

There are a variety of scriptural images that focus on the same realities but in different ways. The Lordship of Christ as head of cosmos and Church is one. "Jesus is *Kyrios*" is the earliest formula of faith in the Christian community. Another equally venerable image connected to the preaching of Christ himself is that of the Kingdom, the Reign of God that has broken into the world in the person of Christ. Like the sovereignty of God over his creation and his people, it too underwent long maturation in the Jewish history. Jesus shared the hopes of Israel as a messianic people, as is indicated in the Lord's Prayer, "Your kingdom come, your will be done, on earth as it is in heaven" (Mt 6:10). The entire Gospel message of Jesus is summarised in Mark's beginning of Jesus' ministry, "The time is fulfilled, and the kingdom of God has come near; repent, and believe in the good news" (Mk 1:15). This saying has a number of elements that are important as a starting-point for Christian morality. First, the time of salvation has arrived. This means that God's grace is already victorious over the power of darkness, that sin is no longer the controlling force of history. It means in a very real sense that time has come to an end in so far as it has reached its term in Christ who is God's final Word on the world. God has fulfilled all his promises. The Messiah has arrived and the final age of the world has been initiated. All subsequent history is catching up with this reality and coming to terms with the Son of God who has visited his people. Secondly, the Kingdom of God is so close to us, we only have to put out our hand to take hold of it. In other words God has made himself personally present to us, he has put himself totally at our disposition though he be Ruler of the world and Lord of the chosen people. This means that Christ has become a challenge of which the chosen people could not remain in ignorance. His presence demands a response, a decisive choice, "Yes" or

"No", for or against the Messiah, belief or unbelief. Thirdly, "Repent" is what a sincere believer does when he acknowledges his Lord. It is not remorse, the acknowledgement of having strayed. That is negative and paralysing. It is the actual turning around, the change of direction in one's life that is effected when one hears a cry of alarm, a shout that catches one's attention, or when a herald proclaims a public message. Repentance is our response to Christ as the Father's herald publicly announcing to the whole universe the time of God's graciousness. Under those circumstances it is not hard to leave behind a godless existence to embrace God in the confidence of faith. By faith the Kingdom of God breaks into the human heart as salvation. The Christian message is "good news". It announces a divine act of healing, reconciliation, forgiveness, of God reaching out to the powerless, of his raising up those without hope and of transforming not only the heart by inward grace but the whole of creation in all its woundedness through its being "subject to futility" (Rom 8:20). The "good news" responds to our wildest dreams for the universe "that the creation itself will be set free from its bondage to decay and will obtain the freedom of the glory of the children of God" (Rom 8:21). The Gospel of the Kingdom therefore arrives as an absolute demand on human freedom: it is God's last, final, complete and unconditional giving of himself. The response must be equally complete and absolute, the commitment of our lives into his hands by faith. The coming of the Kingdom is also an implicit threat, for if it is denied it means that God's absolute love has been lost, even forever. That would be the ultimate work of the powers of darkness.

There are two key moral terms that arise out of the proclamation of the Kingdom. Both of them define specifically Christian characteristics of morality. They are repentance as *metanoia* and discipleship as the *sequela Christi*.

7.1 Conversion

What is this repentance? It is not mere change of behaviour, going down a different road. Indeed, the Greek *metanoia* usually means a change of mind. To the Hebrew it meant turning away from one's former consciousness, now recognised as wrong, and setting out in a new direction. Therefore, conversion or repentance is not just sorrow for sin but a fundamental reorganisation of one's whole life. Christ demanded that his hearers not only repent but believe in the Gospel of forgiveness that he preached (Mk 2:10, 17). He drove his point home with various parables, particularly that of the prodigal son in Luke 15, which should better be called the divinely prodigal Father in his absolutely unconditional forgiveness. He compared conversion to becoming like a little child (Mt 18:3). St Paul describes it as putting on a new self, as being "dead to sin and alive to God" (Rom 6:11). Conversion is essentially that movement from being dead in sin to being alive in God, the transference from the kingdom of darkness to the Kingdom of God's life, truth and light. Now it is only God who can forgive sin. Therefore the power to move from death to life, from darkness to light, is from God as his own personal gift. This gift is called justification, it is totally God's doing and it comes by faith. The first result of God's action is that the Trinity itself comes to make its home in the human heart. We become temples of the Holy Spirit and our consciences sanctuaries where the living God is worshipped. Nicodemus was warned, "No one can see the kingdom of God without being born from above" (Jn 3:3). The second result is that we are empowered to act as God's own children, as citizens of the Kingdom. This involves the exercise of human freedom, a confirmation of our dependence on God in every decision made. This means that conversion is not just a one-off occurrence; it is happening in every positive decision we make. It is permanent and continuous because we are aware of our spiritual poverty and need of God. The antithesis of a repentant heart is an attitude of self-righteousness and presumption. Jesus repudiates the proud Pharisee (Lk 18:10-14), the elder brother who resents his father's benevolence to the prodigal on his return (Lk 15:25-30), and the discontented labourers in the vineyard (Mt 20:1-15). To those who set themselves proudly above others, Jesus declared that harlots and publicans would enter the

Kingdom before them (Mt 21:31-32). He condemned them for trying to shut the doors of the Kingdom (Mt 23:13). All of us, he warned, are unprofitable servants (Lk 17:10), ever in God's debt (Mt 6:12). God will exalt the humble and bring down the proud (Lk 14:11). Each must pray that God will forgive his or her trespasses. And whoever is without sin should cast the first stone (Jn 8:7). The early Church would continue this message, "Repent, and be baptised every one of you in the name of Jesus Christ so that your sins may be forgiven; and you will receive the gift of the Holy Spirit" (Acts 2:38). The sacraments are all directed to conversion, to a life-long process of turning to God till he be "all in all".

Bernard Häring summed up the radicalness of conversion and explained the divine power that brings it about with this simple formula that re-echoes the strength of Catholic belief and tradition. "The powerful and urgent invitation to conversion proceeds from the coming of the Kingdom of God."[6]

7.2 Discipleship

The second effect of God's Kingdom breaking into the world calling persons to conversion is that they become disciples of Christ. In the New Testament discipleship refers to those who have accepted Jesus as their master. Unlike the followers of the rabbis who sought out a master and then had to, as it were, pass an entrance exam, the disciples of Jesus are sought out and called by Jesus himself. "Come, follow me" is Jesus's call. "And immediately they left their nets and followed him" (Mk 1:18). Jesus called his disciples together without any regard to their educational qualification or background. Not only does he call the tax collector Levi to discipleship, but he also calls women who serve him and remain with him to the end. Unlike the rabbis who welcomed students as long as they had something to say to them, Jesus chooses his disciples on the basis of faith in who he is. Faith is the animating force in the relationship between Jesus and his disciples, not the knowledge that gives a teacher authority. For his disciples, then, Christ is master and teacher because he is Lord.

The disciple is a witness to the person of Christ. For that reason Jesus' disciples always remain attached to him. To follow him is to cut all ties with the past in a total act of conversion (Lk 5:11), to give up one's family (Lk 14:26), and to take up the Cross and to share in the very destiny of their master (Mk 8:34). They are to be associated with the poor, the sick, the dispossessed, the outcast, the handicapped and deformed (Lk 4:18-19), and they are to love even their enemies (Lk 6:27-28). The following of Christ means they conform their lives to his instruction. They begin to live in the last days of God's salvation while still immersed in a world subject to the power of sin. Finally, being a disciple means receiving a mission to go into the whole world to call it to conversion in Christ and to call all races, nations and tongues into his Kingdom. Discipleship links conversion as the event of the Kingdom breaking into a person's life and that person being commissioned to call others to share Christ's destiny. Every conversion and every vocation is therefore essentially missionary. And this quality applies to the Church herself, as the Second Vatican Council taught. After the resurrection of Christ discipleship was expressed as imitation of Christ. This was not external conformity but a finding of the will of the Father within the human mind and heart. "Let the same mind be in you that was in Christ" (Phil 2:5). It means a willingness to undergo *kenosis*, that is, to empty oneself so as to be filled and glorified by God as Christ was in his paschal mystery. Devotion to the person and passion of Christ led historically to the *imitatio Christi* as an individual form of piety. But the Scripture does not concentrate on the past, but on the future. "Beloved, we are God's children now; what we will be has not yet been revealed. What we know is this: when he is revealed, we will be like him, for we will see him as he is" (1 Jn 3:2). To imitate Christ means searching by faith to discern how he is actively working to bring about his final Kingdom even here and now. To respond to the call of Jesus with faith is the first meaningful and faithful act of a Christian life. Contemporary theological reflection therefore sees the call-response model of theology being fulfilled in a life of discipleship, of faithful following of the Lord of history. In this way the disciple of

Christ in the community of disciples has become a theme of deep theological significance and the point of reference for the dialogue between faith and culture, economics and politics etc.

7.3 Social ethics

God's Kingdom, according to the New Testament, is first of all eschatological. It pertains to the last day when God breaks into human history and brings about a new heaven and earth. But it is also an essential of Christian faith that in the teaching, healing and the whole ministry of Jesus Christ, especially his resurrection, the Kingdom has already been made present. The Synoptic apocalypses (Mk 13; Mt 24-25; Lk 17 and 21) give a very detailed picturesque account of the inauguration of the Kingdom on the last day. Some elements do appear essential: resurrection from the dead, final judgement, rewards and punishments, and life in God's Kingdom.

What Christians are expected to do in the present can be discerned by looking critically at what identifies God's Kingdom. One strand that runs through Christian history has been a spiritualising, individualistic reading of Luke 17:21 as saying, "The Kingdom of God is within you." Exegetes reject this reading today, preferring to render it as "among you" or "in your midst". These reflect the social nature of God's Kingdom even in the present. God's future Kingdom provides the horizon and goal for action in the present. But it remains always God's prerogative to bring it about in its fullness. We do not bring it about nor do we build it up. The furthest the New Testament goes is to say, in 2 Peter 3:12, "waiting for and hastening the coming of the day of God". We can look forward to, prepare for and remove obstacles to, but we cannot effect that transcendent divine intervention when God's fullness will be manifest and unveiled before us. The biblical writers do not identify God's Kingdom with any earthly empire. In fact Jesus was executed as a political rebel, as "the King of the Jews", at the hands of Pilate, the Roman governor, and the Jewish leaders. St Paul counselled cooperation with the imperial power. The Apocalypse of John criticised the same empire for abusing religious principles by idolatry. The early Christians did not aspire to construct a political order of Christian principles. They had no social teaching as such, but looking to the Kingdom they conceived of Christian life in a social context. From the demands of the Kingdom they discovered doctrines that could be applied with social consequences, e.g., concern for the poor, loving enemies, forgiveness, and criticism of excess wealth.

The Kingdom of God is related to the Church but should not be confusedly identified with it. Daniel Harrington says, "The kingdom of God presupposes a community of faith in which those who already recognise and act on God's sovereignty dwell. The church is made up of those who aspire to the fullness of God's kingdom."[7] Such people have been gathered by the Spirit who leads them in Christ's name. The Church, then, is a sign of God's definitive reign. Modern biblical research has restored the Kingdom of God as the horizon and goal of Christian social ethics. Christ's resurrection, then, is the most brilliantly illumining anticipation of the reality of the Kingdom, when the fullness of Christ has spread to the whole creation. Hope has become the key to understanding both the unfolding of history and its final goal in the Kingdom. The prayer, "Your will be done, on earth as it is in heaven", helps in the formulation and the practice of a social ethic that has to bridge the tension between the "already" and "not yet" of God's Kingdom.

The American Catholic bishops' pastoral letters *The Challenge of Peace* (1983) and *Economic Justice for All* (1986) express the biblical vision of how eschatology impinges on social action.

> The fullness of eschatological peace remains before us in hope, and yet the gift of peace is already ours in the reconciliation effected in Jesus Christ... Because we have been gifted with God's peace in the risen Christ, we are called to our own peace and to the making of peace in our world (CP 55).

Christian social ethics has to find a balance between future hope and present responsibility by reflecting on the demands of faith and love in the present condition of society.

> Although the ultimate realisation of God's plan lies in the future, Christians in union with all people of good will are summoned to shape history in the image of God's creative design and in response to the reign of God proclaimed and embodied in Jesus (EJA 53).

8. Christ's sovereignty over the world

The mission of the Church in the world has really been the principal concern for theology since the Council. This mission has its reference-point in the Kingdom but it is also related to and makes the community of faith, the body of the disciples of Christ in history, present to that history in its secular reality. Since the resurrection of Christ there is no reality that is not sacred to God. All is "in Christ". But still "in Christ" there are two spheres, Church and world, that can be distinguished on the basis of how they relate to the transcendent Kingdom of God. Before God established his covenant with his people he had a plan for the world from creation. He already saw it recapitulated, filled with his fullness in Christ (1 Cor 8:6; Col 1:12-20). Now redemption embraces this plan and brings it into the order of redemption.

The *eschata* therefore mean perfect monotheism for everything belongs to God. Things are good only when they correspond to the creative Word of God, when they realise his will and plan. That is why St James pushed home the message to his community, "Be doers of the word, and not merely hearers" (Jas 1:22). How then is God's creative and redeeming Word realised in the world, or, if you will, in the secular sphere?

The redemption effected by Christ's Pasch transforms the world which exists outside the sphere of the Church as an organised social body. The Pasch fulfils not only God's covenant with his people but also his plan for creation. In spite of sin and even in the conditions of sin, Jesus Christ has put back into the world the energy and dynamism that will allow creation to arrive at the end first willed, the fullness of the Kingdom. That is why created wisdom becomes the wisdom of the Cross (1 Cor 1:18-25). This in fact is the key to understanding Christ's presence and action in the world and to secular reality. The relationship between Church and world is not that between the two power blocks of Church and State as in the Middle Ages. The Church does not claim hegemony over culture as she did then. But this does not mean that she is neutral or indifferent to culture. She cannot be, for she is not indifferent to people's salvation, their belonging and entering into the Kingdom of grace. Nor is the Church's attitude one of hostility, as when she protested last century against the anticlericals' encroachment on her socially organised life of faith because they were denying her freedom of religious practice and expression. These are now usually recognised as rights for all in the constitutions of secular States.

The cosmic value of the redemption means that the created order has its own existence, its own goodness, and along with that a fundamental drive and aptitude to return to God once a way is opened and given to it by the eternal Word, God's Wisdom, through whom all things exist. The work of grace in creation is to remove its being "subjected to futility" and to free it from its "bondage to decay" (Rom 8:20-21). The Kingdom will be the healing of wounds, the reintegration of diminished and mutilated being, the remaking of distorted human likeness to God. It will be the victory over illness, ignorance and finally death itself (1 Cor 15:26, 54). It will be the reconciliation, peace and communion that overcomes all opposition, tension and superficial exteriority of worldly life. The Kingdom will therefore unite two realities now separated, the Church and the world, the order of creation and the order of redemption. When the human community of nations finally becomes the communion of saints, then God's Kingdom has come as the *parousia* and his plan has been perfectly fulfilled. The Church is a sign to the world of this ultimate Kingdom reality. Without the liturgy celebrating the presence of the great High Priest to his people, without the sacraments transforming life's events into occasions of salvation history, without the preaching of the Church to proclaim the truth of Christ, without the visible presence of the mystery of salvation, the world would remain in darkness about her ultimate destiny with God. The Church is "an instrument for the redemption of all" (*Lumen Gentium*, n. 9). The Church is therefore necessary for the mediation of salvation to the whole race. How this can happen in the case of each individual person is often a deep mystery of faith to us. The mission of the Church is therefore essentially religious, that is, to relate all reality including that of the world to God and bring it into the realisation of his ultimate purposes. "Christ did not bequeath to the Church a mission in the political, economic, or social order: the purpose he assigned to it was a religious one" (*Gaudium et Spes*, n. 42). But the light of the Gospel preached by the Church penetrates secular realities as well. The mission of the Church in the world is summed up in this passage: "In pursuing its own salvific purpose not only does the Church communicate divine life to men but in a certain sense it casts the reflected light of that divine life over all the earth, notably in the way it heals and elevates the dignity of the human person, in the way it consolidates society, and endows the daily activity of men with a deeper sense and meaning" (*Gaudium et Spes*, n. 40). The Council invokes a metaphor used in the Scriptures to explain the relationship between Church and world. The Church "is to be a leaven and, as it were, the soul of human society in its renewal by Christ and transformation into the family of God". The Council refers to God's law as the point of reference for the renewal of the social order. The Church, reflecting on her own proper mission, sees the social order from the point of view of God's eternal law. "But this religious mission can be the source of commitment, direction and vigour to establish and consolidate the community of men according to the law of God" (*Gaudium et Spes*, n. 42). The Gospel therefore proves to be a leaven of brotherhood, unity and peace in the world. In the Decree on the Laity, n. 5, the Church's mission in its full range may be said then to include not only the directly religious apostolate but also the penetration of the temporal order with the spirit of the Gospel. This is the function the Church has in the world and for the world in the latter's own structures and activities, but leaving the world as world in its own order.

The Church exists in the structures of the world and she experiences all the ambiguity of human affairs. She renders a service to the world by explaining what is truly human in the light of Christ, revealing humanity to itself as it exists in the plan of God.

The Church in obedience to the voice of Christ can never be absolved from humble service of the world in its needs. The Church's aim, like that of its Divine Master, is to serve and not to be served. She seeks to liberate and not to dominate, to give rather than to take. The Church's mission in the world is not exercised through an established public authority that can impose its law. This is her directly religious mission *ad intra*, that is, in the zone of the public authority over the celebration of the sacraments, the preaching of the Word and the community of love among believers. Her mission in the world is exercised in the domain of consciences and of human freedom so that humanity may listen to the truth, as Christ said to Pilate (Jn 18:37). "The Church is the sphere of Christ's domain where his lordship is recognised and obeyed. The world is the sphere where this lordship is ignored or opposed."[8] The world, therefore, taken in its own right and autonomy, proceeds without any explicit reference to Christ. What results is a great ambiguity in the very definition of the world itself. It can mean the world of God's creation in all its goodness. It can mean the rightful autonomy of the whole terrestrial sphere in contrast to the heavenly reality brought by Christ. It can mean the cosmos as redeemed by Christ. And, finally, it often means all or any of these as they have been set in contradiction with Christ's Lordship. Things that were made in harmony are often found in discord in the world. Sin thus takes God away from the world. It is the battle between the Kingdom of darkness or sin and the Kingdom of God that makes the reality of the world so ambiguous even to the eyes of faith. Christ has already won the victory, but we still wait for him to impose his reign over the total range of creation. He can be said to reign *in* and *over* the Church; he reigns *in* the creation but he is not seen to have any established authority *over* it. He is present to the whole creation, but he is there as yet hidden in grace. As Congar says, "The earthly Kingdom of Christ is still 'occupied' by the enemy."[9] God reigns in humanity through the genuinely and integrally human use we make of the world.

The presence of Christ to the world from Pentecost to the *Parousia* is that of the Suffering Servant of God in service of humanity; his action is that of *kenosis*, the outpouring and emptying of himself with all the love he displayed on the Cross. The standard for the Church's service of the world is given in Christ himself:

> who, though he was in the form of God,
> did not regard equality with God
> as something to be exploited,
> but emptied himself,
> taking the form of a slave,
> being born in human likeness.
> And being found in human form,
> he humbled himself
> and became obedient to the point of death –
> even death on a cross (Phil 2:6-8).

NOTES

1. Cited by Brian Davis, *The Thought of Thomas Aquinas*, Clarendon Press, Oxford 1992, 264.
2. See his *Jesus Christ,* Herder and Herder, New York 1966, 131-166 and 167-223.
3. Ibid., 136.
4. Ibid., 138.
5. Ibid., 151.
6. *This Time of Salvation*, Herder and Herder, New York 1966, 219.
7. "Kingdom of God" in the *New Dictionary of Social Thought*, (ed.) Judith A. Dwyer, Liturgical Press, Collegeville, Minnesota 1994, 512-513.
8. Congar, op. cit., 183.
9. Ibid., 185.

Conclusion

Doers of the Word has proposed a unified vision of human action. Its first concern was to show how we can make sense of human action in the universe we inhabit. Indeed, its thesis has been that it is precisely personal action that makes us dwell in this world, makes us belong to it by participating in its structures so that it belongs to us as our home. Action incarnates our meaning in reality. Theology that reflectively penetrates God's Word is fine. Theology that transforms the person, making him or her an agent of grace and goodness, achieves its complete role of being theoretical explanation that becomes practical realisation. Theology that is genuine changes not just our thinking but ourselves. The deepest change is conversion worked only by God when he calls us to be disciples of the Kingdom.

The conception of the Christian as a *doer of the Word* is essentially eschatological. It means living by the values of Christ as Lord and Master.

The first Word of God that penetrates our silence is the creating Word that makes us his image. We are persons like him who can communicate with him in love and partnership. It is he who inserted us into the human family so that we could have a destiny of happiness with himself. The truth of the person is confirmed by the history of salvation, by the Church's teaching and living tradition of holiness throughout the ages. The Gospel has penetrated human action with new meaning in Christ. The conscience of the true Christian is a redeemed heart, a sanctuary for adoration of the Father. There the Spirit teaches the perfect law of love within. There the believer becomes part of the new creation under the Lordship of Christ. This is, in brief, an outline sketch of the portrait of the *doer of the Word* described in this volume.

Bibliography

NOTE: This bibliography is divided into two parts. The first gives an overview of manuals and reference works in moral theology. The second provides material to fill out the arguments treated under the chapter headings in this volume.

PART I

SPECIALISED REVIEWS IN MORAL THEOLOGY

Journal of Christian Ethics, Georgetown University, Washington, D.C.
Moralia, Instituto Superiore de Ciencias Morales, Madrid.
Rivista di Teologia Morale, Dehoniane, Bologna.
Studia Moralia, Accademia Alfonsiana, Rome.
Studies in Christian Ethics, T & T Clark, Edinburgh.
Supplément, Le: Revue d'éthique et de théologie morale, Cerf, Paris.
Zeitschrift für evangelische Ethik, Gütersloher Verlagshaus, Gütersloh.

The following two reviews provide important information on current literature in moral theology each year.
Ephremerides Theologiae Lovanienses, University of Louvain, Louvain.
Theological Studies, "Notes on Moral Theology", Theological Studies Inc., Washington, D.C.

DICTIONARIES AND REFERENCE WORKS

Becker, L.C. (ed.), Becker, C.B. (assoc. ed.), *Encyclopedia of Ethics*, (2 Vols.), Garland Publishing Inc., New York and London 1992.
Bondandi, Alberto, "Panorama sui manuali di teologia morale fondamentale in Italia (1970-1984)", in *La Scuola Cattolica*, CXV (1987) 5-6, 449-494.

"Allargando il panorama sui manuali di teologia fondamentale (1970-1987)", in *La Scuola Cattolica*, cxvii (1989) 1, 27-76.

"Manuali di teologia morale fondamentale (1987-1994)", in *La Scuola Cattolica*, cxxiii (1995) 1, 91-134.

Brugès, J.-L., *Dictionnaire de Morale Catholique*, C.L.D., Chambray-les-Tours 1991.

Childress, J., Macquarrie, J. (eds.), *The Westminster Dictionary of Christian Ethics*, Philadelphia 1986.

Compagnoni, F., Piana, G., Privitera, S. (eds.), *Nuovo Dizionario di Teologia Morale*, Edizioni San Paolo, Cinisello Balsamo (MI) 1990.

Curran, Charles E., and McCormick, Richard A., S.J., (eds.), *Readings in Moral Theology*, Vols. 1-8, Paulist Press, New York 1979-1993.

Goffi, Tullo, *Problemi e prospettive di teologia morale*, Queriniana, Brescia 1976.

Höffe, (ed.), *Dictionnaire de Moral*, Editions Universitaires, Fribourg 1983.

Lexikon der Ethik, C.H. Beck, München 1980.

Lorizio, G., Galantino, N. (eds.), *Metodologia teologica: Avviamento allo studio e alla ricerca pluridisciplinari*, Edizioni San Paolo, Cinisello Balsamo (MI) 1994; (Moral Theology 359-381).

Macquarrie, J., *A Dictionary of Christian Ethics*, SCM, London 1967.

May, William E., (ed.), *Principles of Catholic Moral Life*, Franciscan Herald Press, Chicago 1981.

Ramsey, Ian T., *Christian Ethics and Contemporary Philosophy*, SCM, London 1973.

Rossi, L., Valsecchi, A. (eds.), *Dizionario Enciclopedico di Teologia Morale*, Edizioni Paoline, Rome 1973.

Supplemento della IV edizione, Edizioni Paoline, Rome 1976.

Rotter H., Virth, G. (eds.), *Neues Lexikon der christlichen Moral*, Tyrolia, Innsbruck-Wien 1990.

Spaemann, Robert, *Basic Moral Concepts*, Routledge, London and New York 1989.

Stoerkle, B. (ed.), *A Concise Dictionary of Christian Ethics*, Seabury Press, New York 1979.

Thévenot, Xavier, "Théologie et agir moral", in *Introduction à l'étude de la théologie 2*, Joseph Doré (ed.), Desclée, Paris 1992, 604-618.

Vidal, M. (ed.), *Conceptos Fundamentales de Etica Teológica*, Editorial Trotta, Madrid 1992.

Diccionario de Etica Teológica, Editorial Verbo Divino, Navarra 1991.

Valori, Paolo, *L'esperienza morale: Saggio di una fondazione fenomenologica dell'etica*, Morcelliana, Brescia 1971.

Wils, Jean-Pierre; Mieth, Ditmar, *Grundbegriffe der christlichen Ethik*, Schöningh, Paderborn 1992.

MORAL THEOLOGY: MANUALS AND GENERAL WORKS

Aubert, Jean-Marie, *Abrégé de la morale catholique: la foi vécue*, Desclée, Paris 1987.

Caffarra, C., *Viventi in Cristo*, Jaca Book, Milan 1981.

Caffarra, Carlo, *et al.*, *Persona, verità e morale*, Città Nuova, Rome 1987.

Chapelle, A., *Les fondaments de l'éthique: la symbolique de l'action*, Éditions de l'Institute d'Études Théologiques, Bruxelles 1988.

Chiavacci, Enrico, *Teologia Morale*, (3 Vols.), Cittadella, Assisi 1980.

Demmer, K., *Deuten und Handeln; Grundlagen und Grundfragen der Fundamentalmoral*, Herder, Freiburg 1985.
Moraltheologische Methodlehre, Herder, Freiburg 1989.
Introduzione alla teologia morale, Piemme, Casale Monferrato (AL) 1993.

Ernst, W. (ed.), *Grundlagen und Probleme der heutigen Moraltheologie*, Echter, Würzburg 1989.

Furger, Franz, *Kinführung in die Moraltheologie*, Wissenschaftliche Buckgesellschaft, Darmsdadt 1988.

Gatti, G., *Temi di Morale Fondamentale*, Elle Di Ci, Leumann, Turin 1988.

Gula, Richard M., *Reason informed by Faith: Foundations of Catholic Morality*, Paulist Press, New York 1989.

Gustafson, James M., *Theology and Ethics*, Basil Blackwell, Oxford 1981.

Guzzetti, G.B., *Morale Generale*, Elle Di Ci, Leumann, Turin 1990.

Haro, Ramón García De, *La vida cristiana: curso de teologia moral fundamental*, Ediciones Universidad de Navarra, Pamplona 1992.

Hauerwas, Stanley, *The Peaceable Kingdom*, SCM, London 1984.

Lobo, George V., *Moral Theology Today: Christian Living according to Vatican II*, Theological Publications, Bangalore 1982.

May, William E., *An Introduction to Moral Theology*, Our Sunday Visitor Press, Huntington 1991.

Moser, Antonio; Leers, Bernardino, *Moral Theology: Dead Ends and Alternatives*, Orbis, New York 1990.

O'Connell, Timothy, *Principles for a Catholic Morality*, Seabury, New York 1978. Revised edition, Harper and Row, San Francisco 1990.

O'Donovan, Oliver, *Resurrection and Moral Order: An Outline for Evangelical Ethics*, Inter-Varsity Press, Leicester 1986.

Pinckaers, Servais, *Les sources de la morale chrétienne: sa méthode, son contenu, son histoire*, Éditions Universitaires Fribourg Suisse, Fribourg 1985.

La morale catholique, Cerf, Paris 1991.

Le renouveau de la morale, Casterman, Tournai 1964.

Privitera, S., *Il volto morale dell'uomo*, Palermo 1992.

Simon, René, *Fonder la morale: Dialectique de la foi et de la raison pratique*, Seuil, Paris 1974.

Tettamanzi, D., *Temi di morale fondamentale*, OR, Milan 1975.

Vidal, M., *Manuale di Etica Teologica I: Morale Fondamentale*, Cittadella, Assisi 1994 (translation from the Spanish original).

Weber, H., *Allgemeine Moraltheologie: Ruf und Antwort*, Styria, Gratz-Wien-Köln 1991.

FESTSCHRIFTS

Boelaars, H., C.Ss.R., Tremblay, Real, C.Ss.R., *In libertatem vocati estis*, EDACALF, Rome 1977 (in honour of B. Häring, C.Ss.R.).

Curran, Charles E., *Challenge for the Future: Essays in Honour of R.A. McCormick*, Paulist Press, New York 1990.

Demmer, Klaus, M.S.C., Schüller, Bruno (eds), *Christlich Glauben und Handeln: Frager einen fundamentalen Moraltheologie in der Diskussion*, Patmos, Düsseldorf 1977 (in honour of J. Fuchs, S.J.).

Demmer, Klaus, Ducke, K.H. (eds.), *Moraltheologie in Dienst der Kirche*, St Benno, Leipzig 1992 (in honour of W. Ernst).

Furger, Franz, *Ethische Theorie praktisch: der fundamental-moraltheologische Ansatz in sozialetischer Entfaltung*, Aschendorff, Münster 1991 (in honour of K. Demmer).

Gallagher, R., C.Ss.R., *History and Conscience*, Gill and Macmillan, Dublin 1989 (in honour of S. O'Riordan, C.Ss.R.).

Holderegger, A., Imbach, R., Suarez R., *De dignitate hominis*, Herder, Wien 1987 (in honour of C.-J. Pinto de Oliveira, O.P.).

Hunold, G.W., Korff, W. (eds.), *Die Welt für morgen: ethische Herausforderungen im Anspruch der Zukunft*, Kösel, München 1986 (in honour of F. Böckle).

Kennedy, Terence, C.Ss.R., *Moral Studies*, Spectrum Publications, Melbourne 1983 (in honour of A. Regan, C.Ss.R.).

Mieth, Dietmar; Weber, Helmut (eds.), *Anspruch der Wirklichkeit und christlicher Glaube: Probleme und Wege theologische Ethik heute*, Patmos, Düsseldorf 1980 (in honour of A. Auer).

Nalepa, Marian, C.Ss.R., Kennedy, Terence, C.Ss.R. (eds.), *La coscienza morale oggi*, EDACALF, Rome 1987 (in honour of D. Capone, C.Ss.R.).

Oliveira, C.J. Pinto de, O.P. (ed.), *Novitas et veritas vitae: au sources du renouveau de la morale chrétienne*, Fribourg-Paris 1991 (in honour of S. Pinckaers, O.P.).

Römelt, Josef, C.Ss.R., Hidber, Bruno (eds.), *In Christus zum Leben befreit*, Herder, Freiburg 1992 (in honour of B. Häring, C.Ss.R.).

Selling, J.A. (ed.), *Personalist Morals*, Louvain 1988 (in honour of L. Janssens).

Verdes, Lorenzo Alvarez, C.Ss.R., Vidal, Marciano, C.Ss.R. (eds.), *La justicia social*, PS Editorial, Madrid 1993 (in honour of J. de la Torre, C.Ss.R.).

Verdes, Lorenzo Alvarez, C.Ss.R., Majorano, Sabatino, C.Ss.R. (eds.), *Morale e redenzione*, EDACALF, Rome 1983.

PART II

Chapter 1: GOD, OUR FOCUS ON DESTINY

1. GOD

Demmer, Klaus, *Gottes Anspruch denken: Die Gottesfrage in der Moraltheologie*, Herder, Freiburg 1993.

Furger, Franz, "Gibt es eine Ethik ohne Gott? – oder: Wie stellt Ethik die Gottesfrage", in *Theologische Berichte*, 12 (1983), 63-93.

Gammwell, Franklin I., *The Divine Good: Modern Moral Theory and the Necessity of God*, Harper, San Francisco 1990.

Gustafson, James M., *Ethics from a Theocentric Perspective*, University of Chicago Press, Chicago-London 1984.

Kasper, Walter, *Jesus the Christ*, Paulist Press, New York 1977.

Kress, H., *Ethische Werte und Gottesgedankee: Probleme und Perspecktiven des neuzeitlichen Wertbegriffs*, W. Kohlhammer, Stuttgart 1990.

Löhr, G., *Gott, Gebote, Ideale: Analytische Philosophie und theologische Ethik*, Göttingen-Zurich 1991.

Pizzorni, R., "In che senso si può dire che 'se Dio non esiste tutto è lecito'?" in *Angelicum* 64 (1987), 247-282.

Römelt, Josef, C.Ss.R., *Personales Gottesverständnis in heitigen Moraltheologie auf dem Hintergrund der Theologie von K. Rahner und H.U. von Balthasar*, Tyrolia, Innsbruck 1988.

Rahner, Karl, S.J., *Foundations of Christian Faith*, Crossroad, New York 1982.

2. HAPPINESS AND SAINTHOOD

Abbà, Giuseppe, *Felicità, vita buona e virtù: Saggi di filosofia morale*, LAS, Rome 1988.

Buckley, Michael J., S.J., *At the Origins of Modern Atheism*, Yale University Press, New Haven 1987.

Bujo, B., *Die Begründung des Sittlichen: Zur Frage des Eudämonismus bei Thomas von Aquin*, Ferdinand Schönigh, Paderborn-München 1984.

Demmer, Klaus, "Das vergeistigte Glück. Gedanken zum christlichen Eudämonieverständnis", in *Gregorianum* 72 (1991), 99-115.

Gilby, Thomas, O.P., "Happiness", in *Encyclopedic Dictionary of Religion*, P.K. Meagher, T.C. O'Brien, and C.M. Aherne (eds.), Corpus, Washington D.C. 1979, Vol. 2, 1608-1609.

Hawley, John Stratton (ed.), *Saints and Virtue*, University of California Press, Berkeley 1987.

Kleber, H., *Glück als Lebensziel*, Aschendorff, Münster 1988.

Korff, W., *Wie kann der Mensch glücken? Perspectiven der Ethik*, R. Piper and Co., München 1985.

Lubac, Henri de, S.J., *The Drama of Atheistic Humanism*, Meridian, New York 1963. *The Discovery of God*, J.P. Kenedy and Son, New York 1960.

The Mystery of the Supernatural, Herder and Herder, New York 1967.

Augustinianism and Modern Theology, Herder and Herder, New York 1969.

La rivelazione divina e il senso dell'uomo, Jaca Book, Milan 1985.

Oliveira, C.J., Pinto de, "La finalitè dans la morale thomiste. La métaphysique de la fin au service d'une éthique de bonheur évangelique", in *Angelicum* 69 (1992), 301-326.

Owens, Joseph, C.Ss.R., *Human Destiny*, Catholic University of America Press, Washington D.C. 1985.

Pinckaers, Servais, O.P., "La beatitude dans l'éthique de Saint Thomas", in *Studi Tomistici* 25, Editrice Vaticana, Vatican City 1984, 80-94.

Spaemann Robert, *Glück und Wohlwollen: Versuch über Ethik*, Glett-Cotta, Stuttgart 1989.

Staley, K.M., "Happiness: The Natural End of Man?" in *The Thomist* 53 (1989), 215-234.

Wyschogrod, Edith, *Saints and Postmodernism*, University of Chicago Press, Chicago 1990.

Chapter 2: THE SENSE OF CHRISTIAN MORALITY

Auer, A., *Autonome Moral und christlicher Glaube*, Patmos, Düsseldorf 1984.

Bastionel, Sergio, "Autonomia e teonomia" in F. Compagnoni *et al.* (eds.), *Nuovo Dizionario di Teologia Morale*, Edizioni San Paolo, Cinisello Balsamo (MI) 1990, 70-82.

Bernasconi, Oliviero, *Morale autonoma ed etica della fede*, Edizioni Dehoniane, Bologna 1981.

Fuchs, Josef, S.J., *Christian Ethics in a Secular Arena*, Gill and Macmillan, Dublin 1984.
Human Values and Christian Morality, Gill and Macmillan, Dublin 1970.
Gaziau, Eric, *Moral de la foi et morale autome: confrontation entre P. Delhaye et J. Fuchs*, Leuven University Press, Louvain 1995.
Gillen, E., *Wie Christen ethisch denken und handeln: Zur Debatte um die Autonomie der christlichen Sittlichkeit im Kontext katholische Theologie*, Echter, Würzburg 1989.
Hughes, Gerard J., *Authority in Morals*, Heythrop Monographs, London 1978.
Leube, J.L. (ed.), *L'éthique: Perspectives proposées par la foi*, Beauchesne, Paris 1993.
MacNamara, Vincent, *Faith and Ethics*, Gill and Macmillan, Dublin 1985.
The Truth in Love, Gill and Macmillan, Dublin 1988.
May, William E., "Christian Faith and its 'fulfillment' of the Natural Law", in *Anthropotes* 7 (1991), 155-169.
Midali, Mario, *Teologia pastorale o pratica*, LAS, Rome 1991.
Oliveira, C.J., Pinto de (ed.), *Autonomie: dimensions éthique de la liberté*, Fribourg-Paris 1978.
Pinckaers, Servais, "Christ, Moral Absolutes and the Good: Recent Moral Theology", in *The Thomist* 55 (1991), 343-396.
Ratzinger, Joseph; Schürman, Heinz; Balthasar, Hans Urs von, *Principles of Catholic Morality*, Ignatius Press, San Francisco 1986.
Richard, Lucien, *Is there a Christian Ethics?*, Paulist Press, New York, 1988.
Schüllor, Bruno, *Wholly Human*, Gill and Macmillan, Dublin 1986.
Stoeckle, Bernard, *Erlöst?*, Katholisches Bibelwerk, Stuttgart 1974.
Walter, J.J., "The Foundation of Christian Moral Experience", in *Église et théologie* 16 (1985) 169-184.
Ziegler, J.G., "Die deutschsprachige Moraltheologie vor dem Gesetz der Polarität von Glaube und Vernunft", in *Studia Moralia* 24 (1986) 319-344; 25 (1987) 185-210.

Chapter 3: THE PERSON DEFINES MORALITY

Berti, Enrico, *et al.*, *Persona e personalismo*, Gregoriana, Padua 1992.
Buber, Martin, *I and Thou*, T & T Clark, Edinburgh 1970.

Clarke, Norris, S.J., *Person and Being*, Marquette University Press, Milwaukee 1993.

"Person, Being, and St Thomas", in *Communio* 19 (1992) 601-618.

Doran, Kevin, *What is a Person? The Concept and the Implications for Ethics*, The Edwin Mellen Press, Queenston, Ontario 1989.

Fabro, Cornelio, *Riflessioni sulla libertà*, Maggioli, Rimini 1983.

Fuhrmann, M., *et al.*, "Person" in *Historisches Wörterbuch der Philosophie*, Vol. 7, J. Ritter and K. Gründer (eds.), Darmstadt, Wissenschaftliche Buchhandlung 1989, 269-338.

Lacroix, Jean, *Le personalisme comme anti-idéologie*, Presses Universitaires de France, Paris 1972.

Macmurray, John, *The Self as Agent*, Faber and Faber, London 1954.

Midgley, Margaret, *The Ethical Primate*, Routledge, London 1994.

Mounier, Emmanuel, *Personalism*, University of Notre Dame Press, Notre Dame, Indiana 1970.

Pavan, A. and Milano, A., *Persona e personalismi*, Dehoniane, Naples 1987.

Ricoeur, Paul, *Freedom and Nature: The Voluntary and the Involuntary*, Northwestern Union Press, Purdue 1966.

Rigobello, Armando (ed.), *Il personalismo*, Città Nuova, Rome 1975.

Selling, J.A. (ed.), *Personalist Morals*, Leuven University Press, Louvain 1988.

Stefanini, Luigi, *Personalismo sociale*, Studium, Rome 1979.

Taylor, Charles, *The Ethics of Authenticity*, Harvard University Press, Cambridge, Massachusetts 1991.

Human Agency and Language, Cambridge University Press, Cambridge 1985.

Philosophy and the Human Sciences, Cambridge University Press, Cambridge 1985.

Sources of the Self, Harvard University Press, Cambridge, Massachusetts 1989.

Wojtyla, K., *The Acting Person*, D. Reidel, Dordrecht/Boston 1979.

Chapter 4: SCRIPTURE: "THE SOUL OF MORAL THEOLOGY"

1. SCRIPTURE AND MORAL THEOLOGY

Adinolfi, Marco, *et al.*, *Fondamenti biblici della teologia morale*, Paideia, Brescia 1973.

Collins, R.F., *Christian Morality*, University of Notre Dame Press, Notre Dame, Indiana 1986.

Cranfield, C.E.B., *The Bible and Christian Life*, T & T Clark, Edinburgh 1985.

Curran, Charles E., and McCormick, Richard A., S.J., *The use of Scripture in Moral Theology: Readings in Moral Theology*, No. 4, Paulist Press, New York, 1984.

Fischer, James A., C.M., *Looking for Moral Guidance*, Paulist Press, New York 1992.

Grelot, P., *Problèmes de morale fondamentale: Un éclairage biblique*, Cerf, Paris 1982.

Hamel, E., "Escriture et théologie morale: Un bilan (1940-1980)", in *Studia Moralia* 20 (1982), 177-192

McDonald, J.I.H., *Biblical Interpretation and Christian Ethics*, Cambridge University Press, Cambridge 1993.

Ogletree, Thomas W., *The Use of the Bible in Christian Ethics*, Fortress Press, Philadelphia 1983.

Spicq, C., *Connaissance et morale dans la Bible*, Cerf, Paris 1985.

Spohn, William C., S.J., *What are they saying about Scripture and Ethics?*, Paulist Press, New York 1984.

2. OLD TESTAMENT

Birch, Bruce C., *Let Justice Roll Down: The Old Testament, Ethics and the Christian Life*, Westminster, Louisville 1991.

Brueggemann, Walter, *A Social Reading of the Old Testament*, Fortress Press, Minneapolis 1994.

Eckart, Otto, *Theologische Ethik des Alten Testaments*, W. Kohlhammer, Stuttgart 1994.

L'Hour, J., *La morale d'Alliance*, Gabalda, Paris 1966.

Testa, E., *La morale dell'Antico Testamento*, Morcelliana, Brescia 1981.

Trapiello, J. Garcia, *Il problema morale dell'Antico Testamento*, Massimo, Milan 1983.

3. NEW TESTAMENT

Chilton, Bruce and McDonald, J.I.H., *Jesus and the Ethics of the Kingdom*, Eerdmans, Grand Rapids 1987.

Kertelge, K. (ed.), *Ethik in Neuen Testament*, Herder, Freiburg 1984.

Lohse, Eduard, *Theological Ethics of the New Testament*, Fortress, Minneapolis 1989.

Meeks, Wayne, *The Moral World of the First Christians*, SPCK, London 1986.

Pinckaers, S., *Morale et Evangile*, Cerf, Paris 1989.

Sanders, Jack T., *Ethics in the New Testament*, SCM, London 1975.

Schnackenburg, Rudolf, *The Moral Teaching of the New Testament*, Herder and Herder, New York 1965.
Die sittliche Botschaft des Neuen Testaments, (2 Vols.), Herder, Freiburg 1986-1988.

Schrage, Wolfgang, *The Ethics of the New Testament*, T & T Clark, Edinburgh 1988.

Segalla, G., *Introduzione all'etica biblica del Nuovo Testamento*, Queriniana, Brescia 1989.

Tremblay, R., "Le Christ et la morale", in *Studia Moralia* 30 (1992), 289-298.

Chapter 5: TRADITION: THE GETTING OF WISDOM

Angelini, G. and Valsecchi, R., *Disegno storico della teologia morale*, Dehoniane, Bologna 1972.

Babcock, William S. (ed.), *The Ethics of St Augustine*, Scholars Press, Atlanta 1991.

Bougerol, J. Guy, O.F.M., *Introduction to the Works of Bonaventure*, St Anthony Guild Press, New Jersey 1963.

Congar, Yves M.-J. O.P., *A History of Theology*, Doubleday, New York 1968.

Copleston, F.C., *A History of Medieval Philosophy*, Harper and Row, New York 1972.

D'Arcy, M.C., *et al.*, *A Monument to St Augustine*, Sheed and Ward, London 1930.

Delhaye, Philippe, *Medieval Christian Philosophy*, Hawthorn Books, New York 1960.

Gallagher, John A., *Time Past, Time Future*, Paulist Press, New York 1990.

Gallagher, Raphael, C.Ss.R., "The Manual System of Moral Theology since the Death of St Alphonsus", in *Irish Theological Quarterly* 51 (1985), 1-16.

Gilson, Etienne, *The Christian Philosophy of St Augustine*, Random House, New York 1960.
History of Christian Philosophy in the Middle Ages, Random House, New York 1955.
The *Philosophy of St Bonaventure*, St Anthony Guild Press, New Jersey 1965.

Jonsen, Albert A., and Toulmin, Stephen, *The Abuse of Casuistry*, University of California Press, Berkeley 1988.

Johnstone, Brian V., "Faithful Action: The Catholic Moral Tradition and *Veritatis Splendor*" in *Studia Moralia* 31 (1993) 2, 265-282.

Leites, Edmund (ed.), *Conscience and Casuistry in Early Modern Europe*, Cambridge University Press, Cambridge 1988.

McAdoo, H.R., *The Structure of Caroline Moral Theology*, Longmans, Green and Co., London 1949.

Mahoney, John, *The Making of Moral Theology*, Clarendon, Oxford 1987.

Murphy, Francis X., C.Ss.R., *Moral Teaching in the Primitive Church*, Paulist Press, New York 1968.

"The Background to a History of Patristic Moral Thought", in *Studia Moralia* 1 (1962), 49-85.

Nedoncelle, Maurice, Is *There a Christian Philosophy?*, Hawthorn Books, New York 1960.

Osborn, Eric, *Ethical Patterns in Early Christian Thought*, Cambridge University Press, Cambridge 1976.

Pieper, Josef, "The Concept of Tradition", in *The Review of Politics* 20 (1958), 465-491. This article is summarised in *Theology Digest* (1960) 1, 3-7.

Ratzinger, Joseph, "La nuova alleanza: sulla teologia dell'alleanza nel Nuovo Testamento", in *Rivista di Teologia* 36 (1995), 9-22.

Verdes, Lorenzo Alvarez, *El imperativo cristiano en San Pablo*, Institutión San Jerónimo, Valencia 1980.

Vereecke, L., "Preface à l'histoire de la théologie morale moderne", in *Studia Moralia* I (1962), 87-120.

"*Moral Theology, History of*", New Catholic Encyclopedia, Publishers Guild Inc., Washington, D.C., Vol. 9, 1119-1122.

"Storia della Teologia Morale", in *Nuovo Dizionario di Teologia Morale*, F. Compagnoni, G. Piana, S. Privitera (eds.), Edizioni San Paolo, Cinisello Balsamo (MI) 1990, 1314-1338.

"Histoire et morale selon *Veritatis Splendor*", in *Le Supplément*, 188-189 (1994), 335-348.

Womer, Jan L. (ed. and tr.), *Morality and Ethics in Early Christianity*, Fortress Press, Philadelphia 1987.

Chapter 6: THE MEANING IN HUMAN ACTION

Anscombe, G.E.M., *Intention*, Oxford University Press, Oxford 1963.

"Modern Moral Philosophy", in *Philosophy* 33 (1958), 1-19.

Autiero, Antonio, "L'agire morale sotto il segno della complessità", in *Asprenas* 41 (1994), 337-348.

Danto, Arthur C., *Analytic Philosophy of Action*, Cambridge University Press, Cambridge 1973.

D'Arcy, Eric, *Human Acts: An Essay in Moral Evaluation*, Oxford University Press, Oxford 1963.

Donagan, Alan, *Human Ends and Human Actions: An Exploration in St Thomas' Treatment*, Marquette University Press, Milwaukee 1985.

Dunne, Joseph, *Back to the Rough Road: "Phronesis" and "Techne" in Modern Philosophy and in Aristotle*, University of Notre Dame Press, Notre Dame, Indiana 1993.

Finance, Joseph De, S.J., *Saggio sull'agire umano*, Libreria Editrice Vaticana, Città del Vaticano 1992.

Frattallone, "Persona e atto umano", in *Nuovo Dizionario di Teologia Morale*, Edizioni San Paolo, Cinisello Balsamo (MI) 1990, 932-952.

Furger, Franz, *Gewissen und Klugheit in der katholischen der letzen Jahrzehnten*, Räber, Lucerne 1965.

Gründel, Johannes, *Die Lehre von dem Umständen der menschlichen Handlung im Mittelalter*, Aschendorff, Münster 1963.

Habermas, Jürgen, *Moral Consciousness and Communicative Action*, Massachusetts Institute of Technology Press, Cambridge, Massachusetts 1993.

McInerny, Ralph, *Aquinas on Human Action: A Theory of Practice*, Catholic University of America Press, Washington D.C. 1992.

Owens, Joseph, C.Ss.R., "Human Reason and the Moral Order in Aquinas", in *Studia Moralia* 28 (1991), 155-173.

Pinckaers, Servais, "Le rôle de la fin dans l'action morale selon saint Thomas" in *Revue des Sciences Philosophiques et Théologiques* 45 (1961), 393-421.
"La structure de l'acte humain suivant s. Thomas", in *Revue Thomiste* 55 (1955), 393-412.

Polanyi, Michael, *Personal Knowledge: Toward a Post-Critical Philosophy*, Routledge and Kegan Paul, London 1958.
The Tacit Dimension, Doubleday, New York 1967.

Quinn, Warren, *Morality and Action*, Cambridge University Press, Cambridge 1993.

Ricoeur, Paul, *Le discours de l'action*, Centre national de la recherche scientifique, Paris 1977.
Freedom and Nature: The Voluntary and the Involuntary, Northwestern University Press, Purdue 1966.

Oneself as Another, University of Chicago Press, Chicago/ London 1992.

Seifert, Josef, *Was ist und was motiviert eine sittliche Handlung?*, Anton Pustet, Salzburg 1976.

Sokolowski, Robert, *Moral Action: A Phenomenological Study*, Indiana University Press, Bloomington 1985.

Tracy, David, "Theologies of Praxis", in *Creativity and Method*, Matthew L. Lamb (ed.), Marquette University Press, Milwaukee 1981, 35-51.

Westberg, Daniel, *Right Practical Reason: Aristotle, Action and Prudence in Aquinas*, Oxford University Press, Oxford 1994.

Winch, Peter, *Ethics and Action*, Routledge and Kegan Paul, London 1972.

Wojtyla, K., *The Acting Person*, D. Reidel, Dordrecht/Boston 1979.

Chapter 7: THE HEART OF CONSCIENCE

Billy, D.J., "Aquinas on the content of synderesis", in *Studia Moralia* 29 (1991), 1, 61-84.

"The authority of conscience in Bonaventure and Aquinas", in *Studia Moralia* 31 (1993), 2, 237-264.

Caffarra, Carlo, "Indicazioni per la formazione della coscienza morale", in *Rivista del Clero Italiano* 57 (1976), 598-603.

Capone, Domenico, "La verità nella coscienza morale", in *Studia Moralia* 8 (1970), 7-36.

"Per la teologia della coscienza cristiana", in *Studia Moralia* 20 (1982), 67-93.

"Legge, coscienza, persona nei moralisti e in S. Alfonso", in *Asprenas* 19 (1972), 133-168.

Chenu, Marie-Dominique, *L'éveil de la conscience dans la civilisation médiéval*, Vrin, Paris 1969.

D'Arcy, Eric, *Conscience and its Right to Freedom*, Sheed and Ward, London 1961.

Delhaye, Philippe, *The Christian Conscience*, Desclée, New York 1968.

Demmer, Klaus, "Coscienza e norma morale", in *Fondazione e interpretazione della norma*, F. Bellino *et al.*, Morcelliana, Brescia 1986, 13-50.

Flick, Giorgio, *Coscienza e sviluppo della personalità*, Dehoniane, Bologna 1971.

Fuchs, Josef (ed.), *Das Gewissen. Vorgegebene Norm oder Produkt gesellschaftlicher Zwänge?*, Patmos, Düsseldorf 1979.

"Conscience and Conscientious Fidelity", in *Moral Theology: Challenges for the Future*, Charles E. Curran (ed.), Paulist Press, New York 1990.

Haro, Ramón García De, "Cristo y la consciencia moral", in *Angelicum* 59 (1982), 475-492.

Hollenbach, Johannes Michael, S.J., *Sein und Gewissen: Über den Ursprung der Gewissensregung: eine Begegnung zwischen Martin Heidegger und thomisticher Philosophie*, Bruno Grimm, Baden-Baden 1954.

Janssens, L., *Liberté de conscience et liberté religieuse*, Desclée de Brouwer, Paris 1964.

Kelly, Kevin T., *The Concept of Conscience and its Place in Moral Theology in the Writings of Bishop Robert Sanderson and other early Protestant Moralists*, Geoffrey Chapman, London 1967.

Magill, Gerard, "Interpreting Moral Doctrine: Newman on Conscience and Law", in *Horizons* 20 (1993), 1, 7-22.

Majorano, Sabatino, *La coscienza: Per una lettura cristiana*, Edizioni San Paolo, Cinisello Balsamo (MI) 1994.

Nelepa, Marian, C.Ss.R., and Kennedy, Terence, C.Ss.R. (eds.), *La coscienza morale oggi*, EDACALF, Rome 1987.

Nelson, C. Ellis (ed.), *Conscience: Theological and Psychological Perspectives*, Newman Press, New York 1973.

Petrà, Basilio, *La coscienza "nello Spirito". Per una comprensione cristiana della coscienza morale*, OR, Milan 1993.

Potts, Timothy C., *Conscience in Medieval Philosophy*, Cambridge University Press, Cambridge 1980.

Rahner, Karl, S.J., "Conscience", in *Theological Investigations*, XXII, Crossroad, New York 1984, 3-13.

Rey-Mermet, Théodule, *Conscience et liberté*, Nouvelle Cité, Paris 1990.

Rossi, Leandro (ed.), *La coscienza cristiana*, Dehoniane, Bologna 1971.

Schnackenburg, Rudolf, "La 'coscienza'. L'assunzione paolina del concetto di syneidesis", in *Il messagggio morale del Nuovo Testamento*, Vol. 2, Paideia, Brescia 1990, 63-76.

Schockenhoff, Eberhard, *Das umstrittene Gewissen: Eine theologische Grundlegung*, Matthias-Grünewald, Mainz 1990.

Srampickal, Thomas, *The Concept of Conscience in Today's Empirical Psychology and in the Documents of Vatican II*, Resch, Innsbruck 1976.

Valadier, Paul, *Éloge de la conscience*, Seuil, Paris 1994.

Chapter 8: CHARACTER, CULTURE AND THE GOSPEL

1. CHARACTER AND VIRTUE

Abbà, Giuseppe, *Felicità, vita buona e virtù*, LAS, Rome 1989.
"L'apporto dell'etica tomista all'odierno dibattito sulle virtù", in *Salesianum* 52 (1990), 799-818.
"Il soggetto e le virtù. Dall'etica di Tommaso all'etica normativa di Duns Scotus e di Ockham", in *Filosofia e Teologia* 5 (1991), 2, 185-206.

Bellah, Robert, *et al.*, *Habits of the Heart: Individualism and Commitment in American Life*, University of California Press, Berkeley 1985.

Casey, John, *Pagan Virtues: An Essay in Ethics*, Clarendon Press, Oxford 1990.

Cessario, Romanus, *The Moral Virtues and Theological Ethics*, University of Notre Dame Press, Notre Dame, Indiana 1991.

Geach, Peter, *The Virtues*, Cambridge University Press, Cambridge 1977.

Haro, Ramón García De, *L'agire morale e le virtù*, Ares, Milan 1988.

Hauerwas, Stanley, *A Community of Character*, University of Notre Dame Press, Notre Dame, Indiana 1981.
Vision and Virtue, University of Notre Dame Press, Notre Dame, Indiana 1974.

Mieth, Dietmar, *Die neuen Tugenden. Ein ethischer Entwurf*, Patmos, Düsseldorf 1984.

Mieth, Dietmar and Pohier, Jacques (eds.), *Changing Values and Virtues*, (the entire issue of *Concilium* 191), T & T Clark, Edinburgh 1987.

Murphy, F.X., C.Ss.R., "Le virtù morali nel pensiero dei Padri", in *Seminarium* 21 (1969), 395-416.

MacIntyre, Alasdair, *After Virtue*, Notre Dame University Press, Notre Dame, Indiana 1981.
Whose Justice? Which Rationality?, Notre Dame University Press, Notre Dame, Indiana 1988.
Three Rival Versions of Moral Enquiry, Duckworth, London 1990.

Pesch, Otto Herman, "The Theology of Virtue and the Theological Virtues", in *Concilium* 191 (1987), 81-100.

Pieper, Josef, *The Four Cardinal Virtues*, University of Notre Dame Press, Notre Dame, Indiana 1980.
Kleines Lesebuck von den Tugenden des menschlichen Herzens, Schwaben, Stuttgart 1988.

Pincoffs, Edward L., *Quandaries and Virtues: Against Reductionism in Ethics*, The University of Kansas Press, Lawrence 1986.

Porter, Jean, *The Recovery of Virtue: The Relevance of Aquinas for Christian Ethics*, Westminster, Louisville 1990.

"The Subversion of Virtue: Acquired and Infused Virtues in the *Summa Theologiae*", in *The Annual of the Society of Christian Ethics* (1992), 19-41.

"The Unity of the Virtues and the Ambiguity of Goodness", in *Journal of Christian Ethics* 21 (1993), 1, 137-163.

Schockenhoff, Eberhard, BONUM HOMINIS: *Die anthropolischen und theologischen Grundlagen der Tugendethik des Thomas von Aquin*, Matthias-Grünewald, Mainz 1987.

2. PSYCHOLOGY AND EDUCATION

Browning, Don S., *Generative Man*, Delta, New York 1973.

Browning, Don S.; Jobe, Thomas; Evison, Ian S. (eds.), *Religious and Ethical Factors in Psychiatric Practice*, Nelson-Hall, Chicago 1990.

Drewermann, Eugene, *Psychoanalyse und Moraltheologie*, (3 Vols.), Matthias-Grünewald, Mainz 1982-1984.

Ellrod, F.E., *et al.*, *Act and Agent: Philosophical Foundations for Moral Education and Character Development*, University Press of America, Washington D.C. 1986.

Guntrip, Harry, *Psychoanalytic Theory, Therapy and the Self*, Basic Books, New York 1973.

Homans, Peter, *The Ability to Mourn: Disillusionment and the Social Origins of Psychoanalysis,* University of Chicago Press, Chicago 1989.

Kiely, Bartholomew M., S.J., *Psychology and Moral Theology*, Gregorian University Press, Rome 1980.

Lakin, Martin, *Ethical Issues in the Psychotherapies*, Oxford University Press, Oxford 1988.

Moore, F.C.T., *The Psychological Basis of Personality*, Macmillan, London 1978.

Noam, Gil G., and Wren, Thomas E., *The Moral Self*, Massachusetts Institute of Technology Press, Cambridge, Massachusetts 1993.

Rieff, Philip, *Freud: The Mind of the Moralist*, Methuen, London 1960.

The Triumph of the Therapeutic: Uses of Faith after Freud, Harper and Row, New York, 1968.

Sheldon, Charles M., *Morality of the Heart: A Psychology for the Christian Moral Life*, Crossroad, New York, 1990.

Terruwe, Anna A., and Baars, Conrad W., *Psychic Wholeness and Healing*, Alba House, New York 1981.

Wallwork, Ernest, *Psychoanalysis and Ethics*, Yale University Press, New Haven 1991.

3. CULTURE AND THE GOSPEL

Carrier, Hervé, *Evangelizing the Culture of Modernity*, Orbis, New York 1993.

Carvalho Avededo, Marcello de, *Inculturation and the Challenges of Modernity*, Pontifical Gregorian University, Rome 1982.

Crollius, Arij A. Roest, *et al.*, *Creative Inculturation and the Unity of Faith*, Pontifical Gregorian University, Rome 1986.
What is so new about Inculturation?, Pontifical Gregorian University, Rome 1984.

Dumais, Marcel, *Cultural Change and Liberation in a Christian Perspective*, Gregorian University Press, Rome 1987.

Gremillion, Joseph (ed.), *The Church and Culture since Vatican II: The Experience of North and Latin America*, University of Notre Dame Press, Indiana 1985.

Ireland, Rowan, *The Challenge of Secularisation*, Collins Dove, Melbourne 1988.

Leavey, Carmel, O.P., and Hetherton, Margaret (eds.), *Catholic Beliefs and Practices*, Collins Dove, Melbourne 1988.

Poupard, Paul, *Église et cultures: Jalons pour une pastorale de l'intelligence*, SOS, Paris 1985.

Quarello, Eraldo, *Morale cristiana e cultura*, LAS, Rome 1979.

Ratzinger, Joseph Card., "In the encounter of Christianity and religions, syncretism is not the goal" [Christ, Faith and the Challenge of Cultures], in *L'Osservatore Romano* [English edition], 26 April, 1995, 5-8.

Silvestri, G., "Antropologia culturale", in *Nuovo Dizionario di Teologia Morale*, Edizioni San Paolo, Cinisello Balsamo (MI) 1990, 35-49.

Waliggo, *et al.*, *Inculturation: Its Meaning and Urgency*, St Paul Publications-Africa, Kampala 1986.

Chapter 9: GUILT AND "THE MYSTERY OF EVIL"

Baum, Gregory, *Religion and Alienation*, Paulist Press, New York 1979.

Cooper, Eugene, "The notion of sin in light of the theory of the fundamental option – The fundamental option revisited", in *Louvain Studies* 9 (1983) 4, 363-383.

Delhaye, Philippe, *et al.*, *Pastorale du péché*, Desclée, Tournai 1961.

Demmer, Klaus, *Entscheidung und Verhängnis: Die moraltheologische Lehre von der Sünde in Licht christologischer Anthropologie*, Bonifacius, Paderborn 1976.

Fenn, Richard K., *The Secularization of Sin*, Westminster, Louisville 1991.

Fuček, Ivan, S.J., *Il peccato oggi: Riflessioni teologico-pastorale*, Pontificia Università Gregoriana, Rome 1991.

Gaffney, James, *Sin Reconsidered*, Paulist Press, New York 1983.

Görres, A., and K. Rahner, *Il male: La risposta della psicoterapia e del cristianesimo*, Edizioni Paoline, Cinisello Balsamo (MI) 1987.

Häring, Bernard, C.Ss.R., *Sin in a Secular Age*, St Paul Publications, Slough 1974.

Hidber, Bruno, C.Ss.R., "Freiheit und Sünde, Zur theologischen Verhältnisbestimmung", in *In Christus zum Leben befreit*, J. Römelt and B. Hidber (eds.), Herder, Freiburg 1992, 84-113.
"Der Mensch als Abbild Gottes und sein böses Tun aus Freiheit", in *Studia Moralia* 30 (1992), 2, 299-320.

Kerans, Patrick, *Sinful Social Structures*, Paulist Press, New York 1974.

Mackey, J.P., "The idea of sin in the modern world", in the *Irish Theological Quarterly* 33 (1966), 309-326.

McCormick, Patrick, C.M., *Sin as Addiction*, Paulist Press, New York 1989.

McHugh, Gerard, *Christian Faith and Criminal Justice*, Paulist Press, New York 1978.

Maly, Eugene M., *Sin: Biblical Perspectives*, Pflaum, Dayton 1973.

Martelet, Gustave, *Libre réponse à un scandale: La faute originelle, la souffrance et la mort*, Cerf, Paris 1988.

Menninger, Karl, *Whatever became of Sin?*, Hawthorn Books, New York 1973.

Monden, Louis, *Sin, Liberty and Law*, Sheed and Ward, New York 1965.

O'Keefe, Mark, *What are they saying about social sin?*, Paulist Press, New York 1990.

Pieper, Josef, *Über den Begriff der Sünde*, Kösel, München 1977.

Pohier, J.M., *Psychologie et théologie*, Cerf, Paris 1967.

Rahner, Karl, S.J., "Guilt and its Remission: The borderline between Psychology and Psychotherapy", in*Theological Investigations* II, Seabury, New York 1975, 265-282.

"Does traditional theology represent guilt as innocuous as a factor in human life?", in *Theological Investigations* XIII, Darton, Longman & Todd, London 1984, 133-151.

"Penance in the early Church", in *Theological Investigations* XV: Darton, Longman & Todd, London 1983.

"Guilt – Responsibility – Punishment within the view of Catholic Theology", in *Theological Investigations* VI, Seabury, New York 1974, 197-217.

"Sin and Suffering", in *Theological Investigations* XIX, Darton, Longman & Todd, London 1984, 179-208.

Ricoeur, Paul, *The Symbolism of Evil*, Beacon, Boston 1967.

Rigali, Norbert, "Sin in a Relational World", in *Chicago Studies* 23 (1984), 3, 321-337.

Rondet, Henri, *The Theology of Sin*, University of Notre Dame Press, Notre Dame, Indiana 1960.

Schoonenberg, Piet, *Man and Sin: A Theological View*, University of Notre Dame Press, Notre Dame, Indiana 1965.

Taylor, Michael J. (ed.), *The Mystery of Sin and Forgiveness*, Alba House, New York 1971.

Tettamanzi, D., "Teologia morale e peccato: alcune discussioni attuali", in *La Scuola Cattolica* 115 (1987), 610-657.

Thevenot, Xavier, *Sin: A Christian View for Today*, Liguori Publications, Liguori, Missuori 1984.

Chapter 10: THE LAW ACCORDING TO THE GOSPEL

NOTE: Information on natural law and legal philosophy is provided by *The Natural Law Forum* which, since 1969, has been renamed *The American Journal of Jurisprudence*. Both are published by the University of Notre Dame, Indiana. See also the volume *Atti dell'VIII Congresso Tomistico Internazionale, Vol. 6: Morale e diritto nella prospettiva Tomistica*, Libreria Editrice Vaticana, Vatican City 1982, as well as *Credo in Spiritum Sanctum: Atti del Congresso Teologico Internazionale di Pneumatologia*, Libreria Editrice Vaticana, Vatican City 1983.

Aubert, Jean Marie, "Herméneutique du droit naturel", in *Recherches de science religieuse* 59 (1971), see Bibliography 490-492.

Per una teologia dell'epoca industriale, Cittadella, Assisi 1973.

Loi de Dieu: Lois des hommes, Desclée, Tournai 1964.

Bastit, Michel, *Naissance de la loi moderne*, Léviathan PUF, Paris 1990.

Battaglia, Anthony, *Toward a Reformulation of Natural Law*, Seabury, New York 1981.

Bobbio, Norberto, *Giusnaturalismo e positivismo giuridico*, Edizioni di Comunità, Milan 1970.

Böckle, Franz, *Das Naturrecht im Disput*, Patmos, Düsseldorf 1970.

Brown, Oscar, *Natural Rectitude and Divine Law in Aquinas*, Pontifical Institute of Medieval Studies, Toronto 1981.

Composta, Dario, *Natura e ragione: studio sulle inclinazioni naturali in rapporto al diritto naturale*, Pas-Verlag, Zürich 1971.

Crowe, Michael Bertram, *The Changing Profile of the Natural Law*, Martinus Nijhoff, The Hague 1977.

"St Thomas and Ulpian's Natural Law", in *St Thomas Aquinas Commemorative Studies*, I, Toronto 1974, 261-282.

Curran, Charles E., and McCormick, Richard A., S.J., *Readings in Moral Theology: Natural Law and Theology*, No. 7, Paulist Press, New York 1991.

Davitt, T.E., *The Nature of Law*, Herder, St Louis 1951.

Delhaye, Philippe, *Permanence du droit naturel*, Nauwelaerts, Louvain 1960.

Le Décalogue et sa place dans la morale chrétienne, La pensée catholique, Bruxelles 1963.

Entreves, A.P. d', *Natural Law: An Historical Survey*, Desclée, New York 1965.

Evans, Illud (ed.), *Light on the Natural Law*, Helicon, Baltimore 1965.

Finnis, John, *Natural Law and Natural Rights*, Clarendon, Oxford 1980.

Fuchs, Josef, *Natural Law: A Theological Approach*, Gill and Macmillan, Dublin 1970.

George, Robert P., *Natural Law Theory*, Clarendon, Oxford 1992.

Grisez, Germain, *Contraception and the Natural Law*, Bruce Publishing Co., Milwaukee 1964.

"The first principle of practical reason: A commentary on the *Summa Theologiae*, question 94, article 2", in *Natural Law Forum* 10 (1965), 168-201.

Hart, H.L.A., *The Concept of Law*, Oxford University Press, Oxford 1961.

Hittinger, Russell, *A Critique of the New Natural Law Theory*, University of Notre Dame Press, Notre Dame, Indiana 1987.

Kaczynski, Edward, *La legge nuova: l'elemento esterno della legge nuova secondo San Tommaso*, LIEF, Rome 1974.
Krapiec, M.A., O.P., *Person and Natural Law*, Peter Lang, New York 1993.
Mahony, J., *Seeking the Spirit*, Sheed and Ward, London 1981.
McCabe, Herbert, *Law, Love and Language*, Sheed and Ward, London 1968.
Maritain, Jacques, *Nove lezioni sulla legge naturale*, Jaca Book, Milan 1984.
Midgley, E.B.F., *The Natural Law Tradition and the Theory of International Relations*, Barnes and Noble, New York 1975.
Newman, Jeremiah, *Conscience versus Law: Reflections on the Evolution of the Natural Law*, The Talbot Press, Dublin 1971.
Nichols, Barry, *An Introduction to Roman Law*, Clarendon, Oxford 1984.
Piana, G., et al., *Ordine morale e ordine giuridico*, Dehoniane, Bologna 1985.
Pizzorni, Reginaldo, *Il diritto naturale dalle origini a San Tommaso d'Aquino*, Città Nuova, Rome 1978.
Rhonheimer, Martin, *Natur als Grundlage der Moral: Ein Auseinandersetzung mit autonomer und teleologischer Ethik*, Tyrolia, Innsbruck 1987.
Rossi, Leandro (ed.), *La legge naturale*, Dehoniane, Bologna 1970.
Theron, Stephen, *Morals as founded on Natural Law*, Peter Lang, New York 1987.
Tuck, Richard, *Natural Rights Theories: Their Origin and Development*, Cambridge University Press, Cambridge 1979.
Urban, Claus, *Nominalismus im Naturrecht*, Patmos, Düsseldorf 1979.
Weinreb, Lloyd L., *Natural Law and Justice*, Harvard University Press, Cambridge MA 1987.

Chapter 11: CHRIST THE "PLEROMA" OF THE KINGDOM

Bastianel S., and Di Pinto, L., "Per una fondazione biblica dell'etica", in *Corso di Morale I*, T. Goffi and G. Piana (eds.), Queriniana, Brescia 1989, 75-173.
Capone, Domenico, *L'uomo è persona in Cristo*, Dehoniane, Bologna 1973.
Congar, Yves M.J., *Jésus Christ notre mediateur, notre Seigneur*, Cerf, Paris 1965.

"Le Saint Esprit dans la théologie thomiste de l'agir moral", in *Atti del Congresso Internazionale Tommaso d'Aquino nel suo settimo centenario*, Vol. 5, Edizioni Domenicane, Rome-Naples 1977, 9-19.

I Believe in the Holy Spirit, (3 Vols.), Seabury, New York 1983.

Desclos, J., *Libérer la morale. Christocentrisme et dynamique filiale de la morale chrétienne à l'époque de Vatican II*, Éditions Paulines, Montréal 1991.

Driver, T.E., *Christ in a Changing World: Toward an Ethical Christology*, SCM, London 1981.

Elders, L.J., and Hedwig, K. (eds.), *Lex et Libertas: Freedom and Law according to St Thomas Aquinas: Studi Tommistici*, 30, Libreria Editrice Vaticana, Vatican City 1987.

Galot, Jean, S.J., *Jesus, Our Liberator*, Gregorian University Press, Rome 1982.

Guidi, Sergio De, "Per una teologia morale fondamentale sistematica secondo la storia della salvezza", in *Corso di morale I*, T. Goffi and G. Piana (eds.), Queriniana 1989, 201-324.

Häring, Bernard, C.Ss.R., *This Time of Salvation*, Herder and Herder, New York 1966.

Himes, Michael J., and Himes, Kenneth R., O.F.M., *The Fullness of Faith: The Public Significance of Theology*, Paulist Press, New York 1993.

Kelly, Tony, *Touching on the Infinite: Explorations in Christian Hope*, Collins Dove, Melbourne 1991.

Mongillo, Dalmazio, O.P., "Potere normativo della 'ratio' nella legge nuova", in *Angelicum* 51 (1974), 169-185.

Piana, G. (ed.), *Cristologia e morale*, Dehoniane, Bologna 1982.

Index